Women
on the Job

The Attitudes of Women to their Work

Judith Buber Agassi

LexingtonBooks
D.C. Heath and Company
Lexington, Massachusetts
Toronto

Library of Congress Cataloging in Publication Data

Agassi, Judith B.
 Women on the job.

 Bibliography: p.
 Includes index.
 1. Women–Employment–Massachusetts. 2. Women–Employment–
Germany, West–Hesse. 3. Women–Employment–Israel. 4. Women–Mass-
achusetts–Attitudes. 5. Women–Germany, West–Hesse–Attitudes. 6. Wo-
men–Israel–Attitudes. 7. Work–Social aspects–Case studies. I. Title.
HD6095.A653   331.4   78-24789
ISBN 0-669-02815-0

Published simultaneously in Canada.

Printed in the United States of America.

International Standard Book Number: 0-669-02829-0

Library of Congress Catalog Card Number: 78-24768

Contents

List of Tables

Preface

This study examines the validity of two groups of theories. The first group of theories is in the field of the sociology of work, and concerns attitudes to work. These theories are well known, and have been discussed in the literature and tested in the field. The second group of theories is part of the same field, and concerns factors that influence women's attitudes to work; the theories are new and at most only adumbrated in the literature. I hope that the empirical results presented here will contribute to the discussion of both kinds of theories and indicate, at least in broad outlines, a few general conclusions in the sociology of work as well as some specific conclusions for women.

The results, in general, are:

1. Less than a quarter of a population of women employed in jobs under the semiprofessional level hold a clear-cut instrumental attitude toward their work roles, where the instrumental attitude comprises the lack of emphasis on the importance of the content of work as employment, the lack of concern about negative task aspects of their jobs, and the lack of readiness to make any effort to advance to a better quality job.

2. The clear-cut instrumental attitude appears as the outcome of resignation, its incidence rising considerably after age thirty-five.

3. The incidence of the instrumental attitude is highest among workers with jobs lowest in content quality, whose initial aspirations were low to begin with (their schooling and vocational training were below their national average), whose employment careers had been static or declining, and who perceive themselves to be in less than good condition of health.

4. A minority of the instrumentally adapted are consistently satisfied with their job, hardly any are openly dissatisfied with it, and the majority are superficially, inconsistently satisfied with it.

5. The level of the task characteristics of the job is the most important factor for the following work attitudes: emphasis on content, concern for content, attachment and commitment to employment and occupation, and the instrumental attitude. It is second in importance for satisfaction/dissatisfaction with work and the full instrumental syndrome. It is third in importance for interest in advancement to more challenging work and for one's self-image as an economically active person. It is fourth for self-confidence in the ability to perform more challenging work and for superficial, inconsistent satisfaction.

6. For two work attitudes that are deemed most problematic for employed women, namely, interest in advancement to more challenging work and self-confidence in the ability to perform more challenging work, the most significant factor influencing them positively is the ideological factor of relative egalitarianism concerning the appropriate work roles of the sexes. This egalitarianism also acts as the third most important factor, raising emphasis on content,

concern for content, attachment and commitment to employment and career, and self-image as basic earner. Also, as the third in importance, it decreases the incidence of superficial, inconsistent satisfaction and as the fourth factor it increases overt satisfaction.

These findings stand in obvious contrast to the theories currently in circulation. According to them, the level of the intrinsic work characteristics of a job is devoid of importance and significance for all unskilled and semiskilled workers (Goldthorpe), for U.S. industrial workers (Dubin), for young city-bred workers (Hulin and Blood), and for employed women, especially married ones. My findings indicate that the present shift toward more egalitarian views and values among employed women can be expected to continually diminish supposedly sex-specific differences in interest in advancement and promotion and in attachment and commitment to work.

This volume reports the results of a study of samples of employed women in three countries and in three occupational clusters of jobs that are below the semiprofessional level. The countries were: the United States (the state of Massachusetts); the Federal Republic of Germany (the land of Hesse); and Israel. The occupational clusters were: sewers and stitchers in the needle trade industry; saleswomen and cashiers in retail trade; and clerical and secretarial workers in banks, insurance companies, universities, and labor union offices. The sample size was 761 women, divided almost equally among the three countries and among the three occupational groups. Each of them was interviewed for between forty-five minutes and one hour. I also interviewed members of management and observed the jobs concerned. A large variety of job characteristics were then correlated with a variety of job attitudes in order to test many hypotheses.

After a few pilot studies in the field, the research began on April 1, 1976. The interviews took place in Israel in July and August 1976 and in February 1977, in the United States from November 1976 to January 1977, and in Germany from April to July 1977.

Acknowledgments

I am grateful to the managements of the participating work organizations for permission to interview, and to the interviewees who freely contributed time and effort—at times at a loss of income—and who often volunteered additional information that they deemed pertinent. The managers also provided information about the history and conditions of their respective organizations and permitted free observation. All these people, as well as members of work councils, showed much kindness and hospitality to the interviewers.

I am grateful to those chambers of commerce, employers' organizations, and labor unions in all three countries which facilitated access to the work organizations and offered moral support to the project.

The student interviewers in the three countries were conscientious and enthusiastic and often worked under trying conditions. I regret that I cannot name them here, but I wish to express my heartfelt gratitude to them nonetheless. I also want to thank those Israeli students who undertook the arduous task of checking and correcting the questionnaire data.

Miriam Tsur and I planned the coding of the questionnaire, the means of testing the accuracy of the recording of the data, and the parameters to be used in determining the rules for constructing the variables used in the quantitative formulation of the diverse hypotheses tested by the available data. David Itzhaky was responsible for all the necessary computer operations, including distributions, cross tabulations, and correlations.

Professor Doktor Helge Pross, *Gesamthochschule Siegen,* the official project head and one of the foremost authorities in the field, kindly undertook the difficult, frustrating, and time-consuming effort of administering the entire project. Her observations helped greatly to clarify the project's initial tasks, and later she offered many insightful suggestions. She also invited me to present the project before her graduate seminar, where a very helpful and challenging discussion took place.

Professor Joseph Agassi has offered much technical assistance and many valuable critical comments. He has also prepared the index.

My gratitude goes to them all.

Finally, I am extremely grateful to the Deutsche Forschungsgemeinschaft, which offered financial support after I failed to obtain it in many other places, and this despite my being neither a German national nor employed by any academic institution in the Federal Republic of Germany. The project is one of a series it sponsored in the area of the integration of women in the labor market.

1

Introduction

The Problem

Work—employment or self employment, other than domestic and child-care work in one's own household—occupies an important part of the lives of the great majority of adult men and, increasingly, women. This growing importance has understandably given rise to a number of questions. Are workers satisfied with their work activity? Do they evaluate its characteristics positively or negatively? Are they concerned with or resigned to its negative aspects? Do they want to advance to more responsible or demanding work? Are they ready to train for it? Do they see their schooling and vocational training as relevant to their current job? Do they see their occupational choice as correct or mistaken? What meaning does work activity have for them? Does it merely support off-work activity, or does it have intrinsic meaning for them? Do they see it as an unpleasant necessity or a voluntary choice?

The answers to these questions are presumably of great consequence both to the workers—their physical and emotional health, personality, and intellectual development—and to the overall productivity of the work place. Indeed, one of the central problems of the sociology of work concerns workers' lack of involvement with their work and their alienation from it. The sociology of work seeks to uncover answers to the following questions in this regard. How widespread is this attitude? Is it on the increase or on the decline? What are its effects on individuals, the economy, and the community? What are the causes or contributing factors? Is this a process; is it reversible? Given the existing differences in the social roles between the sexes and the existing values and norms about their respective work roles in the family and in the economy, what are the sex-specific differences in job attitudes?

This study in particular looks at three typical basic women's job clusters, their characteristics, and their impact on the job attitudes of women working in them. The characteristics of child-care services and of the prevalent value system concerning women's employment, as well as the views and values concerning the proper work role of women, were then correlated with these job attitudes.

Current Theory and Research

Before the 1920s, there was little empirical research into work attitudes. But since then, the unease about the situation, especially that of workers in mass-production industries, has brought about inquiries in many directions, at times with no conspicuous logical connection between them. Concern about the degrees of satisfaction with work and their correlation with output developed into studies of the relative impact of remuneration and of human relations on the degree of worker satisfaction and output. Simultaneously, a long series of educationally oriented sociological and psychological studies emerged, based on the presupposition that the correct "fit" between levels of aspiration and the qualities of the jobs would produce, or at least enhance, worker satisfaction. Next came studies about the correlation between certain characteristics of a job (such as its position on the monotony/variety scale or whether the job is fragmented or meaningful) with the quality and quantity of output. Low task content, especially monotony and pressure, were correlated with leisure time or nonworktime behavior of the workers. Intellectual development and psychosomatic disorders of workers were also correlated to the quality of their work.

The studies of Blauner and Herzberg that followed, and the scores of publications that came in their wake, presented attempts to examine, test, refine, broaden, elaborate, and expostulate on these preliminary studies. Robert Blauner isolated what he considered the most valuable factor in the worker's job. He claimed that the degree of autonomy a worker has on the job contributes the most to the degree of satisfaction with the job; the worker's degree of satisfaction was a measure of alienation. But Blauner's findings are inadequate, as Frederick Herzberg has argued, since dissatisfaction/satisfaction is one scale and alienation/involvement is another. As Herzberg has repeatedly claimed, poor "hygiene characteristics" (such as poor remuneration, physical conditions, and social climate) cause dissatisfaction. Workers become more satisfied as conditions are improved, but they do not necessarily become more involved with their job at the same time. Motivation can be raised only by improving the "task characteristics" (such as autonomy, variety, skill, and challenge) of the job.

The contributions of Blauner and Herzberg and their followers have led to the possibility of developing a much clearer identification of workers who demonstrate the so-called instrumental attitude to work. Those who hold this attitude look at their job, not as a fulfilling activity in itself, but primarily as an instrument for gaining satisfaction or gratification outside the work world (for example, in a hobby or the family). Walker and Guest and Bennett Berger have described workers on the assembly lines of the automobile industry. These workers believe that the quality of the content of their jobs is not important to them. They have no illusions about the negative aspects of their jobs, but say that these do not matter. They are not ready to try to improve these aspects or to seek a more interesting or challenging job either by trying to advance within the work organization or to leave it. They see their job only as an instrument for obtaining rewards in their nonwork life—perhaps drinking and gambling or providing comfort and status to their families through the acquisition of a home and cars. Finally, as long as "hygiene" (that is, working conditions) seems satisfactory, they will declare themselves satisfied with their jobs and will perform their tasks routinely. Yet their satisfaction is shallow; their negative attitude to their jobs expresses itself both in a solemn declaration that they prefer their children not to follow in their footsteps and in their lack of occupational pride. This syndrome also appears in the research of Goldthorpe et al. into the attitudes of "affluent" British workers, as he called them, in the automotive and chemical plants of an English industrial boom town in the late 1950s. Goldthorpe called this attitude "privatization" and considered it typical of industrial workers in all Western postwar societies.

Blauner, Herzberg, and Fürstenberg, however, found that different degrees of involvement and interest in industrial workers were parallel to the quality of certain content characteristics of their jobs. Blauner called this characteristic "autonomy," and found that it exists both in the industrial skilled trades and in the jobs of operatives in highly automated industries. Herzberg pointed to the workers' opportunities to use initiative and to solve problems, and Fürstenberg looked at the differences in the jobs of skilled and semiskilled chemical workers.

Herzberg, following the work of psychologist Abraham Maslow, assumed that normal people desire involvement in work because once their basic needs for food, shelter, and security are taken care of, they look to satisfy their higher needs for ego growth. If frustrated in this desire by the low level of the tasks of their jobs, they may adapt and withdraw, becoming uninvolved and unmotivated.

Herzberg also assumed that jobs can be enriched by introducing elements of initiative, judgment, and responsibility from jobs higher in the job hierarchy to lower ones. He thus studied job attitudes by following up the reactions of workers to planned changes in the content of their jobs. Previously, researchers had usually concentrated on documenting the consequences of such changes for the productivity of labor, and research into attitudes was usually limited to questions about satisfaction with work in general and evaluation of the state of affairs after the reform (whether it is better, the same, or worse than before, for example). The followup studies usually showed a considerable rise in productivity (especially in the quality of the product or service), a diminished waste of materials and instruments (and thus savings in expenses), and most of all, reduced turnover and absenteeism, all pointing to a growth of involvement and of occupational pride. Yet in many of these experiments, the workers under study had not been chosen randomly; they had volunteered for the project because they were interested in more challenging jobs. Wherever the jobs of entire existing work groups were enriched, usually a minority of workers declared that they considered the previous situation "the same" or "better."

Hulin and Blood asked industrial workers in jobs with low-level tasks if they were interested in more challenging work. Examining the demographic data, they found that more of those who answered negatively had spent their childhood in a city, as opposed to a small town or rural area, than those in the group expressing interest in a more challenging job. They suggested the hypothesis that the instrumental attitude to work is not the result of an adaptation of the individual worker to a low-level job but that urban working-class boys are socialized to have this attitude; conversely, the work ethic of small-town and rural folk demands that workers find intrinsic value in their jobs.

Hulin and Blood's contribution is valuable because it points to the fact that different human groups, national as well as socioeconomic, socialize their young to accept different "work ethics," that is, different values and norms concerning work. Differences in childhood socialization may cause some difference in the reaction of adult workers to identical work situations. Unfortunately, Hulin and Blood disregarded the impact of continuing socialization in adolescence and young adulthood, and many other factors as well. Since the 1960s, such values as rejection of arbitrary, hierarchical, and impersonal authority and the quest for "meaningfulness" and "self-realization," have affected many young people throughout the Western world and have changed their expectations of and demands from work.

This widely observed change has expressed itself in different forms of work behavior, ranging from attempts to democratize or humanize work organizations and occupations; to shunning all larger work organizations; to dropping out completely from employment; to reacting negatively to narrow, monotonous, and stressful jobs by strikes and even sabotage. What was clearly observed among the generation of younger workers entering industrial employment in the 1960s is that only a small percentage exhibited both declared satisfaction and an instrumental attitude. The majority of industrial workers declared that aspects of the content of their jobs were of equal or higher importance to them than the actual working conditions.

In spite of all these studies, there remains a multitude of unstudied problems. For example, no one has measured the extent of the relative prevalence of the instrumental attitude in a variety of occupational groups, all belonging to the lower reaches of the occupational scale, or sought to find correlations between various aspects of a job with the rate of incidence of this attitude. And no one has studied whether the initial aspirations of workers are significant in this regard, what impact initial socialization and resocialization may have on the work ethic, what significance this may have in the development of the instrumental attitude, or whether the development of this attitude is a process of adaptation and, if so, whether it is reversible.

Recently, Bruggemann has suggested a classification of kinds of satisfaction with work that is designed to clarify the correlation between the distribution into satisfied and dissatisfied workers and the distribution into active and passive attitudes. It should be possible to differentiate empirically, she thinks, the satisfied and active, the satisfied and passive, the dissatisfied and active, and the dissatisfied and passive workers. If so, it would be important to measure the sizes of these groups and to examine correlations.

Women's Work Attitudes

Early studies of work attitudes did not pay attention to women as a special group with special problems, although the subjects of some of the most famous experiments in the field were women. Thus, an all-woman group in the Relay Assembly Test Room of the Hawthorne experiments (1927-1932) when given permission to talk freely during work, demonstrated that the "informal organization" of workers may decide to raise productivity. A group of women in the British Industrial Fatigue Board experiments (1924) demonstrated that the fragmentation of an assembly job among ten workers has no advantages for quantity or quality of output over letting one woman perform the complete job. Women were the subjects in the Paris cookie bakery experiment (cited by Georges Friedmann in 1952) who responded favorably to rotation among the various departments of the plant. In the U.S. World War II radar-manufacturing plants, it was demonstrated that a group of rank-and-file women assembly workers could design and effect an efficient plan for the assembly of a complicated electronic device. And in Herzberg's job-enrichment experiments of the 1960s, young women office workers demonstrated the benefits to management or entrusting employees with more scope for judgment and responsibility instead of closely and bureaucratically supervising them.

Curiously, while the findings of these experiments contributed considerably to the development of the field of the sociology and psychology of work in general, they made hardly any impact on the researchers' opinions concerning the attitudes of women toward specific characteristics of their jobs.

Since World War II, when it was discovered that women were playing a growing role in the labor market, and when it was noted that both different age groups and different social strata of women entered or reentered employment more than previously, a considerable amount of research about other, apparently sex-specific, problems concerning women's employment has been undertaken. Researchers looked at the statistics of women's labor force participation and examined them according to age, marital status, educational level, occupational distribution, hours worked, absence from work, unemployment, income, contribution to family budgets, and length of working life. Studies about factors influencing women's participation or absence in the labor market were also examined: educational level, marital status, husband's income, number of children, and age of youngest child. Other areas that came under observation included the impact of mothers' employment on children, as well as on the mothers themselves and on their husbands, and the impact of socialization on the occupational choices women make, on their decision to persist in their wish, and on their chances to advance in their occupation. Time-budgeting studies of the population at large revealed that for employed mothers in industrialized nations the "leisure society" had not arrived; these studies also showed that housework tends to expand to fill the day of nonemployed homemakers.

Since the 1960s and the growth of the women's movement, the inferior position of women in the economy and the labor market, exemplified by their lower pay and their concentration in the lower ranks of all occupations, has been raised to the level of a social problem that demands both theoretical explanation as to its causes and effects and suggestions for its solution. Recently, occupational segregation was isolated as one of the central components contributing to this syndrome of inferiority, and a spate of research was begun into the causes, the effects, and the inner mechanisms of sexual segregation.

Researchers found a body of opinions about the specific psychological and sociological characteristics of employed women that serve as an excuse and justification for many discriminatory management policies and that prevented women from recognizing the facts of discrimination. Not only the population at large, but also many sociologists studying work, including empirical investigators who took it for granted that some empirical studies had amply verified their opinions, cavalierly held these views. Serious investigators had neither paid attention to the problem of whether women have attitudes toward work that are different from those of men nor considered the possibility that apparent differences in attitudes are merely differences in job characteristics. Yet they assumed that there were significant differences in job attitudes between the sexes.

The opinions concerning the differences in job attitudes between the sexes were these: women tolerate fragmentation and repetitiveness in work better than men because of their more passive nature; they are more easily satisfied with jobs of low quality; they prefer authoritative and detailed supervision to democratic management more often than men do, as long as their relations with superiors and fellow workers are friendly; like men, they prefer men to women for bosses; unlike men, they are not very good at teamwork; they prefer individual piecework payment to other methods of remuneration more often than men do; their commitment to work is lower than men's; they are less interested than men in rank, promotion, and equitable payment; since society recognizes their domestic role as legitimate, they do not suffer, at least not so much, the psychological strain of unemployment and of retirement which affect normal men. Recently, however, Crewley, Levitin, and Quinn examined the U.S. research literature about work attitudes and sex-specific differences and found the following:

1. The most frequently repeated finding is that women are more concerned with the social aspects of their jobs, especially with good relations with their fellow employees.
2. For the frequently repeated generalization that women put less emphasis on the content of their jobs than men, they found little and mostly contradictory support.
3. Sex-specific differences concerning the attitudes toward other specific job

characteristics, are, if found at all, rather small and tend to disappear with the level of education and/or the level of the quality of the job held constant.

Additionally, Crewley, Levitin, and Quinn attempted to test the validity of the received opinions concerning women's job attitudes. They chose the seven most common stereotypes and undertook a survey of a sample of 1,532 employed Americans (539 women and 993 men) representative of the entire occupational spectrum. The subjects were requested to grade twenty-three job characteristics in order of their importance as job desiderata. Whenever there was a significant difference between the responses of men and women that agreed with one of the following seven stereotypes, they reexamined the difference, controlling for whichever aspect of the job situation or the way of life of the working person that appeared to be the most likely current explanation of the observed difference. The seven stereotypes and the results of the survey test follow.

1. *Women work only for pin money.* Finding: About two of each five employed women in the survey were not economically maintained by an employed man. In the employed population with low family income, the percentage of employed women was higher than in the population at large.

2. *Employed women work only for the money. They are not involved personally, they do not want to do a good job for the sake of doing so, and job content does not motivate them; they will leave the job as soon as the economic need ceases.* Finding: Between single women and men, there was barely a difference in the percentage of those who declared that they would continue in their job even if there were no longer any economic need; half of the married women said they would continue. Apparently, for them, economic necessity was not the decisive motivating factor.

3. *Women are more concerned than men with the social and emotional aspects of their jobs.* Finding: Only one significant difference was found in the answers to questions concerning relations with management and fellow employees: more women than men declared that friendly and helpful relations with their fellow workers were very important to them. One explanation seems to be that in the jobs of 73 percent of the women, but only 55 percent of those of the men, cooperation is necessary.

4. *Women do not like to show initiative in their work.* Finding: Significantly fewer women than men showed interest in autonomy at work and preferred a clear limitation of their tasks. Two explanations for this attitude are women's early socialization and the characteristics of women's present jobs.

5. *Women, more than men, are interested in the hygienic aspects of their jobs.* Finding: There appeared considerable difference in the emphasis women put on convenient working hours, a short journey to and from work, and pleasant physical surroundings at work.

6. *Women are less interested than men in challenging jobs.* Finding: No differences were found in the emphasis put on the development of special skills, on the chances of finding a job for which one is best suited, and on having an interesting job. Moreover, women were overrepresented in jobs that are not intellectually demanding. Whenever the intellectual demand was held constant, the dissatisfaction of women with the nondemanding job equals that of men.

7. *Women are less interested in promotion.* Finding: Most of the complaints about discrimination concerned promotion. Many more women than men expected not to be promoted. Once the expectation factor was controlled, no difference concerning the desire for promotion remained.

Except for this stimulating study, which compares men and women from a wide range of occupations in the United States, most other research concerning women's work attitudes is confined to one occupation and often to one work organization. None of this research examines the characteristics of several jobs—including the task characteristics—or correlates the women workers' attitudes to each of these.

Finally, Helge Pross did the first study to examine both working conditions and life conditions of seven thousand employed women, as well as a number of their work attitudes—an analysis of an extensive survey conducted in six Common Market countries. Pross's work is very important as the first multinational comparative study. It differentiates between groups of factors that determine women's work life that are national specific from other groups that are not national specific. The other factors—for instance, the difference in physical conditions between blue-collar and white-collar jobs and the difference in chances for promotion in small and large firms, segregated or mixed—are universal. The factors that are national specific pertain especially to the image of women's proper and desirable social role and to the public child-care services available in the country where she lives. Yet the central concern of the study is not women's work attitudes but the status of women in the labor market of six European countries. It is, therefore, largely a detailed study of conditions of work, the division of labor in the household, and the educational and vocational level of the employed woman. The common questionnaire for the six countries, the results of which were analyzed, contained few items eliciting attitudes to work.

2 General Description of the Study

Plan of the Work

This study reports tests of hypotheses concerning women's job attitudes in three job clusters—industrial, commercial, and clerical—in the lower levels of the occupational scale in three countries. Some of these hypotheses concern job attitudes of men and women alike, some are specific to women; all of them, whether true or false, are admitted by all students in the field to be of rather high significance for anyone concerned with the welfare of the working person in the modern world.

First, I will present demographic data, such as age distribution, marital status, and details about children, education and vocational training, occupation of parent and spouse, health, and so on. Data about the interviewees' job careers follow. Statistics about the characteristics of the jobs of the women interviewees follow, mainly regarding their perception of the hygiene and task characteristics of their jobs. Here, hygiene concerns remuneration and fringe benefits, physical conditions, hours of work, social climate, quality of supervision, and freedom of movement and communication. Task characteristics concern the degree of monotony or variety of the job, the degree of pressure exerted on the worker, the skill level required and available, the degree of initiative and responsibility required, and the opportunity for the acquisition of further skill and advancement to more responsible work or to a higher position in the work organization.

Next follow distributions of reactions to questions concerning attitudes according to nine groups—the three national groups and the three occupational groups in each. I will present conclusions from the analysis of the data (which are found in the appendix tables). An example is the emerging clear scale between the three occupational clusters, such as the fact that the degrees of composite satisfaction, emphasis on content characteristics, concern for content, self-image as an independent bread winner, and self-confidence, are all lowest in the industrial cluster and highest in the clerical one.

For the processing of the data, as well as for the purpose of testing the hypotheses, I have postulated the existence of certain variables and offered some sufficiently clear-cut operational definitions for them. For example, one hypothesis holds that when the level of a worker's aspiration fits the level of the task characteristics of her job, then and only then will her degree of satisfaction be high. The problem here is in defining and measuring any of these three related variables: degree of aspiration, level of task characteristic, and degree of

9

satisfaction. Clearly, they are not as obvious as level of remuneration or even degrees of political popularity. It is imperative to define the variables from the data available by means of a questionnaire study. It certainly would have been preferable had I been able to ask each individual interviewee at the outset of her working career what her aspirations were in a manner that would have elicited a clear-cut, reliable, quantifiable answer; yet this method is possible only in a followup study. Therefore, I had to construct the variable as best I could from the information about each interviewee's years of schooling and courses of vocational training completed. Concerning the variable "satisfaction," it is well known that people tend to respond to direct questions about their satisfaction with any major area of their life in an exaggeratedly positive manner. For this reason, this variable is a weighted sum of the answers to one direct question and six additional control questions probing different aspects of satisfaction. Finally, the variable "level of task characteristics," which is supposed to express the quality of the content of the job, is a composite of each interviewee's answers to a number of questions about different aspects of her job. In short, I shall describe the elements included in each variable and give my reasons for constructing it thus and for assigning the relative weights to each component.

The central part of the work is the stating of each hypothesis, its background, and the variables correlated in order to test it; analysis of the results; and attempts to explain the results and their significance. In all those cases where I have tested several hypotheses explaining the same phenomenon, I will try to point out the hypothesis that I would recommend as the most plausible because it has the greatest explanatory power.

Method

The data were gathered with the help of a questionnaire, comprising 282 questions, that was addressed to all interviewees. The items about the characteristics of the job include a considerable number of questions that depend on responses to previous questions. Thus, no interviewee was ever asked all 282 questions.

The questionnaire was prepared after a few field studies. It is a corrected and somewhat enlarged version of the original Hebrew questionnaire that was tested in a final pilot study on about thirty employed women in Israel. (These interviews were used solely for the purpose of testing and correcting the questionnaire and were not included in the sample presented here.) The corrected questionnaire was then used in Israel and translated as exactly as possible into American English and into German. Several minor corrections and clarifications in the instructions for the coding were made during the course of the interviewing process, in each of the three countries, upon observation of simple difficulties in comprehension or of omission of a frequent factor. For example, among family reasons for quitting a job, the category "divorce" was added. In addition, all those who had begun work while they had a child under ten years of age were asked questions about the child care they used. The tables permitted room for nine children, and for each child, information on four age periods could be gathered. All those who had worked in another job before the current one were asked twenty-one questions as to each of their previous jobs (nine possible previous jobs could be registered). Finally, all employees fifty years of age and over were asked twenty questions about their attitude to retirement.

The questions were read carefully to the interviewees. Whenever there was doubt about an answer, the interviewers were instructed to write the full answer in longhand. Answers were coded immediately. During sessions I had with the interviewers, all of the problematic responses were discussed and then coded. Interviewers were also instructed to note down additional information which interviewees had volunteered whenever it seemed relevant.

Since questions concerning child care and job history demanded of the interviewees a considerable effort to remember and to present information in chronological order, I first used tape recorders to gather these data and had the interviewers code the tables, on the basis of the recording, after each day of interviewing. The major purpose of this procedure was to shorten the time of the already lengthy interview. I also had hoped to gather additional information by this method through the use of the typed transcripts of the recordings. But recording proved unsatisfactory, and I abandoned it in each of the countries after a short trial period. The main trouble was that the interviewers disliked it as it did not shorten the interview time. In addition, some interviewees disliked speaking into the tape recorder and transcription proved difficult, expensive, and hardly informative.

After discarding the transcription technique, I used a precoding sheet on which the information on job history could be noted in longhand, and the coding was completed after each interview. The sheet proved extremely informative and valuable later for clearing up and correcting dubious or erroneous coding of the job histories.

I started with the interviewers working in pairs. They alternated; one asked the questions, and the other coded the responses and took notes in longhand when necessary. This method served as a good way of induction for new interviewers, as well as a check against omissions and inaccuracies. The main reason for using it was to shorten the length of each individual interview so as to avoid tiring the interviewee and exasperating management. In the course of the interviewing period, several of the interviewers who had become rather proficient asked to administer the questionnaire alone and did so successfully. The method of remuneration to the interviewers was by hour worked and not by interview completed, so that there was no danger of their filling out the questionnaire just to be paid.

The great majority of interviewers were second- and later-year social science women students of Tel Aviv University, Boston University, and Frankfurt University. There were a few exceptions. A young interviewer in Israel was not yet a student, and in Boston and in Frankfurt, there were several graduates as yet without regular employment. The use of student labor complicated the coordination of the limited and irregular free time available to students with the time slots for interviewing, which were fixed according to the decisions of management. This scheduling necessitated the recruiting and training of teams of about ten students in each of the three countries. The complex logistics worked well only because of the genuine and admirable interest shown by most of the interviewers toward the study.

In all but two situations, interviews were carried out at the work places. One exception was for fifteen stitchers in a factory in Israel where management—after giving permission for interviewing, supplying lists of employees, and agreeing to ask for volunteers—stipulated quite unexpectedly that the interviews take place after work hours. The women were thus interviewed in their own homes shortly after their return from work. The second exception was for ten bank employees in Boston who preferred to be interviewed during their lunch hour in a neighboring coffee shop. Management was informed about the project and a management interview took place as usual, but the choice of the sample of interviewees was arranged without the knowledge of management, according to the workers' own wishes.

The three occupational clusters were chosen on the assumption that among industry, retail trade, and office work, there are specific differences in job characteristics. In addition, in all three, large concentrations of women can be found. In industry, for example, I chose to examine the needle trades, although two other branches—electronics and food—have a high concentration of women. Originally, my intention had been to choose two branches in each of the three areas, but I lacked enough financial support, so, for industry, I chose the branch in terms of number of employees in the three areas with concentrations of women. For services, I also chose the first of retail trade, waitressing, and personal services; and for office work, the first out of lower secretarial jobs, including typing, lower computer services (mainly card punching), and lower clerical work (including mainly filing). Regarding the office cluster, however, I did not succeed in my attempt to isolate one of these groups; instead my sample includes all sorts of secretarial and clerical work, excluding keypunching and higher administrative- or executive-secretarial jobs.

I tried to stay within the limits of the lower occupational categories throughout the study. Nevertheless, 50 of the 761 interviewees at the time of the interview had acquired somewhat higher positions, usually the lowest ranks of supervision, although most of them were (at least partly) still performing production, retail, or office work, respectively. In my statistics, I took account of this fact whenever it seemed pertinent because excluding these women from the sample would bias it post hoc, particularly with regard to the question of real chances of women workers in these kinds of work organizations for promotion and for the acquisition and use of skills.

My decisions about the kinds of occupations to study and the importance of including women with similar job characteristics precluded the search for a sample in the population at large—for example, through the offices of trade unions—and forced me to turn to the managements of work organizations for permission to interview samples of workers identified by task characteristics. This technique also enabled me to check workers' evaluations of their jobs and tasks by observing the work organizations myself and by interviewing at least one member of management in each organization in which the interviewees were employed at the time. Most organizations were of medium size, but I also interviewed in a few rather large ones and took care to balance my sample by also choosing some smaller ones. My samples ranged usually from five employees in the smallest organization to twenty-five in the largest.

The reason that almost all interviews were conducted in the work organization, during the work day and primarily during work hours, is that physical proximity to the job helped interviewees concentrate on job characteristics and prevented the interference of opinions of others. Each interviewee was questioned out of earshot of her colleagues. Of course, interference in the work place is possible too, and there were some minor attempts of management personnel to be present during the interviewing process, but in all cases we objected to interviewing in the presence of members of management. I instructed the interviewers to stop interviewing and contact me if they could not correct the situation. Although I had always explained this condition to central management when requesting permission to interview, sometimes it was not clear to local managers. Similarly, I had to explain that no data in the study would be presented in such a way as to enable anyone to identify an individual interviewee. Management of each firm was asked if it wanted the name of the firm mentioned or preferred to remain anonymous. Because about half the firms chose anonymity, I decided not to mention any firm by name. A list of names of suitable employees was usually provided by management, together with their location within the firm and the time allotted for the interview. Each person was approached personally and was interviewed only if she voluntarily consented. Two women chose to stop the interview in the early stages of questioning; I think their concern was embarrassment, not confidentiality.

The interviewers explained at the beginning of each interview that it was confidential and academic (commissioned by neither management nor labor union), that it was not a test but a survey of opinions, and that its purpose was to find out what they thought about their jobs, so as to find out how matters could be improved. In several plants where individual incentive pay (piecework) was an important part of remuneration, I was requested either by management or by interviewees themselves to recompense them for lost income, and I did so.

In some places, the local union representative expressly requested that I not pay a recompense because the union itself wanted to take care of the matter. No interviewee made any material gain whatsoever from being interviewed, and quite a few sustained a minor loss.

In designing the questionnaire, my chief concern was to avoid prying into potentially embarrassing topics. The questionnaire was also examined to this end by a considerable number of union officials, managers, and even by one special committee from an institution of higher learning in the Boston area, which expressly checked for possible invasion of privacy. Generally, the response, a bit cautious at the beginning, was quite enthusiastic. Many worker interviewees and most management ones asked if the results would be published and available and requested to see them. In many work organizations, additional employees wanted to be interviewed.

Gaining permission to interview was perhaps the most frustrating task of this project. My first step was to approach the appropriate labor union offices, inform them of the intended interviewing, and request a list of plants, stores, and banking and insurance offices in the area. Response was uniformly friendly, and in some cases enthusiastic, and everywhere union officials were ready to supply information concerning conditions of work and special problems of women employed in their branch. The ability of the unions to help with introductions to the firms was limited, however. In Israel, unionization is almost universal in firms of all three occupational areas of this study, but the unions' activity and interest in the retail trade are very low. In the United States, needle trade workers are divided between two unions, and some plants are not organized at all. In stores and offices there, unionization is very partial, and attempts at unionization in banks and in academic institutions are now underway, emphasizing equal opportunities for women. The top management of larger U.S. banks and insurance companies considers unionization a threat and suspects any outside gathering of information about their women employees of being in collusion with unions. In the Federal Republic of Germany, unionization is fairly high, although not universal in all three areas, yet the information available concerning membership in stores and offices was rather sketchy.

My next step was to contact employers' associations and local chambers of commerce to explain the purpose of the research and to request lists of firms and introductions. The proportion of entries gained in this way was extremely small, yet the information I received and the personal contacts I established in this way were very helpful. In Boston, for example, I initially was unable to gain permission to interview from managements of area banks. I turned to the Massachusetts Banking Commissioner, a woman, who contacted several women in higher-middle management, and thus succeeded in opening up three medium-sized banks for interviewing. In two cases in southern Massachusetts, the appeal of the local union secretary to the plant manager was sufficient to open a plant for interviewing. But most often, the obtaining of permission was a lengthy and frustrating process. I contacted and often negotiated for weeks with more than double the number of firms than desired. Finally, employees in seventy-two firms in three countries were interviewed.

One problem that needs to be considered is whether this way of selecting the work organizations biases the sample as to the quality of their jobs. Was permission perhaps granted only by managers who were certain that conditions in their firms were comparatively rather favorable? A slight bias of this kind seems possible; it is likely that owners and managers of firms with considerably below-average physical conditions and pay would be reluctant to permit any inquiry. Yet the level of conditions was certainly not uniform for each of the nine national-occupational groups. My impression is that the wish not to have bad conditions inspected was not an important element causing management opposition to interviewing. The main cause—especially in industry and retail trade—was the fear of sustaining a loss in income through a cut in production or sales. To counteract this anxiety, I offered to interview in plants during coffee and lunch breaks and in stores during slack early morning hours. Yet some loss and at least some inconvenience to management was entailed by the interviewing. So perhaps those firms where top management had the most pronounced and exclusive profit motivation were excluded from my sample. Others were excluded simply by being large, bureaucratic, centralized, and by having their top management offices at a distance (a problem that required too long a time to solve).

I visited each work place personally. I usually introduced the interviewers and often took part in the interviewing. With the permission of management, I then proceeded to observe the entire work process, especially the special group of employees. Often interviewers were given permission to tour the work place, and their observations were also noted. Almost all management interviews were conducted by me, sometimes with a student taking notes.

All of the questionnaires were collected and were examined and corrected before the coded information was transferred to punch cards. In particular, all cases that were coded as "other" and reported in detail in longhand had to be recoded after due deliberation.

There were details to correct in the questionnaires, especially concerning jobs of parents and spouse, since the grading of these jobs had to be done differently in the different countries. Other systematic errors had to be corrected too; all were minor.

3

Statistics Concerning the Sample

The sample is divided into the following groups:

Group 0: Israeli industry
Group 1: Israeli retail trade
Group 2: Israeli office

Group 3: U.S. industry
Group 4: U.S. retail trade
Group 5: U.S. office

Group 6: German industry
Group 7: German retail trade
Group 8: German office

My comments in this chapter chiefly highlight the data that appear in the appendix. I elaborate on points that deserve special attention and present and discuss explanatory hypotheses when these are called for.

Demography

The chief characteristics of the sample concern age, marital status, number of children, children at home, age of youngest child, ethnicity or immigrant status, age of entry into the labor market, years employed at current work place, educational level attained, occupational status, educational level of both parents and spouse, and interruptions in employment.

Of the 761 employed women interviewed, 250 live in Israel, 253 in the United States, and 258 in the Federal Republic of Germany. The women comprise three occupational groups: 255 work as stitchers in the needle trades, 251 as saleswomen and cashiers in retail trade, and 255 as office workers, ranging from typist to secretary. Table 3-1 presents the data.

There is one instance of possibly deviant cases. Fifty women in the sample had achieved supervisory status by the time that the interviews took place. In six of the nine subgroups studied, there were four or five such cases, yet in the U.S. industrial group there were none, in the Israeli retail group there were eight, and in the U.S. retail group, fourteen. My explanation for there being none in the U.S. industrial group is that even the lowest supervisory positions there are well

Table 3-1
Nationalities and Occupations of Sample

Occupation	Israel	United States	Germany	Total
Industry	85	86	84	255
Retail trade	82	84	85	251
Office	83	83	89	255
Total	250	253	258	761

differentiated from the rank and file, since these people do not belong to the union. As to the larger number of women with supervisory functions in the Israeli and American retail groups, the reason may be the practice of assigning a head of department to even the smallest department in a store. Indeed in Germany, such a position is usually given to a senior saleswoman, who is responsible to a department head.

I have drawn general conclusions from the study, although I have not tested my samples for randomness. (I suspect some deviation from randomness because of the choice of location and the limitation to work places whose managements had granted permission to study them, as well as the limitation of the interviews to the employees who had consented to be interviewed.) I assume, nevertheless, that the localities are representative for the selected branches and the conditions there are slightly above average. I assume, further, that some of the conditions in those work places to which I gained entry were deemed by their management as better than average or that some showed more concern for the conditions of their employees than average, although in some other work places the management was rather indifferent. Finally, I realize that employees who consented to be interviewed did so for diverse motives. I made some effort to maintain a broad age distribution for each work place in the occupational group studied. Thus, the average age of each group differs; the lowest is in Israeli industry, where 29 percent are in the lowest age group (sixteen to twenty-five years old) and the highest is in U.S. industry, where 36 percent are in the next to the highest age group (forty-six to fifty-five years old).

Israeli industry (Group 0) is the youngest group and has the largest percentage of unmarried women of the nine groups (table A-1). The reasons for this are as follows. The old needle trade plants, which were located in or near Tel Aviv, have transferred most of their sewing and stitching operations to Arab and Druze villages and keep in their central locations only small nuclei of older employees, who usually reside near the plant. In these locations, age is usually high, and the few new recruits are young relatives who are not representative of the city population. The average urban woman worker refuses to accept the low wages and poor physical conditions offered here if she has any choice. The newer needle trade plants, which are no more than eleven years old, were opened in development towns and in small towns where the general level of education for women is elementary or elementary plus a little secondary vocational. These women have a very small range of choice of work place and kind of employment. Additional sources for young, cheap, female labor are the cooperative small-holder farming villages, whose members are of Oriental origin, whose educational level is usually below average, and whose marriage age is also below average. Between completing elementary school (at age fifteen or sixteen) and marriage (at age eighteen), the custom is to work in a local factory. Therefore, the women production workers in these new plants are overwhelmingly young. There is also a group of older women stitchers in development towns, but they were excluded from interviewing by the decision to exclude members of clear-cut subcultures who are likely to have attitudes that differ considerably from those of the national culture. Representatives from a group of older recent-immigrant women from Soviet Georgia who do not yet speak Hebrew and who live in an extreme patriarchal family system were therefore excluded from the sample. Also excluded were Israeli Arab and Druze women and kibbutz women from the Israeli sample, southern black women and recent Portuguese immigrants from the U.S. sample, and guest workers (nationals of other countries) from the German sample.

The second youngest group is Israeli office women workers (Group 2), with only 20 percent of the group thirty-six years old and over; of these, 41 percent were unmarried. Age is not always exactly concomitant with marital status and number of children, however. The U.S. group of office workers, for example, has a higher percentage of unmarried women, and the groups of U.S. retail and office workers have a higher percentage of childless workers.

An explanation for the relatively low age of the Israeli office workers is the need for a high degree of Hebrew literacy, the higher age groups comprise a higher proportion of recent immigrants who lack this specific skill. By contrast, in the group of Israeli retail workers, the age distribution is most even among the Israeli groups, since the linguistic proficiency required here is different. There is less need for a knowledge of written Hebrew, whereas the proficiency in both a foreign—especially European—language and arithmetic skills are in demand. Both skills characterize women in the middle age group, especially immigrants from Europe.

The oldest of the three groups in the United States is that of the industrial workers; 38 percent are in the age group thirty-six to forty-five and nearly 70 percent are thirty-six and over. Three factors are responsible. First is the traditional stability of this population. Second, a considerable number of these women do not stop working (or stop only briefly) when they have children. Third, in some of the work places, management reported difficulties in recruiting young workers. There is an obvious divergence between places where management reported that working mothers bring their daughters to work and those that find no young recruits.

Among U.S. retail workers, the average age is lower than in the other two national groups. Perhaps the high level of unemployment in the United States brings young women with a relatively high level of education into retail jobs; they may hope to stay there only temporarily until they find a more suitable job but end up remaining longer than they expected.

In the U.S. office group, only 20.4 percent of the women are age thirty-six and older. Most of these jobs—particularly those above the lowest level—are held by women with a partial or complete college education; 68.7 percent of these women have thirteen or more years of formal education.

The age distribution of the German industrial group (Group 6) is nearest to a gradually decreasing distribution; 33.3 percent are in the sixteen to twenty-five age group, 25 percent in the twenty-six to thirty-five age group, 22.6 percent in the thirty-six to forty-five age group, 15.5 percent in the forty-six to fifty-five age group, and 3.6 percent in the fifty-six and over age group. These statistics indicate a relatively stable industrial population that has become increasingly feminized. In the 1950s and earlier, many more men than women were employed in the ready-made clothing industry, working in stitching and sewing, and their work was more skilled and tailor-like. Today, such work is deskilled, except for the older tailors still kept in the industry, and feminized. The ready-made clothing industry in Germany before World War II centered on men's clothing; a large portion of women's and children's clothing was made by women dressmakers. In Germany, too, because of the relatively low wages and relatively unattractive conditions, this industry reaches out to relatively more rural regions where the local female population has a much smaller range of choice of employment.

The largest age group of German retail workers—65.3 percent—is between twenty-six and forty-five. The reason seems to be that the German retail trade more often uses a work week that is shorter than the standard eight hours a day, which makes it easier for mothers of school-age children to work.

Office workers in Germany comprise a group of relatively fewer young people, with a slowly declining number of women of higher age groups; 27 percent are in the age group forty-six and over. Whereas in Israel the greatest group of older women is in retail trade and in the United States it is in industry, here it is in office work.

The relatively small number of women fifty-six years of age and older in all groups except U.S. industry is explained by the fact that the official pension age for women—sixty—is lower than for men in these national and occupational groups and that early retirement is fairly common and readily attainable from the age of fifty-five onward, especially for reasons of health. The fact that the highest concentration of older women is in U.S. industry is explained by the fact that in this group pension funds are held by one of the two unions; in order to qualify for a full pension, a woman has to be a paid-up member for twenty years. Because of interruptions in her work life or of periods of working in nonunion shops or in those organized by the other union, many women have to work until they are sixty and over in order to qualify.

Marital Status

I divided the population into the following categories: unmarried, married, living with male friend or fiancé, divorced, separated, and widowed. (See tables A-2 and A-3.) In the entire sample, 30.4 percent are unmarried, 53.1 percent are married, 9.2 percent are divorced, 5.1 percent are widowed, 1.2 percent are separated, and 1.1 percent are living with a friend or fiancé. In the questionnaire, I did not include the category "living with a friend" so as to avoid embarrassment. To my surprise, eight young interviewees volunteered the information that they belonged to this category. It may, of course, include many more interviewees now classified as unmarried, separated, or divorced. It reflects the state of the prevalent sexual norms much more than the state of the prevalent marital practices.

The proportion of unmarried women in the sample is not equal in all nine groups. In four groups—0, 3, 4, and 5—40 percent or more are unmarried. This high percentage is easily explained by the fact that these groups have the highest percentages of women up to twenty-five years old. Only for one of them is the high rate not so easily explained. Group 4 (U.S. retail) has only 36.9 percent in the youngest age group, compared with from 45.8 percent to 58.8 percent in the other three groups. The peculiarity is that Group 4 includes more women age twenty-six and over who are not yet married and also a larger group of divorced women than most of the other groups (except for Group 8, German office, which has a considerably higher age composition).

The percentage of divorced and separated women is low in all industrial groups—in Israel apparently because the group is so young and in the United States and Germany because these groups there have a high percentage of Roman Catholics. (I had no item in the questionnaire about religious affiliation, but this information can be deduced from the high proportion of first- or second-generation Portuguese and Italians among the U.S. groups and from the preponderance of Roman Catholics in the population of Aschaffenburg and especially of the rural area to the east of this town where most of the members of the German industrial group live.) Groups 2 and 5 (Israeli and U.S. office), whose age composition is very similar and very young, include more divorced women than the industrial groups—6 percent in Group 2 and 8.4 percent in Group 5, which also has three separated women. The number of divorced women is considerable in Groups 4, 7, and 8 ranging from 12.9 percent in the German retail group to over 20 percent in the German office group. Only Group 1 (Israeli retail) has a large number of widows. The group includes a considerable number of middle-class women who entered employment rather late in life or reentered it after a rather long absence.

Age at Marriage

The figures concerning the distribution of those ever married among the nine subgroups into those married before eighteen, between nineteen and twenty-one, between twenty-two and twenty-five, and twenty-six and over reflects the tendency in the recent past of members of the groups toward early or late marriage. The very young members of the groups are obviously excluded from the ever-married category and may reflect newer dispositions. It is generally held that very early marriage tends to limit a woman's growth, both educationally and professionally. Our sample shows a concentration of early marriage—61.6 percent were married by age twenty-two—but indicates neither agreement nor refutation of this supposition. Admittedly, the groups with a higher educational level are also those that have relatively fewer women married while teenagers, yet the distribution of all women married between the age of nineteen and twenty-two is even.

Number of Children

Almost half of the women in the sample (48.9 percent) have no children, although only 30.4 percent are unmarried and our sample also includes a small number of unmarried mothers (table A-4). These data show that there is a larger percentage of childless women in the labor force than in the population at large. The percentage of childless women varies from 71 percent in Group 5 (U.S. office) to only 23.3 percent in Group 3 (U.S. industry). In the overall study, 18.3 percent have one child, 21.7 percent have two children, 6.3 percent have three children, and 4.9 percent have four or more children. Two groups deviate considerably from this average: 52.4 percent of Group 1 (Israeli retail) and 38.4 percent of Group 3 (U.S. industry) have two children.

If we subtract the number of childless women from the sample total, we will see that the average number of children per mother is slightly above two children for five groups. Only in Group 4 (U.S. retail) is it as high as 2.9 children per mother. Only 85 of the 389 mothers in the sample—21.85 percent of mothers and 11 percent of all the women in the sample—have more than two children. Only Group 4 has as many mothers with three or more children than with one or two children. Therefore, with this one exception, the norm is two children for the three national groups.

The order of groups by the number of children per married woman is this: Groups 1, 4, 3, 6, 0, 7, 5, 2, and 8. Group 1 (Israeli retail) has almost two children per married woman and Group 8 (German office) has one per married woman. The order of the groups by the number of children at home at the time of the interview is somewhat different: Groups 4, 1, 2, 0, 3, 6, 7, 5, and 8. Group 4 (U.S. retail) has little less than one child per married woman, and Group 8 (German office) has just over one child at home per two married women. The change of order indicates that Group 4 (U.S. retail) contains the highest number of mothers of large families. The order of the groups with preschoolers (children under five years old) is still different: 6, 0, 2, 1, 7, 8, 4, 5, and 3. Group 6 (German industry) has over one preschooler per three married women, and Group 3 (U.S. industry) has one preschooler for twenty married women. (See table A-5.)

The total number of children per national group shows that the U.S. sample has the highest birthrate and the German, the lowest. The higher number of children at home reflects both the presence of larger families and the fact that women's careers are interrupted less, especially in the three industrial groups, in which the number of children at home is largest next to Group 4 (U.S. retail). The presence of preschoolers reflects the availability of child-care arrangements of different kinds during working hours (table A-6). This does not mean that the situation regarding the care of babies and infants is satisfactory in Israel. Most Israeli crèches do not take infants before the age of six months, and in these there are not sufficient places. Furthermore, only a minority of employers pay part or all of the expenses of day care for its women employees. Only employed mothers with relatively high salaries can afford to employ nursemaids. The institution of a day mother (a woman who has received some basic training in child care and looks after a small number of infants in her own home) is not common in Israel. The child care reported by the women in the Israeli sample shows that they neither use more modern kinds of child care than the women in the other two national groups nor interrupt their employment careers less during the infancy of their children. (See table A-7.) Therefore, the relatively greater number of children for the industrial and the office groups of the Israeli sample seems more likely to be a reflection of the relatively higher birthrate in the 1970s among younger Israeli women than among American or German women, whose birthrate has recently declined.

Employed Mothers of Young Children

The percentage of mothers in each of the nine groups deviates considerably from the 51 percent average of mothers in the entire sample (table A-8). It is as low as 28.9 percent in Group 5 (U.S. office) and as high as 76.7 percent in Group 3 (U.S. industry). The percentage of mothers in a group does not indicate the extent to which mothers carry a double burden of job and home responsibilities and are in need of child-care services during their work careers. A considerable number of the mothers stayed outside the labor market as long as at least one of their children was under ten years of age. Assuming that most children ten years old or older are looked after for a considerable part of the day by public educational institutions and can manage independently for the rest of their mothers' workday, the study of child care for employed mothers whose children were not below the age of ten during the period of employment is not really to the point. Therefore I have recorded how many women in the sample were employed while having at least one child under ten at home (table A-8).

About half of the mothers in four of the groups and about 70 percent of those in two other groups went to work in spite of the problems of arranging for the care of young children during their absence from home and in spite of the double burden of the domestic work involved in providing services for one or more young children. Two groups deviate. In Group 3 (U.S. industry), the rate of intensity of participation in the labor force is as high as 95.4 percent, and in Group 1 (Israeli retail), it is as low as 38.1 percent. In all three national samples, the participation rate of the retail group is the lowest of the three occupational groups, but in the German sample the difference is insignificant.

In none of the three national samples is it the norm for married women to interrupt their employment for ten to fifteen years upon the birth of their first child, as Myrdal and Klein posited. In the United States and in the Federal Republic of Germany, the opposite pattern of employment—significantly shorter interruption of work—is equally high (82.7 percent), and in Israel it is lower (67.3 percent). These statistics are in keeping with the generally lower labor force participation rate of Israeli women as compared with the Americans and the West Germans.

In examining the factors that are likely to cause lower intensity of participation in the labor force in retail trade, it seems likely that wherever saleswomen are obliged to work a long workday (interrupted by a long midday closing), or very irregular hours, it is very difficult for the mothers of young children to be in the retail trades. Therefore, retail jobs in such places attract either women who have no child-care obligations or who no longer have them.

Immigrant Status and Ethnicity

Any woman who showed difficulties in understanding and speaking the national language was omitted from the sample, a provision that excluded most recent immigrants. Recent immigrants were also affected by the provision excluding members of subcultures. Nevertheless, immigrants were not totally left out of the sample because they comprise a significant part of the populations under study. As U.S. studies have shown, immigrants tend to occupy the lower levels of the occupational ladder and to rise only with time, especially in the second generation: this has become an accepted expectation. The questionnaire therefore included an item about native versus immigrant status. The results are shown in table 3-2. The data indicate that only the U.S. sample behaves as expected. The German sample is the reverse of the expected, and the Israeli sample shows the expected characteristic when we compare industry or retail workers with office workers.

The expectation can be revised to hold that immigrants from favored countries need not conform to that view and that second-generation immigrants from less-favored countries are still at a disadvantage. For Israel, the favored

Table 3-2

Percentage of Immigrants According to National and Occupational Groups

Occupational Group	Israel	United States	Germany
Industry	60	20	8
Retail	72	11	19
Office	29	5	22

countries are Europe and America; for the United States, they are Western Europe and Canada; and for Germany, any German-speaking population in Europe. The less-favored countries for Israel are Asia and Africa; for the United States, any countries other than the favored ones; and for Germany any non-German-speaking populations. Table 3-3 shows the percentage of women in the sample who are either native born with a father from a less-favored country or are themselves from a less-favored country. (The details are in table A-9.)

In Israel, there is a very pronounced positive correlation between occupational status and ethnic origin. Industry overwhelmingly recruits either first-generation or second-generation girls or women of Afro-Asian origin. In retail work, there are a number of middle-aged women who have immigrated from Western, especially European, countries. Finally, the Israeli office group is composed overwhelmingly of young native-born women whose fathers have come from favored countries.

In the United States in the industrial group, the percentage of immigrants is by far higher than in the two other groups, and nearly all of them are immigrants from less-favored countries. In addition, 31 percent of the native-born members of this group are daughters of immigrants from less-favored countries, mainly Italy and Portugal. This trend is also visible in the retail and office groups, though it is less pronounced; the great majority are third-generation Americans.

In the German sample, the situation is contrary to the one that might be expected. The population working in the needle trades is mostly from small towns or rural areas and is established. The other two groups comprise members of the mobile city population and therefore also refugees who came to West

Table 3-3

Percentage of Women Who Are Native Born with a Father from a Less-favored Country or Are Immigrants from a Less-favored Country

Occupational Group	Israel	United States	Germany
Industry	79	48	2
Retail	35	17	6
Office	38	14	8

Germany after World War II, mainly from areas previously under German rule or from East Germany. They had few or no language or educational handicaps as compared with the indigenous population.

Years of Employment at Current Work Place

The answers to the question concerning length of employment at the current work place tell us something about the degree of stability of the employment of women in the sample. If we exclude from the sample all employees under nineteen and on their first job, a population of employed women whose length of current employment cannot as yet indicate what tendency they have toward stability, these data might be more representative. But even without this omission, the data indicate different tendencies in the different groups, both national and occupational. (For more detail, see table A-10.)

The averages for the whole sample of nine groups are: worked up to one year at the current job, 25.6 percent; worked over one and up to five years at the current job, 33.8 percent; worked over five and up to ten years at the current job, 19.8 percent; worked over ten and up to twenty years at the current job, 15.9 percent; and worked over twenty years at the current job, 4.9 percent. The deviations of the national groups from this average are displayed in table 3-4. They show clearly that the German sample is the most stable.

Three groups—0 (Israeli industry), 4 (U.S. retail), and 5 (U.S. office)—have a disproportionately large concentration of women working under one year at the current job; these are also the groups with large numbers of employees under the age of twenty-five, but there is no complete positive correlation between these two characteristics. Thus, Group 5 has the largest percentage working in the same job under one year—nearly half of the group—yet it has only the third largest percentage of employees under the age of twenty-five.

An entirely different profile is apparent in Groups 3 and 6 (U.S. and German industry, respectively). Group 6 has a normal distribution of length of work in the current job; only 10.7 percent have worked under one year and 23.8

Table 3-4
Deviations of National Groups from Average Years Employed at Current Work Place

Years Worked	Israel	United States	Germany
0-1	+7.5	+6.7	−4.5
1-5	−2.5	+1	+1.3
5-10	+0.8	−9.6	+7.6
10-20	−5.5	+1.2	+4.9
20 or more	−1.3	+0.6	+0.6

percent, between ten and twenty years. At the other end of the scale is Group 3, which shows signs of an aging population and where management finds recruiting new employees difficult. In this group, 51 percent of the employees have worked over ten years in the same work place and only 7 percent under one year. Group 3 is also the only one with a large proportion of women—12.8 percent—who have worked over twenty years.

Years of Schooling

Years of schooling are defined as full-time attendance at any school, vocational school, or college. I did not count the standard three years' attendance (of one day per week) in the schools that working youth in Germany and Israel under the age of seventeen or eighteen must complete after leaving the basic obligatory schooling. (These schools are known in the German Federal Republic as *Berufsschule* and in Israel as apprenticeship schools.) Whenever the full course at this kind of school for apprentices had been completed, this was recorded and counted as vocational training.

The educational systems of the three countries differ from each other. In Israel at the time of the interviews, obligatory and free schooling began at age five with one year of obligatory kindergarten and continued through nine years of elementary school. In parts of the country, a tenth year was also free but not obligatory. School attendance during the final years is not fully enforced, especially in areas where the population is of Afro-Asian origin. Legally, youngsters under age eighteen may not be employed for more than seven hours a day, five days a week, and are required to attend an apprenticeship school one day a week in order to improve the level of their general education and to receive specialized training in one of the trades. Apparently, many young employed girls do not attend regularly but work a full six-day, forty-five-hour week. On the other hand, attendance at a vocational high school, usually up to age sixteen or seventeen, has become much more common for urban girls in the lower socioeconomic strata. Most of these schools are not coeducational and train mainly for such typical women's occupations as domestic science, sewing, hairdressing, and typing. The Israeli middle classes consider a full twelve-year secondary schooling with matriculation as the desirable norm for boys and girls alike, in spite of the relatively high cost of this education, and in fact, more girls than boys complete academic high schools and pass the final examinations. The high school leaving certificate is necessary not only for higher education but also as the key for training for the semiprofessions and the newer technical occupations.

Of the women who have immigrated to Israel after school age, those coming from Middle Eastern countries are often illiterate or almost illiterate, and they tend to remain so. But they seldom enter employment, and when they do, they usually work as domestics, or as cleaning workers in offices, stores, restaurants, and hotels. Some of the older immigrants from Europe attended secondary schools, but their education was affected by World War II, the holocaust, and the aftermath. If, after immigrating, they did not acquire a good knowledge of Hebrew and did not retrain for their desired occupation under new circumstances but became housewives for a longer time, then their schooling and skills became rather useless.

In the United States, all children can attend twelve years of secondary education without fees or special entrance examinations. Employment becomes legal only at age sixteen; a special permit is needed for temporary or part-time employment at a younger age. Therefore, school attendance for ten years has become almost universal. Although completing the entire twelve years of high school and graduating are not obligatory, graduation has been the accepted norm since the end of World War II for the stable industrial working class. For the middle classes, the desired educational norm for both sons and daughters has become a college education. Thus for younger Americans, the average level of education is now over twelve years. There are, of course, older Americans in the labor market who have attended only eight years of grade school, and some immigrants in our sample had only four years of schooling.

In the Federal Republic of Germany, obligatory education of nine years, usually followed by an apprenticeship and attendance at an appropriate *Berufsschule,* is still the norm for most young people. A minority attend school for an additional tenth year and pass examinations for the *Mittlere Reife* or attend a *Fachschule;* another minority finish the twelve to thirteen grades of academic secondary school, take the *Abitur* and usually attend a university. The system of vocational training in the Federal Republic of Germany is still based largely on apprenticeship. This applies not only to the skilled crafts and industrial skilled trades—as in Israel and the United States—but also to mass-production, commercial, and even insurance and banking jobs. (Table A-11 shows the complete educational data for all nine subgroups.)

In all three national samples, an obvious grading of educational level for the three occupational groups clearly exists. This grading is not very steep in Israel. In the United States, there exists a considerable difference between the industrial and the retail groups but not between the retail and the office groups. In the German sample, the difference between the industrial and the retail groups is not very large, but it is still significant. That not one woman in the industrial group had completed secondary schooling points to a rather unitary utilitarian class character of their education. In the retail group, 9.4 percent completed twelve years or more of schooling, and in the office group, 32.6 percent did. The office group includes a number of women who came from middle-class families.

The Israeli group has the widest spread in the three occupational groups, ranging from near illiteracy to college. Of the Israeli sample, 38 percent have completed twelve years of schooling, which is remarkable for a country where secondary schooling was neither obligatory nor free until fall 1978. Our sample is in accord with recent statistical findings about the relatively high educational level of employed women in Israel. On the average, their educational level is higher than that of employed men by more than one year of schooling.

The U.S. group has the highest level of formal education. Because of its higher age and its ethnic characteristics, our American industrial sample has an educational level considerably lower than that of the other two occupational groups. A considerable proportion—26.7 percent—had only grade school education, and 47.7 percent had nine to eleven years of schooling. Yet even in this group, 25.6 percent had finished high school, compared with only 14.1 percent in the Israeli industrial group and none in the German industrial group. Six women in this group had at least one year of college as compared with one in the Israeli industrial group and none in the German industrial group. In both the U.S. retail and office groups, the level of education is higher by far than in any other group: 85.7 percent of the retail group finished high school and 47.6 percent had some college; 98.8 percent of the office group finished high school and 68.7 percent had some college. Because 92 percent of the two groups had a full secondary education and more, it is to be expected that the aspirations and intellectual skills of most members of this group go beyond the execution of routine functions. Because of these characteristics, we should investigate whether management in retail and office work organizations have taken account of this situation and enriched the jobs of these women, whether these women are less satisfied with routine jobs, whether they put more emphasis on the content of their jobs, whether these aspects matter to them, and whether they are interested in advancement to more challenging jobs.

In the German group, only 9.4 percent of the women working in retail have slightly more schooling than the low upper limit of schooling of the industrial group. In addition, 57 percent of the entire German group had completed a formal course of vocational training of some kind, compared with 32.4 percent in the entire Israeli group and only 15 percent in the entire U.S. group.

Vocational Training and Its Use

The German system of early and thorough preparation for a specific occupation might seem more functional than a school system that gives young women a nonspecific liberal education except that 39 percent of those who have completed a vocational training course do not make use of the specific skills for which they have been trained. Indeed, 34 percent of the entire sample have completed such courses, yet only 18 percent make use of them (table A-12).

The situation concerning training is especially unfavorable in all three industrial groups and in the Israeli retail group. In these groups, more of those who have completed training make no use of it than do. By contrast, the record of the German retail and office groups is impressive; the great majority of those who have training are also using it. The obvious explanation for this contrast (beyond the difference between national systems of education) is that the systematic vocational training for production jobs in the needle trade industry is usually fictitious. Most of the girls who take a two-year course in sewing or in dressmaking in a vocational school and who enter industry do not use these acquired skills at all, not even progressively. Currently, there is no progressive occupational or skill ladder that might lead from the operation of an industrial sewing machine to the use of such skills as cutting and designing. Even the more limited skills acquired in the German shortened—one and a half years—apprenticeship (*Anlehre*), the use of different kinds of machinery and accessories common to the needle trade industry, are used only by a minority of women production workers. The great majority work each at one machine and do not rotate. The position of a woman who regularly stands in for absentee operators, which exists in nearly every large plant, is not made attractive enough, either by added pay or by higher status, for more women workers to invest the additional effort it requires, especially since it does not lead to a better position. In addition, quite a few of the women who work in industry have completed training (either in a vocational school or during apprenticeship) in hairdressing, domestic science, or millinery, which is useless. After training, they realize that the hours of work demanded in hairdressing are incompatible with their domestic duties and that millinery is a dying occupation. As to domestic science, it is hardly more than training for private household jobs, which have been increasingly unpopular since World War II.

The relatively small number of women who have completed vocational training and are using it within the retail and office groups, both in Israel and in the United States, reflects the situation in these countries, where little systematic and specific preparation for these jobs is offered except for relatively brief courses in bookkeeping for cashiers or in typing for office workers.

Vocational Training on the Job

The overwhelming majority of the interviewees—76.9 percent—have received no vocational training since they started work in their current work place or had been trained for a period of less than one week. Training of more than a week was received by 23.1 percent of the entire sample. Germany has the lowest percentage (19.4), Israel is second (23.6 percent), and the United States has the highest (26.5 percent). These data are clearly inversely correlated with vocational training not on the job. This does not mean that the inverse correlation holds also when the sample is split nine ways; it does not. (See table A-13.) The total may be somewhat misleading, since one woman may be recorded twice, and since in Israel, more so in the United States, young women acquire in high school the basic arithmetic, typing, and language skills they need in retail and in office work.

Occupational Status Compared with Father's

The occupational status ranks used here are blue collar, sales, white collar (including highly skilled and small independent blue collar), and managerial and professional. The occupation of housewife was left outside the scale, although two husbands and one father were house husbands. The occupations of the interviewees were then correlated with those of their fathers. The ranking of occupations used makes it impossible for my interviewees in industry to have attained positions higher than their fathers have, except when the former are supervisors or trainers and the latter are rank-and-file blue collar workers. It also makes it impossible for female retail workers to have achieved the same status as their fathers except when the fathers were salesmen, which is rare in the three countries studied. (Table A-14 presents data on father's occupation and table A-15 presents the correlation.)

In the entire sample, 30.6 percent are occupationally downward mobile in comparison with their fathers, 38.3 percent are equal to their fathers, and 31.0 percent are upward mobile in comparison with their fathers. The most conspicuous fact is that in all three countries, the industrial groups show a high degree of continuity: most blue-collar interviewees are blue-collar daughters. The most conspicuous groups regarding upward mobility are two in which over half are upward mobile: Group 7 (German retail) with 60.7 percent being daughters of blue-collar workers, and Group 5 (U.S. office) with 53.7 upward mobile.

Occupational Status Compared with Husband's

Our sample here is women who were ever married: 504 interviewees. The fact that there are few men sales people is conspicuous. Overall, 36.3 percent of the wives have an occupational status below that of their husbands, 39.7 percent are equal to them, and 24 percent are above them (table A-16). This is quite remarkable because it indicates that the supposition no longer holds that the norm is for wives to have an occupational status lower than their husbands'. Since most members of Group 0 (Israeli industry) are unmarried, it is hardly a reliable sample, yet all three industrial groups show a high level of social stability. The most upwardly mobile group in all three countries is retail, evidently because retail jobs are considered suitable for any working-class women who possess the necessary basic skills. Retail jobs are also deemed suitable for middle-class women, of course, even without any specific vocational training.

Occupational Status Compared with Mother's

Mothers of 69.2 percent of the entire sample were reported as housewives. Correlating occupations thereby becomes pointless. In addition, some interviewees were disposed to ignore any occupation that their mothers had held in their own youth. Our interviewers made some effort, with some measure of success, to draw attention to this possible omission and to elicit information on very early employment of mothers unless it had been for periods that were too short. (Complete data appear in table A-17.)

The overall picture is that 69.2 percent of the mothers were housewives, 14.9 percent blue collar, 1.2 percent saleswomen, 9.5 percent white collar, and 5.2 percent managerial or professional. The U.S. sample, surprisingly, has the highest percentage of economically active mothers in all groups, in spite of the great age difference between the older Group 3 and the two younger Groups 4 and 5; at least 44 percent of mothers were employed. In the German sample, only 26.75 percent of mothers were employed, and for the Israeli sample, the figure is as low as 20 percent.

It is generally assumed that in Europe, the employment in industry of the wives and daughters of industrial workers has been much wider spread and generally accepted than in the United States. It is further assumed that the wages of industrial workers there were sufficient for raising a family and that, until World War II, wives of steadily employed blue-collar workers tended to be employed only sporadically. Our data, however, indicate that this supposition is not true, at least for the needle trade industry in the 1940s and possibly earlier. The needle trade is the continuation of the well-known textile workers' communities for which the generalization has never held. Almost all employed mothers of our blue-collar workers were blue-collar workers themselves. The other, much younger, U.S. groups reflect the doubling of labor-force participation among young women between the 1940s and the 1960s.

Group 6 (German industry) also fails to reflect the situation typical among German blue-collar workers. It has the highest percentage—85.4 percent—of mothers who were housewives. The reason is that these women come from small-town and rural families that have no tradition of industrial work for wives. Most of these mothers were not solely housewives; more likely they were also unpaid workers in family farms, shops, or workshops.

Educational Level Compared with Mother's

An additional measure of social mobility is the comparison of educational levels between generations. The figures for the entire sample show that 6.2 percent have less schooling than their mothers, 32.1 percent have the same, and 61.7 percent have more. This picture is explained by the fact that in both Germany and Israel the level of compulsory education was raised just at the right moment to be reflected in our statistics for the younger members of our sample. Four groups have exceptionally high numbers of educationally upward mobile: 0 (Israeli industry) with 78.1 percent, 3 (U.S. industry) with 77.5 percent, 2 (Israeli office) with 73.1 percent, and 8 (German office) with 72.2 percent. The two industrial groups include a large number of daughters of immigrants from countries with low educational levels, particularly for women, and the two office groups include primarily middle-class women whose education was much less disturbed by large-scale political events than was that of their mothers.

Health

The interviewees were asked to evaluate their own state of health as very good, medium, or not so good and to tell whether they suffer from any of thirteen symptoms listed in the questionnaire. When an answer was in the affirmative, they were also asked whether they thought that their ailment was caused by their work, aggravated by it, had nothing to do with it, or was improved by it.

The distribution of the answers to the general question about state of health appears in table A-18. Sixty-six percent of the sample answered "very good," 30 percent "medium," and a mere 3.4 percent "not so good." But many who described their health as very good also listed several ailments (in the same way that many who described themselves as satisfied with their job also said that they would not want their daughters to work in such a job). Just as there is a strong tendency to answer affirmatively to direct questions about satisfaction with work, marriage, or other major areas of life, so there is a tendency to answer affirmatively to direct questions about one's well being. In all three languages, the question, "How are you?" is a standard formula of daily polite conversation eliciting, nearly as a reflex, the affirmative answer, "Thank you, very well." Our question was intentionally worded differently, but nevertheless the norm carried over, and more women answered "very good" than really consider themselves to be in very good health.

Even taking the answers to the direct question about health at their face value, there were significant variations among the different groups. The answers "medium" or "not so good" are both to be understood as expressions of a negative evaluation or assessment of one's health. The data show a decisive rise in negative responses to questions about health on a national scale, from U.S. to Israel to Germany, and a decline in the negative responses on the occupational scale from industry to retail to office. (See tables A-19 and A-20.) The difference in the self-evaluation regarding health between the U.S. and the German sample is extreme. Since it is unlikely that the objective state of health of the German sample is so much inferior to that of the U.S. sample, the variance has to be ascribed to the difference in norms in the two national cultures. It could be argued, of course, that the variance in age differences caused the responses, but this explanation is not valid. Among the nine groups, the one with the highest average age—Group 3 (U.S. industry—had 70.9 percent positive responses, and the group with the lowest average age—Group 0 (Israeli industry—had only 64.7 percent. Group 6 (German industry), whose average age is the lowest among the German groups, had only 38.1 percent positive responses. (See table A-21.)

The difference among the three occupational groups is conspicuous. We may assume that this is the outcome of two factors: first, physical conditions are worst in industry and best in offices; second, the demands on the worker's body, senses, and nerves are highest in industry and lowest in offices.

There is a strong correlation between the perceived state of health of the interviewees and their age; generally health is reported as declining with age (see table A-21). For example, in the group of those under age twenty-six, 78 percent answered "very good," and only 56.9 percent of those between fifty-six and sixty-five answered in this way. Yet the decline is not even. The group aged thirty-six to forty-five perceives its state of health the most negatively, more so than the two older groups; only 50.7 percent answered "very good," 42.1 percent "medium," and 7.1 percent "not so good." The data about different symptoms or ailments indicate that this age group may suffer from relatively early symptoms of menopause; the highest percentage of them in the sample reported suffering from nervousness, tired eyes, backache, stomach and digestive problems, abnormal blood pressure, and feminine complaints. It is also likely that this age group suffers from the combined effect of the double burden of employment and a still considerable domestic and child-care work load and the onset of menopause.

The details of the complaints are presented in table A-22. With the exception of tired eyes and skin trouble, the German sample has the highest frequency of complaints of all eleven ailments. And excluding headaches, tired eyes and painful legs, they also have the highest frequency of those perceiving their condition as having been caused or aggravated by their work.

An obvious explanation would be that this information has little to do with the objective state of health of the interviewees but is decisively influenced by national norms that either favor complaints about aches and pains or prescribe profession of excellent health. But this explanation is contradicted by the uniformity of a higher frequency of complaints about eleven of the ailments by the industrial workers in all three national samples. The exceptions, too, are rather uniform. Only in the case of varicose veins do the retail workers, many of whom are not allowed to sit down during working hours, complain more frequently than do the stitchers. In the case of hemorrhoids, more office workers connect this condition with their work, although more stitchers complain about it. More office workers complain about heart conditions than do stitchers. Finally, the same percentage of industrial and office workers report feminine complaints, but more stitchers consider them caused by their physically more demanding work.

Assuming that the information concerning the complaints serves as a valuable addition to the direct answer about the state of health, I have constructed from the interviewees' answers a composite variable, "health condition," classified by three levels: good (33.2 percent of the sample), medium (26.9 percent), and poor (39.8 percent). (See table A-23.) The decline of health with age is very apparent again.

When asked if they ever had a work accident, only 13.6 percent of the entire sample answered affirmatively. Obviously, the chance that an older person would have experienced such a mishap is greater. There is no difference among the three national groups, but among the occupational groups the difference is striking and illuminating. In both the industrial and the retail groups, 18.1 percent reported accidents. The most frequent were a needle through a finger or a mishap with ladders and heavy merchandise, respectively. The safer conditions in the office environment produced accidents for only 7.4 percent.

Domestic Work Load

The interviewees were asked how many hours they usually worked per week in their household and looking after their children. The interviewers helped by adding up hours routinely worked on weekdays and during weekends. The general tendency was to underestimate, by overlooking work performed in the morning before going out to work or on weekends.

Mean hours of domestic work load for the three national samples, the three occupational samples, and the nine groups are shown in table A-24. Table A-25 shows the distribution of women with light, medium, and heavy domestic work loads in the nine groups. The German sample has the highest average domestic work load in the nine groups, and the U.S. sample, the lightest. The three office groups are the least burdened in all three national samples. In the U.S. and in the German samples, the industrial groups are by far the most burdened. The reason for the deviation of the Israeli industrial group is that the overwhelming majority in this group are young unmarried women living with their parents. Only twenty-one women in this group have at least one child at home, yet twenty-seven have a heavy domestic work load.

The size of the average domestic work load of the women in the nine groups ranges from 12.7 weekly hours for Group 5 (U.S. office) to 23.8 hours for Group 6 (German industry). It could be argued that this difference may reflect simply the different composition of the groups' marital status. That is, unmarried women usually have a very small domestic work load, since they either run their own very small household or participate in their parents' household chores, or they may be free of it altogether. Whereas, in the socioeconomic strata to which the samples belong, there would hardly be a mother with at least one child living at home who would not have at least a medium-sized domestic work load. Nevertheless, the variation in average domestic work load is only partly explained this way.

I have compared the number of unmarried women in each group with the number of women in them who have low domestic work loads, and I have also compared the number of women with children at home in each group with the number of women in them with heavy domestic work loads. The comparison shows a high correlation, but not as high as the hypothesis in question suggests. Thus, in two groups—0 (Israeli industry) and 6 (German industry)—there are considerably more unmarried women than women with light domestic work loads, whereas Groups 3 (U.S. industry) and 5 (U.S. office) have considerably more women with light domestic work loads than unmarried women. Similarly, in three groups—0 (Israeli industry), 1 (Israeli retail), and 6 (German industry)— there are far more women with heavy domestic work loads than mothers with at least one child living at home. And there are six groups with more such mothers than women with heavy domestic loads; prominent among them are Groups 5 (American office) and 4 (American industry). The differences in average domestic load reported, therefore, seem to be a national characteristic no less than an occupational one. The average national domestic load is 16.4 hours for the United States, 17.7 for Israel, and 21.5 for Germany. The average domestic work load by occupational groups is 15.0 hours for office, 19.5 for retail, and 21.0 for industry.

Comparing each of the nine groups with the national average, as well as with the occupational average, and taking the marital status of individuals into account is instructive. In Israel, there are ten more unmarried women than women with low domestic loads and four more mothers than women with high work loads. Similarly, the U.S. sample has the least domestic work load both ways and the Israeli the most; in Germany, the rejected hypothesis—that domestic work load relates to marital status—works well enough on the national average.

The same comparison can be made for occupational groups. Clearly, the difference between office workers and the rest of the population in domestic work load is most pronounced even after taking into consideration the fact that generally marriage and children increase a woman's domestic work load. Even between the retail and the industrial groups, there is a significant difference.

The higher domestic work load of the German sample might be explained as the result of the high housekeeping standards accepted in Germany. Similarly, the lower domestic work load of the U.S. sample may be attributed to the widespread use there of labor-saving devices and the prevalence of the use of semiprepared or even restaurant food.

Finally, high domestic work load correlates with poor health. (See table A-26.) The heavier the domestic work load, the poorer the state of health, both as reported in the response to the direct question and in the detailed composite response.

Work Career

Age at Start of Employment

Age at start of employment of the interviewees largely complements the length of schooling. The correlation is not exact, however, since it is possible to avoid both schooling and a job (say, as an unpaid family worker), and since it is possible to both hold a job and attend school.

Groups 4 and 5 (U.S. retail and office) have a considerable overlap of schooling and job. This is explained by the fact that in the United States all but the lowest socioeconomic strata accept the norm of a full high school education and most seek employment during the long summer vacation from age sixteen to the end of their schooling. More than 15 percent of the entire sample reported that they entered the job market at the age of fourteen or below; these were often older women (and in the United States, more often immigrants) who had never combined job and schooling (table A-27). The fact that the largest number of women in the sample started work between ages seventeen and twenty reflects the improving state of education for women.

Very few women in the sample entered the labor market after age thirty-one and after having raised their family. Those who did so are over fifty years of age.

Previous Jobs and Interruptions

The mean number of jobs, prior to and not counting the current job, is shown in table A-28. In the national samples, the Israeli group held an average of 1.4 jobs (1.3 excluding summer jobs); the American, 3.4 (2.6 excluding summer); and the German 2.1 (2.0 excluding summer). Among the occupational groups, those in the industrial sector held an average of 1.6 jobs (1.5 excluding summer); those in retail, 2.6 (2.3 excluding summer); and those in office, 2.7 (2.2 excluding summer).

The strikingly high rate of change of job in the United States is partly explained by the American custom of having a summer job during education from age sixteen up. In the retail group, over 25 percent of all previous jobs were summer employment and in the office group over 29 percent. But even if we ignore these data, the U.S. sample remains the most mobile. Perhaps the practice of temporary employment that is so widespread in the United States is not always consciously turned into a mode of preparing oneself for a career, yet it enables young people to acquire skills that help them familiarize themselves with the labor market, compare jobs, and rule out jobs they find unsuitable to their own temperament. (My overall impression is that, of the three national groups, the American working woman is by far the most sophisticated and occupationally mobile, over a broader spectrum of kinds of employment.)

Clearly, in all three countries, the industrial group is the most restricted in the range of previous employment experience.

The questionnaire divided the causes for leaving a job into family reasons and other reasons. Of the cases of leaving a job, 19 percent were reported as due to family reasons, and of these, 47 percent were related to motherhood and child care. The other family reasons included marriage and divorce, care of sick husband or parent, and in a few cases (twelve) husband's opposition to interviewee's employment. The other reasons were divided into change of residence location (which may indeed be a covert family reason), 12 percent; too heavy load, too distant workplace, or inconvenient hours (which may also be covert family reasons), 4 percent; personal reasons, including study, illness of interviewee, reduced economic need (the last item is often a covert family reason), 15 percent; economic reasons, such as dismissal from work, closing of workplace, or completion of a project (mainly projects employing student labor), 17 percent; and finally, the largest group, voluntary change of workplace, which means that the interviewee disliked her previous job, wanted a change, found a better job, or had other reasons (in the United States, forty-one women wanted to travel, and in Israel, seventeen girls were drafted into the army), 31 percent.

The chief significance of this category is that although declared family reasons are small in number (19 percent), they are the causes of the largest portion of absences from the job market. The average length of period of absence in each of the two groups of job interruption because of family reasons is over 4 3/4 years. Surprisingly, children take hardly more time on average than the rest of the family. The complete data are shown in table A-29.

Although the overt family reasons cover less than 20 percent of the interruptions, they cover 69 percent of the time of absence due to interruption. No doubt, ignoring such reasons like return to studies, which should really not be counted as interruptions at all, and adding the covert family reasons, the conclusion is inescapable that almost all of the prolonged interruptions are due to family reasons.

Absences for family reasons have been very protracted—nearly five years on the average. If this were representative, it would amount to the claim that hardly any woman in our sample was employed while having preschool children at home. This is not the case. Rather our sample belongs here to two distinct populations, only one of which is composed of women who interrupt their work career until their children are independent (that is, they need no supervision during the workday beyond the one provided by ordinary public schools). I separated all the cases of women who interrupted their work career for ten consecutive years or more; all of them did so for family reasons alone. The group data are shown in table A-30.

When these cases are excluded, the average interruption due to family reasons declines sharply (despite the relatively small number of women who have interrupted their work career for ten consecutive years or more) from 59.8 to 27.7 months. Of the seventy women who interrupted their work careers for ten consecutive years or more (their interruption lasted on the average for over fifteen years), most are in the retail sample, and they are almost evenly divided among the national groups, although the United States leads. These seventy women comprise 9 percent of the entire sample, 18 percent of the 389 mothers, 21 percent of the 330 women thirty-six years old and over, and 25 percent of the 282 ever-married women thirty-six years and over in this sample. Few have arranged their lives according to the pattern that Myrdal and Klein had expected, in 1956, to become universal.

Part-time Work

Although part-time work is supposed to be much more prevalent among employed women than among employed men, only 12.9 percent of the sample (ninety-eight women) work less than the full workday customary at the current work place. (Complete information is shown in table A-31.) These data may be not fully representative of the incidence of part-time work in the nine occupational groups, however. When I arranged for the interviews, I specified that I had no objections to the inclusion of part-time workers as long as part-time work was not a rare exception in their work place. Therefore, the data reflect the differences in the use of part-time employees by the three economic branches in the three countries.

The only U.S. sample in which part-time work plays a role is retail. Part-time shift work in supermarkets in particular, affords employment to mothers with three or more children at home. In the other two national groups, part-time employment plays a role in all three occupational groups, but it is significant only in retail, where management expects and uses it (often in conjunction with shift work) to staff counters in late afternoons on which late closing is practiced and on the sixth workday.

In Israel, the widespread practice of the prolonged midday closing of stores and banks makes managements employ extra part-time employees who work five or six hours a day. Since this divided workday causes full-time employees to be absent from home for too many hours, women with heavy and time-bound domestic obligations are usually constrained to work part time.

In the German retail trade, the managements of some department stores have instituted a system of flexible part-time work. Each saleswoman has an agreement about the minimum and maximum hours she works each month.

Many saleswomen, especially veterans, are dissatisfied with this arrangement: they prefer regular full-time employment.

Temporary Employment

I cannot claim that my data on temporary employment are representative. My specifications as to the suitability of temporary employees for interviewing were the same as for part-time employees. Eighty-two interviewees (10.8 percent of the sample) were temporarily employed. In the three groups—Group 5 (U.S. office), Group 6 (German industry), and Group 8 (German office)—temporary employment was rare.

I expected to find significant differences in the incidence of temporary employment among the younger employees and the older ones. I also expected to find more young employees in Israel being temporarily employed before being drafted into the army and more young vacation workers in all three national samples. I have separated the data for interviewees up to age twenty-three and those twenty-four and over. As many as 22 percent of the young group are temporary workers, however, of the bulk of the sample, only 6.5. percent are not regularly employed. In Israel, 33 percent of the young group are only temporarily employed. In industry, these are all unmarried women under age nineteen, who could be employed only temporarily because of the draft. Some of these predraft girls also tended to work temporarily in the retail trade or in offices, but because these girls most often had completed twelve years of schooling, the period between leaving school and the draft was much shorter for them, and the incidence of this kind of temporary employment was also much smaller. Some of the young temporarily employed in the Israeli office group are college students who have completed their military service. Students working temporarily in offices may also be among the older Israeli group because studies usually start at a considerably later age than in both other countries and because most students there are employed at least part time or temporarily.

In the other two national young groups, there is only one sizable group of temporarily employed workers, saleswomen in the American group (42.3 percent). These were students working during college winter vacation, which coincides with the peak sales season. Store managers are interested in this kind of temporary employment as a means of recruiting better-educated young women, a considerable number of whom subsequently become regularly employed. Among the older groups, there is only one other sizable group of temporarily employed: American industrial (14.1 percent). At the time of the interviewing, business in the manufacture of women's clothing was rather slack, and the management of some of these plants tried to reduce their permanent work force and to employ additional stitchers on a seasonal temporary basis only.

Advancement

Table A-32 sums up the information regarding the overall instances of job advancement versus stationary position and decline during the entire previous job careers and the present jobs of the women in the sample. It takes into account only improvement in job content or status (not in pay or fringe benefits) within each previous job as well as between any two previous jobs. Whenever instances of decline are more numerous than instances of progress in one and the same career, the career is considered declining.

Half of the interviewees (50.1 percent) are stationary, 5.1 percent have declined, and 44.8 percent have advanced. As to the distribution according to national groups, the U.S. sample has progressed the most and the Israeli the least. As to occupational groups, the office group has progressed the most and industry least. In three groups, over 50 percent have experienced progress in their work careers: Group 5 (U.S. office), 77.1 percent; Group 2 (Israeli office), 61.4 percent; and Group 4 (U.S. retail), 58.3 percent. These three groups also have had the most years of schooling.

Characteristics of the Job

The interviewees were requested to describe and evaluate the characteristics of their current jobs according to task characteristics or content of the job, and hygiene characteristics or working conditions. Several other items were included that are neither task nor hygiene characteristics: personal freedom on the job, including freedom of movement and communication, and evaluation of union performance in the present work place. By content or task characteristics one usually means: quality of product or service and skill needed; degree of variety; repetitiveness, speed, and strain; degree of autonomy; and degree of responsibility. By hygiene characteristics one usually means: material rewards, physical conditions, work hours, and social relations in the work place.

Together these two variables (task characteristics and hygiene characteristics) describe the current job of the interviewee. These variables, as well as the majority of the variables expressing the interviewee's work attitudes, will be structured on three graded levels—low, medium, and high—and will be correlated later with other variables. To facilitate comparison between different groups, the average of each group will be computed as follows. For each group, I shall take the difference between the high and the low level. To avoid negative numbers, I shall add to this difference the figure 100, so that a figure above 100 will signify a higher incidence of the high level and a figure below 100 a higher incidence of the low level. For the national and occupational groups I will take simple averages of the values for the three appropriate groups computed as described here.

Task Characteristics or Content

The interviewees were asked thirty-eight questions about the task characteristics of their jobs, some of them eliciting simple information and others calling for evaluation or grading. The questions are grouped along the following lines: quality and skill level; variety versus monotony; repetitiveness and speed; and autonomy and responsibility. Responses to thirty of these questions were weighted and used to construct the variable "level of task characteristics or content of the job." (The detailed results for the composite variable are in table A-33, and the results for the five subgroups are in tables A-34 through A-41.)

I have graded the content of the jobs into three levels: low, medium, and high. There is little doubt that taking the world of work as a whole, the grade of the majority of the jobs in question is low, but I took the accepted low standard of the part of the world of work in which the present study is situated, and I have graded the content of jobs as high or low by that given standard. I found that 32.9 percent of the entire sample reported low content, 45.1 percent medium, and 22.1 percent high.

Here follow the average level figures for the nine groups, computed in the above mentioned method:

Group 0	43.5
Group 1	97.6
Group 2	121.7
Group 3	50.0
Group 4	96.7
Group 5	147.0
Group 6	26.2
Group 7	84.7
Group 8	136.0

There are only slight differences in the average levels of the content of the jobs of the three national groups: Israel, 87.6; United States, 97.8; Germany, 82.3. The U.S. average is the highest. There is, however, a pronounced occupational scale: industry, 39.9; retail, 92.2; and office, 134.9. Since there are such pronounced differences between the occupational groups, assuming that the level of the task characteristics of the job is important for employed women, all pronouncements to the contrary notwithstanding, then attitude measures should show significant differences between attitudes of the members of the three occupational groups.

Repetitiveness, Speed, and Strain

This is a composite variable, comprising a question about the length of time needed for the completion of the central activity, a question about the speed of work required, and a question about whether the interviewee feels she is under strain (table A-35). Because the data regarding the length of time needed for the completion of the central activity are the most objectively reliable, I have included information on their distribution. (The information about repetitiveness and speed has been included in the construction of the variable, task or content characteristics. The response to the question about the feeling of strain was not included because of its subjective nature. [See tables A-36 and A-37.]) The degree of breaking a task into small, fractionated jobs usually is reflected also in speed demanded. The more broken down a task is, the greater the tendency of management to demand speed of performance, with strain following suit, although not always. At times, strain is due to other forms of frustration.

Of the sample, 37.6 percent described and evaluated their jobs as being fractionated, high speed, and causing strain. We graded these characteristics as high (that is, negative), medium, and low (that is, better) and found, for the entire sample, 37.6 percent high, 32.6 percent medium, and 29.8 percent low. There is a considerable variation among occupational groups. Industry is by far in the worst position: 72 percent evaluated their jobs as negative in this respect. Retail trade followed with 29 percent negative and office with 13 percent negative. Less significant are the national grouping, with Israel at the bottom. The U.S. sample contains both the most-favored group—Group 5 (U.S. office), the only group with well over 68 percent in the best position, far ahead of all other groups—and the least favored group—Group 3 (U.S. industry), which has only 7 percent in the better category.

Nearly half of the sample perform tasks that are not highly repetitive; their central activity lasts ten minutes or more and includes tasks that last hours or even a whole day (table A-37). For the other half, their jobs consist of repetitive tasks; no fewer than 14 percent perform tasks that last one minute or less. This worst-off group is concentrated in industry. The best off are distributed over the three occupations, with industry having the least share and office having the greatest share. The extreme division of labor in industry is traditionally tied to the piecework method, the so-called individual incentive pay. There seems to be a vicious circle here, with fractionating and piecework reinforcing each other. Nevertheless, in one plant in the United States, I saw women work according to the piecework method, yet each made full garments. The plant was divided into two equal sections—one working by the "detail method" and the other by the "full garment method."

Fractionating has serious negative consequences, such as monotony, severe eye and nervous strain, the limiting of the use of skills, and the blocking of advancement opportunities. By contrast, the individual incentive pay method may also have some positive consequences. The worker can plan periods of higher or lower investment of effort, and if management notices that workers plan their investment of effort well, it may conclude that workers can be granted a high degree of personal freedom and even elastic work hours without loss of productivity.

Chances of Promotion

In answer to the question, "Do you think that the chances of promotion for women employees in your kind of job here are good, medium, poor?" 25.4 percent answered "good"; 21.6 percent, "medium"; 50.2 percent, "poor"; and 2.9 percent, "don't know." (See table A-41; in that table the "don't know" were included as "poor.") The national distribution is significant; Israel has the most optimistic evaluation and Germany the most pessimistic (see table 3-5).

The table shows evaluations and does not necessarily reflect the objective situation accurately. The concept of promotion may have a different meaning for different groups because of different practices. In Israel, many work organizations have rigid systems of rank that are maintained by agreement with the unions and serve as standards for pay increases. Therefore, the "promotion" that Israeli employees refer to often does not reflect change in the quality of the task characteristics or in the status of the "promoted" employee; it is instead almost an automatic by-product of seniority. The pessimistic evaluation of so many of the German interviewees is founded on the difference in the methods of training and recruiting for professional and middle-management positions in industry and in office jobs. In industry, a completed apprenticeship after elementary education rarely qualifies a production worker for the position of department head, production manager, or branch manager; these positions are attained only after completion of a technical school (*Fachschule*). And in office work, even the most experienced and highly qualified secretary tends to arrive at a barrier above which the positions are reserved for persons with academic or higher technical education.

These data are included in the composite variable "level of task or content characteristics of the job." I have discussed them separately here because they will serve as a separate variable for the purpose of examining factors influencing interest in advancement and promotion.

Hygiene or Working Conditions

Hygiene characteristics comprise material rewards, physical conditions, work hours, social relations, and unionization. I combined these into one composite

Table 3-5
Evaluation of Chances of Promotion

Evaluation	Israel	United States	Germany
Poor	31.9	45.2	72.5
Medium	27.6	27.3	16.3
Good	34.9	30.5	11.2

variable and asked twenty-one questions, some of which elicited straight information and some evaluation or grading. Details of the composite variable are in table A-42 and its subgroups in tables A-43 through A-46. The hygiene characteristics of their jobs were evaluated as low by 27.3 percent of the interviewees, as medium by 36.9 percent, and as high by 35.7 percent.

Here are the average level figures for the nine groups, computed in the same method as before.

Group 0	96.4
Group 1	131.7
Group 2	148.0
Group 3	82.6
Group 4	86.9
Group 5	106.0
Group 6	97.6
Group 7	99.9
Group 8	126.9

There are modest differences in the average levels of the work conditions of the three national groups: Israel, 125.4; United States, 91; Germany, 108.1. The differences among the three occupational groups are of the same order of magnitude and on the expected scale: industry, 92.2; retail, 106.2; office, 127; The interviewees' overall evaluation of their work conditions is more favorable than that of the task characteristics of their jobs.

Some work conditions were evaluated more negatively than others: 39.3 percent of the sample describes the material rewards (pay, social benefits, and fringe benefits) as poor; 36.1 percent described physical conditions as unsatisfactory; and 31.7 percent described social relations as unsatisfactory; but only 19.8 percent of the interviewees criticized work hours (inconvenient working hours and inflexible attitudes toward part-time work). The Israeli sample evaluates material rewards and physical conditions higher than the other two national groups. For material rewards and physical conditions, the industrial group considers its situation worst. This is obviously correct, as comparison of objective conditions clearly indicates. Admittedly, it is more difficult to compare objectively physical conditions than to compare material rewards, and the grading of these variables also reflects workers expectations. For example, all Israeli interviewees found strong neon lighting and air conditioning to constitute a high level of physical conditions, but the U.S. retail and office groups prefer natural daylight and complain that air conditioning causes cold symptoms.

The "social relations" variable is also a composite, since it includes relations with female and with male coworkers and with management. I found a strong tendency to answer questions about social relations of any kind in the affirmative, perhaps more so because of the expectation set by accepted norms for women. Nevertheless, differences did appear, both among occupational groups and between attitudes to coworkers and to management. In four of the nine groups, more than forty percent evaluate social relations between women workmates as less than "very friendly" (answers included "medium," "poor," and "don't know"). Furthermore, the attitudes to management are usually less favorable than to workmates in seven out of the nine groups. Group 5 (U.S. office) is particularly outstanding for its high worker solidarity and critical view of relations with management.

The three industrial groups complain the most about social relations with management; more than 50 percent refrained from the highest evaluation. And in one of them, Group 6 (German industry), relations with coworkers are more cordial than in the other German groups. The only office group where relations between coworkers are unsatisfactory is Group 8 (German office).

Union Performance. The interviewees were asked whether the union and the work councils or shop stewards in their current work organization look after the interests of the employees well, medium, or poorly; whether they have women representatives; whether the representatives look after the interests of the women employees as well, less well, or better than the interests of the men employees; and whether they further the advancement of women employees. (The composite results are shown in table A-47.)

The number of women who answered these questions (604) is considerably smaller than the total number (761). The other 157 women either reported that their work place was not unionized or that there were neither local work councils nor shop stewards. Of those who did answer, 63 percent gave their unions and local representatives high marks, 32 percent medium, and only 5 percent low. These results are far from having uniform significance because of different situations regarding unions, especially in the different national groups. Israel and Germany are highly unionized, and almost all but the smallest work organizations there also have representatives. The American situation is much more complicated. In New England, the needle trade industry is very highly organized (only one stitcher in the sample worked for a fur store that was not unionized) by two unions, yet the unionization of retail employees is only partial and that of clerical workers in the very earliest stages.

In all three countries, individual union membership is not necessarily identical with the unionization of the work place. Only in the American needle trade is there a perfect "closed-shop" system. There a plant is either organized or not, and never by more than one union. All production workers (except foremen and "floor-ladies") belong to the union, which bargains for them (especially about the norms determining the piece rate) and administers their health services and pension funds. The workers tend to identify with their particular union, not with the umbrella organizations, and also with their local functionaries. Of the eighty-five organized women in this group, only three rated union activity as poor. Some Boston-area retail stores are also closed shops, but the management of some other stores, large and small, is strongly opposed to unionization. The higher-quality stores have been particularly successful in keeping unions out by providing their own personnel with favorable health, accident, and retirement insurance coverage. Most small-store employees, however, have neither union protection nor in-firm or in-house services.

For Boston-area clerical workers, unionization is still fairly rare. Many large organizations, such as banks and insurance companies, are openly opposed to it. In institutions of higher education, clerical workers are free to unionize provided a majority votes in favor of this move. At the time of our interviewing, unionization among clerical employees was a controversial issue. Because of this late arrival of unionization and the fact that most clerical employees are women, there is a strong link between attempts at unionization and the goals and ideology of the women's movement regarding equal pay, unbiased hiring practices, and equal opportunities for promotion through professional development or into managerial positions. In the absence of unionization, this struggle is also carried out by informal women's organizations and institutions that attempt to enforce equal-rights or affirmative-action programs in the diverse work places.

Israel also has different unions for different occupational branches. There is no specific union for industrial stitchers, only one for textile and clothing workers in general. Israeli retail workers have no union of their own; they are a minor subdivision of the large white-collar union. Bank clerks are another subdivision of the same union. Most individual workers or employees are barely aware of the existence of their specific union and identify instead with the general trade union federation, which both bargains with the government collectively for all its members and administers a multitude of services, including health services and pension funds, for all its members. Theoretically, union membership is voluntary and individual. Yet because union membership goes with sick fund membership, many workers are members involuntarily. When many of the less-educated Israeli interviewees were asked, "Are you a union member?" they responded, "Do you mean the sick fund?" Others explained that they had to pay union dues—usually automatically deducted from their pay—but did not pay the higher sick fund dues because their husbands were members of a competing nonunion sick fund. In short, there is little union consciousness in Israel. Identification is usually with the work councils there, whose members are all union members. Most interviewees knew who the council's chairperson was, and questions on evaluation were answered largely concerning the council's or the chairperson's performance.

In Germany, the unionization of work places is almost universal, but individual workers in unionized work places need not be unionized even to be elected members of works' councils. The union institutions complain that a smaller percentage of women than of men is organized.

Because of these large differences in the objective situation concerning unionization and the role of the union for the working conditions of our interviewees, I decided to include only the fact of unionization or its absence as one point on the scale in the evaluation of the level of the hygiene characteristics of the job. The data on the level of union performance were not included.

Personal Freedom. Personal freedom is a composite variable comprising the permission, or its absence, to do the following: move from time to time from one's designated position, whether sitting or standing; use the toilet when desired; hold conversations; drink tea or coffee; smoke; telephone home; and receive phone messages. This is the only item on which a whole occupational group—the office group—had no sizable negative evaluation. The great difference within the industrial group probably indicates the backwardness of arrangements in the Israeli industry, which still considers restrictions on personal freedom as an essential precondition for productivity. Within the Israeli and the U.S. retail groups, cashiers especially are restricted in their freedom of movement. Details on this characteristic are given in table A-48. The evaluation of the level of personal freedom on the job is on the borderline between working conditions and the task itself. It was not included in the general evaluation of the hygiene characteristics of the job.

Attitudes toward Work

Questions eliciting attitudes toward work either focused on the current job or on a specific aspect of the job or requested the interviewee to draw conclusions from the experiences of a previous job, career, or work experience. The questions were asked to elicit information concerning the following attitudes:

1. Attachment and commitment to employment and occupation.
2. The significance of the earning activity.
3. The meaning of work.
4. Concern or the lack of concern toward negative task characteristics (that is, poor content quality of the job).
5. Concern or the lack of concern toward negative hygiene characteristics (that is, towards poor work conditions).
6. Interest in advancement.
7. Self-confidence as to the ability to perform more challenging work.
8. Satisfaction with work.

None of these attitudes is uncomplicated; all but self-confidence contain several aspects. Thus, to elicit information about each of these attitudes, several questions were asked and/or several responses to the same question were offered. Each attitude variable used for the purpose of testing a hypothesis is composite and based on several answers. Obviously, all these attitudes toward work are interconnected; both the defining of individual attitudes and the drawing of borderlines between them cannot be done without some subjectivity and arbitrariness. I shall now describe the structure of each of these attitude variables and my data concerning it.

Attachment and Commitment to Employment and Occupation

When the degree of attachment or commitment to work is measured for men, the usual procedure is to ask them about their plans concerning work and employment should there be no financial need for them to be gainfully employed or after they have reached retirement age. Often, such questions are considered to be just one of the questions meant to elicit the meaning of work to the working person. It is assumed that normal men in Western society have internalized the norm of their society that all healthy adult men are supposed to be continuously gainfully occupied. (This assumption, however, has been shaken somewhat by the behavior of considerable numbers of young men in the West since the mid-1960s who no longer seem to follow this norm.)

For women, the situation is different. Until recently, continuous employment for pay outside the home was definitely not the norm for women in general, and even less for married women, for mothers in general, and especially for mothers of small children. Two widely accepted suppositions about the work attitudes of women are that women's commitment to employment is lower than that of men and that women work only because of the money, (the financial aspect of work is much more important to them than the vocational one). The apparent assumptions behind these suppositions are that women prefer the domestic role, or perhaps the parasitic glamour girl role, to the employment role and that they enter the employment role only temporarily for purely material purposes and do not become strongly attached to it.

I attempted to elicit information about the degree and the nature of the interviewees' commitment to work outside the home by the questions: "What are your plans as to work in the future?" and "If your father/husband would earn more, or you or he would inherit enough (or you would win in the lottery), to make up for your pay, you would . . . ?" Five alternative answers were offered for each question and two choices were offered. In both cases, there was also the possiblity of a write-in choice. The possible answers concerning work in future were: "until marriage," "until birth of children," "until sufficient income of husband," "until achievement of specific economic goal," "up to retirement," "to take up an activity that is neither housework nor employment," and "no plans." (The Hebrew questionnaire also included the choice "until recruitment to the army.") Forty-one women had no plans, and forty-nine women offered two choices, usually reflecting ambivalence. Tables A-49 and A-50 show both the number and the percentage for all answers given by the women in each of the nine groups. The most frequent answer—56.7 percent—specified "up to retirement"; that is, 60.3 percent of the women declared that their intention was to work until retirement age. (Among these was a small number of women over fifty years old who qualified this answer by saying that because of health reasons or general fatigue, they might prefer early retirement.) The second most frequent answer was "until the birth of children" (12.6 percent of the answers and 13.4 percent of the women). The third was "until the achievement of a specific material goal" (10.9 percent of the answers and 11.6 percent of the women). And the fourth was "until sufficient income of husband" (6.8 percent of the answers and 7.2 percent of the women).

In six of the nine groups, between 56 and 67 percent of the women plan to work continuously. Only the three industrial groups deviated. In Group 6 (German industry) and in Group 0 (Israeli industry), only about one-third of the women plan to work until retirement (34.5 and 35.3 percent, respectively), and in Group 3 (U.S. industry) as many as 87.2 percent do. Group 0 is the youngest and has the highest percentage of unmarried women, who therefore still have the domestic and maternal role in front of them; they also lack experience in mastering both the domestic role and the employment role at the same time and have many illusions about the earning capacity of their future husbands.

Commitment to employment tends to be higher for women whose children are no longer infants and who are still employed or who have returned to work. Yet this commitment to employment is not correlated simply to age and family status. The relatively low commitment to employment of women in Groups 0 and 6 has to do with their views regarding their proper roles. Many of the women in Group 0 hold a mixture of traditional views about the primacy of marriage and motherhood (this is the only group where 20 percent plan to work only until marriage) and have a considerable amount of confusion and ambiguity, which is common to young women in Israel. Over 12 percent of the Israeli sample have no plans about the extent of their future employment career. This is not true of the women in the German industrial group. Most of these do not plan to stop working because of marriage or maternity; they see their employment as temporary and auxiliary to the role of their husbands as chief breadwinner. Nearly half the women plan to stop working as soon as they reach a specific material goal (usually the acquisition or building of a family home) or when their husbands' income becomes sufficient.

At the other end of the scale is the American industrial group. These women are the oldest and most experienced. They are also members of communities with a well-established tradition of employment of women in industry. An additional factor in their decision to work until retirement age is the nature of their provision for retirement, which is paid by the union's pension funds. In order to qualify, the worker (and her employer) is required to have contributed for at least twenty years to the same pension fund. Thus, it seems that this group of women has concluded that in order to live at a standard of living desired by them through their adult married life, as well as in old age, they have to be continuously employed until retirement.

This seemingly high commitment to employment is only one aspect of the attitude; it is not identical with attachment to a career or occupational pride. A second question isolates this aspect: "What would be your choice or alternatives to regular employment should the present financial need for your income cease?" (See table A-51.) Nineteen did not answer, and 294 (38.6 percent) gave two answers each. The first two options appearing in the questionnaire—"gladly stay home" and "continue at my present job"—appeared nearly always as first choice. Double choice usually was not an expression of ambivalence, nor was it usually the grading of first and second priority. Most double choices were considered combinations, such as "part-time employment" plus "back to study or vocational training" or "back to study" plus "looking for more interesting job." The two write-in choices were hobbies and voluntary work. The order of relative frequency of choice of options, once financial need is removed, follows:

1. Further study or training: 23.9 percent of answers; 32.2 percent of women.
2. Part-time work: 22.9 percent of answers; 31.1 percent of women.
3. Present job: 21.6 percent of answers; 29.4 percent of women.
4. Stay home: 13.8 percent of answers; 18.8 percent of women.
5. More interesting job: 12.8 percent of answers; 17.2 percent of women.
6. Hobby: 4.5 percent of answers; 6.2 percent of women.
7. Volunteer work: 0.6 percent of answers; 0.8 percent of women.

The option "back to study" had a somewhat different meaning to different groups of women. Those who had some college education interpreted it as completing their first degree; a few even specified the desire to enter medical school, law school, or some other higher professional training, such as finance. But most of the younger women in industry and retail work understood it to mean specific vocational or diploma courses. Some of the older women, especially in Israel, specified adult education of a general cultural nature, such as literature.

The differences among national groups and among occupational groups are fairly marked. (See table A-52.) The choice of the option to stay home is highest in industry—over one-third of the women—whereas, in the two other groups, it is only over one-tenth. In the German group, over double the percentage want to stay home than in the Israeli group, with the U.S. group in between (although nearer to the German group). For the retail and the office groups, staying at home is the fifth option. To me this choice indicates that the purely domestic role is unattractive to most working women. Nevertheless, the attachment to the present job is the choice of over two-fifths of the retail group only; one-quarter or fewer members of the other groups make this choice. The choice of the option to stay in the present job may signify, however, in addition to the preference of employment over staying at home, a certain degree of vocational pride. This would explain why women in industry show so much less readiness to stay in the present job than do the retail workers; saleswomen are known to have much more occupational pride. Moreover, the choice of the option to stay in the present job does not correlate with the level of the task characteristics of the job. Only 26 percent of the office workers choose to stay on the present job, despite the fact that office jobs are the highest in quality as compared with the other two groups. In addition to the difference between the retail and the industrial groups (fewer saleswomen want to stay home than industrial workers and more want to stay in their present job), there is another noticeable difference: twice as many retail as industrial workers consider it feasible to look for a more interesting job. This readiness is still more marked in the office group. The degree of willingness to entertain the idea of returning to studies or training is much higher in the office group than in the other two. It may be assumed that the studies intended are generally employment oriented. Also it may be assumed that the even choice of between 20 and 25 percent in each of the nine groups of part-time employment signifies a mixture of the expression of the wish to reduce the double load of job and home duties with a bid for a chance to attempt an improvement in their work life by either studies or the search for a more interesting job.

There is a significant difference between the commitment and attachment to work as expressed by answers to the question, what would the interviewee do were she not constrained financially to stay in her present job, and the commitment and attachment to work as expressed by plans for future work. Group 3 (U.S. industry) has the highest percentage of women declaring an intention to work until retirement age; yet it also has the highest percentage of women who prefer to stay home were the financial need removed. This answer shows that attachment to employment as a means of income is not identical with the attachment to employment as an occupation or a career. For the purpose of testing hypotheses concerning commitment, I therefore composed a variable—"degree of commitment to work/employment"—based on the indication of low commitment to work as transpired from the answers to both the question of alternative options and the question concerning future plans.

The compound variable "commitment to work" indicates the degree of commitment to work/employment in each of the nine groups (table A-53). It shows that only 15.6 percent of the sample have a low commitment to work/employment, 34.6 percent have a medium commitment, and 49.8 percent a high commitment.

Here are the average level figures for the nine groups, computed in the above mentioned method.

Group 0	116.5
Group 1	158.5
Group 2	125.3
Group 3	151.2
Group 4	151.2
Group 5	156.7
Group 6	83.3
Group 7	114.1
Group 8	150.5

With the exception of Group 6 (German industry), in all groups, the percentage of women with high commitment is considerably greater than of those with low commitment. The average level figure for the national groups is: Israel, 133.4; United States, 153; and Germany, 116. For the occupational groups the figures follow the usual scale with industry as the lowest (117), then retail (141.3), and office a little higher (144).

Self-Image as an Economically Active Person

This attitude toward work is especially problematic because of considerable differences in the norms of different national cultures in the Western world, as well as differences in norms among different socioeconomic groups within the same national culture, concerning women as breadwinners. The egalitarian views concerning the proper social roles of both sexes propagated by the modern women's movement have changed the attitudes of some national cultures more than others. This kind of attitude change tends to start from circles of college-educated youth and to spread only gradually to occupational groups that have little contact with campus life, as well as to older age groups.

I tried to elicit the self-image of the women interviewees as economically active and earning regular income by asking whether the interviewee considers herself as basically earning her own living, as a breadwinner for her family, as contributing to the satisfaction of the essential needs of her family. Or alternatively, whether she considers her earning as secondary or even marginal, adding to those of her husband as the chief breadwinner, providing the family with extras, providing herself with pocket money and clothes, permitting herself to pay for the services of household help or babysitter. Or alternatively, whether she considers her economic activity as not permanent but aimed at the achievement of a larger but temporary economic goal, such as a dowry, a college education for herself or her children, a house, a car, or something similar.

Interviewees were asked to choose at least one of the seven possible options or, if desired, two or three in order of priority. Many interviewees were considerably ambivalent; half of the sample chose two answers, and one-fifth chose three. Table A-54 shows the percentage of each of the seven possible answers. The answers were weighted, giving all first-choice answers three points, second-choice answers two points, and third-choice answers one point. The four first answers were chosen most often as the first choice; the fifth, sixth, and seventh answers appeared more frequently as the second or third choice. Many women chose two or three answers that are not quite consistent with each other. The use of the answers for the exact evaluation of the attitudes of the nine groups is complicated by the fact that age and, even more, marital status influenced the choice of certain answers, while the composition of the nine groups with regard to age and marital status was not uniform. Thus, single, divorced, separated, and widowed women were not likely to answer that they earned in order "to add to the income of my husband," even if they considered this the proper aim for a married woman. Few nonmothers chose the answer "to permit my family to live at a standard I think essential" or "to earn my own and my family's/my children's living." Most mothers who are without a present and earning husband may choose one of those two answers, even if they consider a secondary economic role more proper for women. It could also be assumed that young single women, especially those still living in their parents' households would be likely to answer "to earn enough for pocket money and clothes." Thus, the answers would reflect the diverse situations of different age and marital status groups more than an attitude.

In order to examine this point, I correlated the number of currently married women in each group with the number of answers "to add to my husband's income" and found it most imperfect. In different groups, between 56.7 percent and 84 percent of the married women gave this answer, and as first choice, the groups ranged from 32.2 percent to 71.7 percent. Even in a group that comprises mainly older and married women, eighteen answers specified "pocket money and clothes." Thus, all single and currently married women, young and old, in the sample seemed to have felt free to choose between answers specifying either a role of basic earner or a role of secondary, marginal or temporary earner. Yet it is to be assumed that nearly all of the 118 divorced, separated, and widowed women in the sample saw little reason to choose answers other than those specifying a basic earning role.

Clearly, not all women who did not answer "to earn my living" necessarily saw their contribution as secondary or marginal. In Group 0 (Israeli industry), for example, only 20.2 percent of all (weighted) answers were "to earn my living," whereas 23.8 percent of the answers were "to earn my family's living." It can be assumed that in this group many husbands and fathers have incomes that are not sufficient to provide for their families, and the answers realistically reflect this situation.

Those answering "providing my family with extras" or "to earn to finance a specific goal" were also asked to choose from a list of extras or specific goals. The most popular luxuries were, first, holiday trips and, second, a car. The most popular specific goal—and nearly one-fifth of the women chose this answer—was a house or an apartment. In the German industrial group, twenty-six women of the thirty-three women who chose this answer specified this goal. It transpires that in this group, which is overwhelmingly rural and small town, the building of a family-owned home is a central goal of women's employment and earning. This goal is also important for women in the German retail and the Israeli office groups. The second most frequently mentioned specific goal is "to save toward getting married." Characteristically, thirty of the thirty-eight women specifying this rather traditional goal belong to the Israeli sample, and sixteen of these belong to Group 0 (Israeli industry).

In order to measure the incidence of individual consciousness of economic independence together with a clear self-image as a basic provider for her family, I combined the weighted choices two and three and arrived at the following distribution: Group 0, 44 percent of all responses; Group 1, 30.8 percent; Group 2, 27.7 percent; Group 3, 37.8 percent; Group 4, 49.8 percent; Group 5, 52.3 percent; Group 6, 24.6 percent; Group 7, 25.1 percent; Group 8, 54.4 percent. The nine groups range from the very low incidence of one-quarter of the responses to a high incidence of over one-half of the responses. The average level of the national groups of Israel and Germany and of the occupational groups of industry and retail are very similar. In the United States, and in the office group, the level is higher.

To facilitate the correlation of the attitude variable "self-image as economically active person" with other variables, a simpler distribution of the sample was used: those who chose either "to earn my living" or "to earn my family's living" as first choice will be considered as having the attitude of a basic earner, the others will not. Of the sample, 46.3 percent chose either answer as first choice; only 5.7 percent chose either as second or third choice; and 48 percent did not choose them at all.

Meaning of Work

The meaning that work has is a central aspect of the research into work attitudes. The decision as to whether a given worker has an instrumental or an autotelic attitude to work depends on her answer to the question about what she finds important in work and in her present employment. The researcher then has to determine what qualities indicate an instrumental attitude and what qualities an autotelic one, which depends on her or his division of the qualities of work to the different categories. There are, indeed, two different problems here. The first is to determine whether these two attitudes are clearly definable, homogeneous, exclusive, and exhaustive categories. The second is to decide what different ingredients and what emphasis on them indicates the adoption of each of these two attitudes. The instrumental attitude includes a low (but not necessarily no) appreciation of the task characteristics of the job. There are also workers who, when asked to grade different qualities, do not pick any content characteristic as important, but they are very few. Yet the autotelic worker, or the worker who emphasized the task characteristics of the job, will naturally not ignore the hygiene conditions, the attention to which is usually taken to be characteristic of the instrumental attitude. The assumption behind the study of the instrumental attitude is that the person who adopts its uses work as a mere instrument for attaining gratification or satisfaction outside his work world.

The current approach—broadly endorsed here—is that of Herzberg. He divides the qualities of jobs into two categories—the task qualities, which are allegedly valued by the autotelic workers, and the hygiene conditions, allegedly valued by the worker adopting the instrumental attitude. The task category contains such qualities as skill, variety, autonomy, and responsibility; the hygiene category contains such qualities as pay, fringe benefits, physical conditions, work hours, degree of physical effort, and the proximity of work place to home. Herzberg also includes all of the social relations in work—with management, with supervisors, and with workmates—in this latter category. The quality of supervision seems to me, however, to belong clearly to task characteristics and not to hygiene, since it has a direct impact on the degree of both the skill and the autonomy of the job. I have also included the fact of the unionization of the work place or its absence as a minor component of the level of hygiene characteristics, but have excluded the evaluation of union performance from it because one national sample included a considerable number of nonunionized work places.

I have included the chance for promotion as a component of the level of the task or content characteristics of the job, but not interest in advancement and promotion. Instead, I have constructed a separate variable of the attitude "interest in advancement and promotion." Finally, I have studied the quality of personal freedom of movement and communication during work time but have counted it as neither a hygiene nor a task characteristic.

In order to ascertain the relative emphasis on the different aspects of work, I asked two questions. First, "What do you consider most important for you in a job?" And second, "If you left your job and stayed home, what would you miss?" In each case, I gave a list of options (tables A-55 and A-56). I asked the interviewees to grade answers in accord with degrees of importance while looking at the list of optional answers to choose from. On the first question, the interviewees were requested to choose eight of fifteen options, but this turned out to be too complex a task for some of them and the less sophisticated interviewees tended to decide on their answers without much concern for precise grading. Therefore, I decided not to give much weight to the precise order of the answers. Instead I gave the first four answers a weight double that of the last four. Also, the question pertained to a job in general, and interviewers were asked to stress and explain this point to the interviewees.

Some interviewees, however, could not easily abstract from the present job to jobs in general. The second question refers to the present job, and therefore, answers to it diverge more significantly from answers to the first one with the more sophisticated interviewees. For them, answers to the first question reflect aspirations and, to the second question, the gap between aspiration and a realistic assessment of present job; they noticed the difference between the two. Most members of Group 5 (U.S. office), for example, rated interesting work as first, yet they put interest in work as only sixth on the list of what they might miss most if they left their present job. The interviewees had much less difficulty in answering the second question concerning the meaning of work to them, since they had less abstractness and a simpler task to handle. I therefore graded the four options with four diminishing weights.

I have used the composite answer to both questions to design and evaluate the variable of emphasis on content. I have not done the same with hygiene characteristics because they are much more varied than the task characteristics, and their high appreciation is much less indicative of the instrumental attitude than the low appreciation of the task characteristics.

The literature holds that certain hygiene conditions are particularly important to women workers. I have examined this assumption and found intriguing results. The sample does not particularly stress good physical conditions such as cleanliness (it is put as the sixth degree of importance), proximity of work place to home (twelfth), and physically easy work (fifteenth and last), although these are the characteristics claimed to be highly valued by women. The characteristic that is more justly claimed to be valued by women is convenient work hours (fifth), since most employed women have maternal and domestic commitments that are often tied to certain hours, which may easily conflict with hours of employment. Only Group 2 (Israeli office) counted convenient work hours as high as second in importance. The reason is simple. The Israeli banks and offices often have very long workdays with long midday breaks, and many Israeli women seek offices where the workday is short with no, or almost no, lunch break.

The literature, including some comparative studies, also deems good social relations on the job (harmonious relations with both management and work-mates) as significant to women, and indeed the sample considers these two characteristics to be first and second in degree of importance. Yet when the sample is broken down, only three of the nine groups consider good relations with management of top priority, and for two groups, it is second in importance. For three groups, good relations among employees follows second after good relations with management, and for one other group (German office), good relations among employees is even first choice. The Israeli and U.S. office groups show a completely different pattern. Their first choice is interesting work, independence in work is third and second, respectively, good relations among employees is fourth, and relations with management comes only seventh (Israel) or fourth (United States). So there is a considerable similarity among the three industrial groups, the three retail groups, and two of the office groups. The German office group stands out: here relations among employees comes first, but they are followed by independence in work, interesting work, and use of skills (in that order).

In all three national groups, the industrial workers give pay a higher priority than do the retail and the office groups (the last gives it the lowest priority). The U.S. office group stands out. For them, pay is fourth priority, reflecting the struggle for a real implementation of equal pay that American women are now engaged in. Since the same group also ranks high in emphasizing the importance of task characteristics, the view of the emphasis on pay as a reflection of a mere instrumental attitude is refuted.

I combined several task characteristics—independence in work, interest in work, opportunity to use skills, opportunity to perform high-quality work, and having a boss who knows his or her job—and listed the nine groups in order of degree of emphasis on content characteristics based on answers to the first question on the meaning of work:

Low emphasis on content
    Group 6 (German industry)
    Group 0 (Israeli industry)
    Group 3 (U.S. industry)

Medium emphasis on content
    Group 1 (Israeli retail)
    Group 7 (German retail)
    Group 4 (U.S. retail)

High emphasis on content
    Group 8 (German office)
    Group 2 (Israeli office)
    Group 5 (U.S. office)

The division of national and occupational groups concerning high emphasis on task characteristics follows (the numbers signify priorities as explained above and as extracted from table A-57):

Israel	31.6 percent
United States	33.6 percent
Germany	28.1 percent
Industry	24.2 percent
Sales	30.3 percent
Office	38.9 percent

Clearly, there is a scale of the three occupational groups regarding emphasis on content. As to the national groups, the German has the lowest emphasis on content and the American the highest.

The answers to the second question concerning the meaning of work go in a somewhat different way. In all nine groups, missing the money if one stayed at home turned up as first priority, although in each national group there is a decline in emphasis on money from industry to retail to office groups. Of the weighted answers, 33 percent concerned missing the money. The next two highest choices—each with 15.6 percent of the answers—were, "If I stayed home, I would miss most the feeling of independence" and "the company of my fellow workers." Next were the importance of "the feeling of being useful" (13.7 percent), "interest in my work" (11.6 percent), "the chance to use my skills/occupation" (6.3 percent), and "the chance of advancement" (4.8 percent).

Again, good social relations in work appear as an important aspect of work for women, yet they appear more realistically as a second priority to money and even then for only four of the nine groups; the others grade them as third, fourth, or even fifth in importance. The feeling of independence in the second question is different from the independence in work presented in the first question and signifies a radical change in the self-image of the employed woman. The fact that four of the nine groups chose this feeling of independence as second in priority seems very significant.

Priorities in the answers to the second question on the meaning of work appear in table A-58.

The differences in the results concerning the emphasis on content characteristics between answers to the first question, on the meaning of work in the abstract, and the second question, on the meaning of work in the current job, are nearly exclusive due to the fact that members of Group 5 (U.S. office) have graded the loss of their "interest in work" as of little importance if they left their current job, as compared with Group 8 (German office) and more so with Group 2 (Israeli office). Group 5 was by far the highest in answer to the first question about the importance of intersting work. My explanation for this fact is that for this group there is a particularly large gap between their aspiration as to what their job should be and their assessment of their actual job.

On the basis of the answers to the first question, good relations with management and with fellow employees appear as the two characteristics of the job most valued by the sample as a whole, although not very emphatically. This preference for good social relations is nearly the only sex-specific difference that agrees with conventional allegations substantiated in the small amount of comparative literature on the topic. The simplest explanation for this attitude of women is their sex-specific socialization toward tension avoidance, compromise, and peace making, and even toward passiveness and submission. Yet the literature also claims that there is more need for cooperation among women in the course of their work than among men, even in the same work organization and for similar activities. This claim seems unexamined; examining it requires not only comparative studies concerning men and women but also studies concerning the degrees of cooperation that different jobs require. As far as the present study can illuminate the situation, it does not indicate any correlation between good relations and the need for cooperation.

"Missing the company of my fellow employees" was one of the aspects of the job the interviewees were asked to grade in the second question, but it is not the same as "good relations with my fellow employees," which the interviewees were asked to grade the importance of in the first question. The second question reflects the meaning of work vis-à-vis nonwork, whereas the first one reflects just the emphasis that the worker puts on different aspects of her job. Thus, if an interviewee rated highly "missing the company of her fellow employees," then she apparently lacks social relations outside work. This void may be the consequence of a low level of education, shyness, or social isolation resulting from divorce or widowhood. But even women who have easy access to social contacts outside work may value those with fellow workers because of common occupational or professional interest, comradeship in union activity, or other common efforts to improve the quality of their jobs. The comparison of the two kinds of emphasis on good social relations with workmates is shown in table A-59.

The classical characterization of the instrumental attitude is Dubin's claim that the worker's central life interest lies outside the work place. This is also reflected in his opinion of the worker's lack of interest in personal relations on the job. By contrast, according to Herzberg's classification of workers into those who pay attention to task characteristics and those who pay attention to hygiene characteristics, good social relations belong to hygiene characteristics. The interviewees' emphasis on good social relations on the job, then, may make them less alienated for Dubin and more for Herzberg. Just as I could not accept the emphasis on pay as an overall indicator of an instrumental attitude, so I cannot agree that the accent on good social relations indicates the same choice between the instrumental and autotelic attitudes equally for all cases. Of course, if an interviewee puts her emphasis solely on hygiene and expressly disregards content characteristics, then her attitude should be considered eminently instrumental, but such cases are rare. What the data indicate to me is what the priorities given in the diverse groups to the task characteristics are. Ignoring hygiene altogether, I have composed a variable from these priorities that should give an overall measure on three levels of the emphasis on task or content characteristics of the job, as given by each interviewee. The results are shown in table A-60.

The women in the three office groups put the highest emphasis on content. In each national group, by far the smallest number of women who put high emphasis on content is in the industrial group. Those who put high emphasis on content range from 11.8 percent in Group 0 (Israeli industry) to 50.6 percent in Group 5 (U.S. office); those who hardly emphasize content range from 13.5 percent in Group 8 (German office) to 66.7 percent in Group 6 (German industry). Using average level computation as before we get the following figures:

Group 0	49.4
Group 1	78.0
Group 2	131.3
Group 3	60.4
Group 4	96.2
Group 5	126.5
Group 6	45.2
Group 7	83.6
Group 8	130.1

The figures for the national groups are: Israel, 86.2; United States, 94.4; and Germany, 86.4. For the occupational groups they are: industry, 51.7; retail, 85.9; and office, 129.3—a most striking occupational scale.

Concern about Negative Task Characteristics

A worker may want very much, or somewhat, to try to change her work situation, to improve the quality of her work role, or she may be resigned to its limitations. I have tried to probe the strength or weakness of such intentions by enquiring after concern or its absence. I asked every interviewee who had described any task or content aspect of her job as inferior whether the problem mattered to her, and if so, how much. One might claim (with some justice) that there is a difficulty here in assessing the answers, because the interviewees answering the question regarding the degree of their concern about content were referring to different numbers of items from a list of up to eighteen items. Nevertheless, the picture drawn from the answers to the question about concern about content is significant. (See table A-61.)

The figures for the average level of concern for the nine groups computed as before are these.

Group 0	77.0
Group 1	103.0
Group 2	116.0
Group 3	32.6
Group 4	75.0
Group 5	97.6
Group 6	41.7
Group 7	52.9
Group 8	122.5

The figures for the national groups are: Israel, 98.7; United States, 68.4; and Germany, 72.4. Israel has the highest level of concern for content, the United States the lowest, but the difference is slight. The differences between the occupational groups are much more pronounced and the scale is the usual one: industry, 50.4; retail, 77; and office, 112.

This attitude variable seems to be of importance in conjunction with others. In my opinion, a worker who indicates a low emphasis on the task (the content of the job) as the meaning of work need not necessarily exhibit an instrumental attitude to work; only if she also indicates a low concern for task characteristics that she declares inferior, will she be likely to exhibit the instrumental attitude. If in addition, she also indicates lack of interest in advancement to a position of higher content quality (see below), then it is very likely that her attitude to work is instrumental indeed. I shall therefore examine later whether this attitude of lack of concern, of indifference, toward the poor quality of the job tends to appear together with these other two attitudes.

Concern about Hygiene

Although neither Maslow nor Herzberg ever said so explicitly, it has been deduced from their theories about the worker and his needs that as long as the worker is concerned highly with the hygiene of his job he will not start being concerned about its content. This would mean that the two concerns exclude each other, that it would be likely to find that those workers who are "instrumentally" indifferent toward inferior task characteristics of their jobs will be highly concerned with hygiene characteristics.

In order to test this hypothesis, which seems to me most unlikely to be true, it was necessary to determine the degree of concern about inferior hygiene characteristics and to correlate this with the already determined degree of concern about inferior task characteristics. In other words, I wanted to find out which part of the sample is concerned about inferior content but indifferent to inferior hygiene characteristics, or vice versa, or concerned about both or indifferent to both.

The data about the subsections of this attitude, "concern for hygiene," appear in tables A-62 through A-65. Those who did not answer any question in a subsection because they considered the hygiene conditions in their jobs favorable appear as "neutral." Those declaring some or much concern appear as "concerned." The data of the composite attitude appear in table A-66; here the data are added up and graded into three levels, low concern, (or indifference), medium concern, and high concern.

Overall concern about inferior financial benefits is the strongest (74 percent). About half the women express some concern about physical conditions; only 26.9 percent express some concern about unfavorable work hours, and even fewer, 20.6 percent, about social relations.

The composite data show that high concern about negative hygiene or working conditions is considerably higher, 42.2 percent, compared with only 25.6 percent for concern about negative task characteristics. Indifference to negative hygiene conditions is not much lower, 38.8 percent compared with 45.9 percent for indifference for negative task characteristics.

Here are figures for the average levels of concern for hygiene for the nine groups, computed as before.

Group 0	117.7
Group 1	109.8
Group 2	110.8
Group 3	54.6
Group 4	75.0
Group 5	89.1
Group 6	115.0
Group 7	123.5
Group 8	133.7

For the three national groups, the figures are: Israel, 112.8; United States, 72.9; and Germany, 124.2. The level of concern of the U.S. group is considerably lower than of the other two. The occupational groups are ranked as usual, but the difference is slight: industry, 95.9; retail, 102.8; and office, 111.2.

Concern about Union Performance

The questionnaire also included questions about concern about negatively evaluated union activity. I did not include these data as a component of the attitude "concern for hygiene" for two reasons. First, although the activity of the unions mainly concern working conditions, it may touch upon matters of the content of the job, such as arrangements for on the job training and, especially important for women, the struggle for equal hiring and promotion. Thus, some expression of concern about inferior union performance may reflect concern for the task characteristics of the job! Second, because of the low degree of unionization in the U.S. retail and office groups, about 50 and 90 percent of these groups, respectively, did not answer any questions on the assessment of the union performance. Therefore, they did not answer questions about their concern. These two groups had to be excluded from my consider-ations of concern about negatively evaluated union performance. The remaining data, although rather defective, appear in table A-67.

Within the six unionized groups, 38 percent of the women showed some concern about minor matters of union performance. It should be noted that there were almost no complaints about union discrimination against women. Yet many of the women noted that the unions had no say in such matters as promotion anyway, and therefore, also had no say regarding equal promotion.

Concern for Personal Freedom on the Job

As I mentioned before, I have not used the details on freedom of movement and communication on the job for the purposes of determining the level of either hygiene or task characteristics. Likewise, I did not use details on concern about inferior conditions of personal freedom on the job for the purpose of determining the level of concern about hygiene. A total of 37.5 percent of the women in the sample described these conditions as medium or low. Of those, 60 percent (22.7 percent of the sample) showed some or much concern for inferior conditions of personal freedom. This concern is very unequally distributed; it is very high in the Israeli industrial group, somewhat less in the Israeli retail group, even less in the German industrial group and plays a minor role in all others. (See table A-68.)

Already in the early seventies, when it was first suggested that modern industrial workers are dissatisfied with the poor content or task characteristics of their jobs, Dubin and Schrank countered by claiming that what young industrial workers and women workers missed most was not the challenge in their jobs but more personal freedom.

In order to test Dubin and Schrank's assumption it would be necessary to examine the correlation of concern for inferior task characteristics with that for inferior personal freedom. Unfortunately, my data are insufficient for such a correlation, since too many interviewees had no chance to express any concern about personal freedom, whereas all had a chance to express concern about some inferior task characteristics. It would therefore be extremely difficult to ascertain here the exact facts of the matter.

Interest in Advancement

Interest in advancement is of special importance for the chances of women to improve their career position. The conventional assumption is that employed women's interest in advancement is very weak, much weaker than that of employed men, and that this is a major factor responsible for their present inferior position as to responsibility, power, status, and pay. I have attempted to explore several aspects of this attitude with the help of questions concerning: readiness to apply for a more responsible job in the same work place or elsewhere; readiness to apply for a supervisory/managerial job; readiness to undergo training leading to a more responsible job during or outside of work hours; emphasis on good chances for promotion as an aspect of a job;

considering the chances for advancement as one of the aspects of one's job that one would miss; and concern (or lack of concern) about the absence of good chances for promotion in one's job. The attitude "interest in advancement" is a composite of the readiness to accept positions of higher skill, more responsibility, authority, or status if offered; to seek such opportunities actively; and to make efforts to acquire the additional skills required for that end together with emphasis on and concern for chances for advancement.

To the first question, "If a more responsible job were available in your work place would you apply?" 59.9 percent of the whole sample replied affirmatively; the rest answered negatively (except for the less than 3 percent who said they did not know or who declined to answer). (See table A-69.) The lowest in readiness to apply were Groups 1 (Israeli retail), 7 (German retail), and 3 (U.S. industry); the highest was Group 5 (U.S. office). A similar pattern occurs with a similar question regarding possible advance through leaving the work place. Here both the risk and effort are higher, and consequently the number answering affirmatively declined to 45.3 percent. Group 5 once again was the most interested, but otherwise the order is different, without either a national or an occupational pattern. Apparently, considerations against changing the current work place interfere with interest in advancement. Nearly the same number of interviewees answered that they would apply for a supervisory position. The ranking of the groups in order of number of affirmative replies to the question, "Would you apply for a more skilled or more responsible job in the same work place?" is almost the same as the ranking of the same regarding the question, "Would you apply for a supervisory position?" The difference indicates the significant number, especially in the industrial groups and in Group 2 (Israeli office), of women willing to take a more skilled job and more responsibility but refusing to enter minor management positions, which would uproot them from their milieu and might cause a rift between them and their workmates. In the United States, it would also disqualify them from continued membership in their union. This last fact explains why the decline is strongest—from over 50 percent to under 20 percent—in Group 3 (U.S. industry). By contrast, the decline is small in the three retail groups and in Group 5 (U.S. office), in which as many as 70 percent declared interest in a managerial position. This answer reflects the struggle of office workers in the United States to break down the traditional barriers between clerical and administrative jobs. The subsequent question, "If management were suggesting that you take training courses that would prepare you for more skilled/professional, more responsible or supervisory work, would you be ready to do so?" produced the following distribution of answers: 52.3 percent said, "yes, also outside working hours," 24.3 percent said, "yes, only during working hours," and 20.4 percent said, "no." (In addition to the 1.4 percent who declined to answer, eleven women said, "no longer," explaining that they were too old for training, eight answered thus to the question about applying for a more responsible job in another firm, and eight answered thus in the case of the question about applying for a supervisory/managerial job.)

The U.S. and the Israeli groups are equally eager for training; over 70 percent are ready to train outside working hours. The Israeli industrial group, which comes third, is also ready for training. This overwhelmingly young group evaluates its chances for promotion as much better than do the other two industrial groups, but this evaluation is certainly overoptimistic. That there exists a positive correlation between evaluation of chances for promotion and interest in it is well known. The question about concern or its absence concerning poor chances for promotion in the current work place was answered only by the 48 percent of the sample who evaluated their chances as poor. Of those, 29.8 percent professed much concern; 21.9 percent, some concern; and 48.1 percent, no concern.

The distribution of the composite variable "interest in advancement and promotion" is displayed in table A-70. It shows that 52.2 percent of the entire sample have high interest in advancement. The three office groups are highest by far in each of the national groups, but there is no overall grading of the industrial and retail groups. The industrial group in Israel is much more interested than the retail group, in the United States much less interested, and in Germany about the same. Comparing the national groups, the level of interest of the Israeli and the U.S. groups is about the same, with that of the German group being considerably lower. As this variable has been computed for two levels only, I give the average figures for the percentage of high interest. First, the three national groups: Israel, 57; United States, 56.8; and Germany, 42.8. For the occupational groups the figures are: industry, 42; retail, 43.8; and office, 70.9.

Self-Confidence as to Ability to Perform
More Challenging Work

Self-confidence reflects interest in advancement but is not identical with it. Interest in advancement here means not only an emphasis on the importance of advancement in a job but also the readiness to take a step in order to advance by gaining a job that is more skilled, challenging, responsible, or of a higher status. Self-confidence (or self-worth) means a person's evaluation of her own capabilities to advance. Here she is not limited by current restrictions on her time or energy that may make her say that she would not apply for a more responsible job or undertake further training. The interviewees were asked, in an attempt to elicit their own assessment of the degree of their worth, "Do you think that you are capable of doing more difficult work (more skilled, more responsible, or supervisory) that pays more?" It seems very likely that such a question would elicit a positive answer from the greatest majority of interviewees, especially if their current jobs are not very skilled, responsible, or supervisory. Yet assumptions in the literature make us expect a negative response from women, or at least a less frequent positive response than from men. These assumptions are that women shrink from accepting responsibility and from exercising authority because of their socialization to be passive and submissive and to follow orders and that their self confidence is low because of a relatively poor education and a defective vocational training or because of their frequently interrupted and static work careers.

The results contradict the current assumption. (See table A-71.) Of the whole sample, 83.4 percent answered affirmatively, and only 13.4 percent negatively; 3.1 percent answered "don't know" or "no longer" or gave no answer. There were slight differences among the groups. Only Group 5 (U.S. office) was nearly unanimous, with only three women—3.6 percent—responding negatively. Group 4 (U.S. retail) and Group 2 (Israeli office) each had four women—4.8 percent—who said "no," but in each of these, another four women replied "don't know" or gave no answer. In Group 8 (German office), 9 percent said "no," and one did not answer. In all three national groups, the office subgroup has the highest average self-confidence. The average for all office subgroups is 92.2 percent, and the averages for the industrial and retail groups are 79.3 percent and 78.8 percent, respectively. Of the national groups, the U.S. group is the highest, with an average of 91.4 percent. Those of the Israeli and the German groups are 76.8 percent and 82 percent respectively.

Satisfaction with Work

Satisfaction or dissatisfaction with work was the first work attitude to be researched extensively by psychologists and sociologists. The concept of satisfaction with work and the assumptions behind it became increasingly confused to the point that many practical researchers have dropped it altogether. I wish first to describe the confusion, then to explain why I consider the concept still a useful instrument, and finally to describe the methods used here to construct and measure the variable "satisfaction with work."

The starting point was the assumption that the worker's expressed satisfaction with his or her job and "motivation" to work well are closely connected, if not identical, work attitudes. They were supposed to have common causes that were empirically researched. Herzberg challenged this assumption by claiming that dissatisfaction is not the lower end of a single scale that has high satisfaction at its other end. Declared dissatisfaction with the job, he thought, is caused by inferior hygiene conditions and can be removed through the improvement of these hygiene conditions, which thus act as "satisfiers." But this satisfaction, he said, is merely a removal of dissatisfaction; it will not "motivate" the worker. Motivation is connected with (or caused by?) a kind of positive satisfaction, a deeper satisfaction derived from the content, the task itself, that can occur only if and when the worker meets a challenge and solves a problem in his job. The general idea that was behind Herzberg's claim is based on Maslow's theory of the hierarchy of needs: the modern worker is in need of a work role that has task characteristics of a considerably higher quality than is offered by the mass of modern industrial and service jobs. He will respond favorably to the enrichment of the content of his job to include challenge.

Academic management scientists have criticized Herzberg's ideas because of the obvious difficulties involved in empirically measuring the two different kinds of satisfaction that he spoke of and in testing his rather unsharp hypothesis. Others saw his idea of motivation as consenting to the managerial manipulation of the worker. Even those practical researchers who specialize in the restructuring of the work organizations and who accept the general Maslow-Herzberg approach prefer to drop silently the use of the concept of satisfaction with work. Einar Thorsrud explains his own preference to do without this concept thus: a worker's declared satisfaction changes with new opportunities; the worker's very perception of his previous job changes as he notices inferior aspects he had not noticed before; in short, he is no longer satisfied with the job he was satisfied with before. Therefore, a declared high degree of satisfaction with work is neither an asset nor is it significant.

Most psychologists and sociologists of work have not dropped the concept, and many of them coupled it with the concept of the instrumental attitude to work or with the concept of alienation from work. The way satisfaction with work was supposed to correlate with the instrumental attitude to work, or to alienation from work, was far from clear. Is the instrumentally adapted worker or the alienated worker satisfied or dissatisfied with his work? Do rising percentages of declared dissatisfaction with work signify a rise or a decline in instrumental adaptation or alienation? The literature is not at all clear about these vital questions. John Goldthorpe has observed a special kind of superficial satisfaction that may well go together with instrumental adaptation. Bruggemann and her coworkers have distinguished kinds of satisfaction and dissatisfaction, which they class as active and passive, and they suggest that the different kinds of satisfaction and of dissatisfaction have to be understood as resultant from different kinds of processes of assimilation of work experiences. Clearly, anyone who still speaks of satisfaction with work had better take all this into account.

I want to describe my own attempt to construct a serviceable variable "satisfaction from work." I have three alternative variants, and I shall use them all, to various purposes. The first is "overt satisfaction or dissatisfaction," the second is "levels of composite satisfaction," and the third is "superficial satisfaction."

The interviewees were asked seven questions. The first was a direct one, and the answer to it served as the measure of overt satisfaction/dissatisfaction: "What is your feeling about your present job? Are you very satisfied, somewhat satisfied, somewhat dissatisfied, or very dissatisfied?" (table A-72). The other six questions served to control and to explore different aspects of satisfaction.

Control was needed because direct questions about satisfaction with a central area of life, such as work, may make the interviewee feel defensive and thus unwittingly invite overoptimistic evaluations.

The exploration into the different aspects of satisfaction or dissatisfaction with the current job was designed with the help of the following six questions: (1) "Compared to your previous job, do you like your present job more?" (2) "Compared to housework, do you like what you do in your job more?" (3) "Would you advise a good friend to apply for a job like yours?" (4) "Would you advise your daughter to apply?" (5) "Your son?" and (6) "If you could start your work life over once, would you choose the same kind of work?" It is likely that the first direct question would elicit the interviewee's judgment, given her awareness of her own limitations as to knowledge, skills, age, seniority, and the limitations of time and place caused by familial and domestic obligations. Her direct answers should often read, under the given circumstances, "I assume that I have done fairly well and so ought to be fairly satisfied with my current job."

The other questions were attempts to help the interviewee answer the question as meant. For example, when an interviewee was asked whether she would recommend the current job to her daughter, it was a request to examine her current job as against the job she desires or aspires to. When she was asked to compare her current job with a previous one, she was requested to view jobs in general or in a comparative way, although on the basis of her own experience. When asked to compare her current job with housework, she was requested to abstract the content of the job from other job characteristics. When asked whether she would recommend her job to a friend, she was requested to view its degree of desirability from the outside, in an objective, abstract manner. Finally, when she was asked whether she would choose the same kind of job if she were given the opportunity to start all over again, it was in the hope to discover whether she has developed attachment and pride—whether, in other words, she has developed an attitude to her job as a vocation. The answers to the seven questions are shown in tables A-73 through A-85.

Overt Satisfaction and Dissatisfaction

To the direct question, "What is your feeling about your present job; are you very satisfied, somewhat satisfied, somewhat dissatisfied, or dissatisfied with it?" 39.6 percent of the whole sample replied "very satisfied." Two groups deviated. Only 28.6 percent of Group 6 (German industry) were very satisfied, and 57 percent of Group 3 (U.S. industry). Nearly half of the whole sample—46.4 percent—answered "somewhat satisfied." But 30.2 percent of Group 3 (U.S. industry) and 64.3 percent of Group 6 (German industry) answered in this manner. Taking both answers together—"very" and "somewhat" satisfied—we get a very uniform result of 86 percent on the average; Group 0 (Israeli industry) is at the bottom with 75.3 percent, and Group 1 (Israeli retail) is at the top with 93.9 percent. The national group that does not overwhelmingly declare satisfaction is the American, with an average of 81.4 percent satisfied; the highest is the German group with 90.4 percent satisfied, and Israel is in between with 86.1 percent satisfied. Yet for many women, the simplest way to answer the question was to exclude the expression of full satisfaction by choosing the second best; it is not an overtly critical attitude but not enthusiastic either and so seems neutral and noncommital. The U.S. and the Israeli groups are very similar in this respect—between 30 percent and 46.3 percent of the six groups in these two countries declare that they are somewhat satisfied. The three German groups give the following answers: Group 6, 64.3 percent; Group 7, 55.3 percent; Group 8, 58.4 percent. The average for the German groups is 59.3 percent, compared to the average of 39.8 percent for the rest.

Only 7.9 percent answered "somewhat dissatisfied" and even fewer—5.4 percent—answered "dissatisfied." Another six women—0.8 percent—did not answer, certainly not a sign of an especially high feminine satisfaction. Thus 13.3 or 14.1 percent of the reactions were expressions of overt dissatisfaction. This can be compared with the average rate of dissatisfaction with work of 11 percent found in recent University of Michigan surveys of a representative national sample of employed men and women.

There are considerable differences among the nine groups in direct expression of dissatisfaction, from a low of 6.1 percent for Group 1 (Israeli retail) and 7.1 percent for Group 6 (German industry) to over 21 percent for Groups 4 (U.S. retail) and 5 (U.S. office) and as much as 24.7 percent for Group 0 (Israeli industry). The average percentage of overt dissatisfaction is lowest in the German group—9.6 percent—and highest in the U.S. group—18.6 percent—with the Israeli in between (13.9 percent). The differences among the three occupational groups are slight.

Assuming that the answer "somewhat satisfied" implies some covert dissatisfaction, I combined all the answers except those stating "very satisfied" and got a rather different picture (see tables A-72 and A-73).

It became apparent that the difference in the rate of absence of pronounced satisfaction between the American and Israeli groups is small—55 percent for the U.S. group and 57.1 percent for the Israeli—and it is considerably higher in the German group—69 percent. The range of difference among the averages of the three occupational groups is insignificant (1.6 percent). The figures might seem to indicate that these answers have nothing to do with the characteristics of the jobs of our interviewees and that all that they signify is a difference in national temperament; the German interviewees, perhaps, are more cautious and have a more subdued view of life than the Israeli and the American women. Yet combining the answers to the direct question about satisfaction with those of the six control questions shows that the level of declared satisfaction with their jobs—plus the valuation of these jobs—follows an obvious occupational pattern. Let us examine the results from each of the six control questions.

Indirect Expressions of Satisfaction

The first control question asked, "Compared to your previous job do you like your present job more, the same or less?" (See tables A-74 and A-75.) The purpose of the question was to cause the interviewee to state her liking of her job relative to another job she has known. One hundred sixty-seven interviewees did not answer this question because they were holding their first job; I disregarded these in my calculations. Of the 594 interviewees who answered, 66 percent consider their current job as better, 22.9 percent as the same, and 11.3 percent as worse than the previous one. The U.S. office and retail groups have the highest level of feeling of improvement, and the Israeli industrial and retail groups have the lowest level; the range of difference among the groups is not very large, however. Averaging the figures for the national groups shows that this aspect of job satisfaction is lowest in Israel (59 percent) and highest in the United States (70 percent). Among the three occupational groups, industry is the lowest (61 percent) and office the highest (70.8 percent).

The second control question, "Compared to housework, do you like what you do in your job more, the same, or less?", was meant to elicit the degree of satisfaction or liking for the content of the present job, the task, or the activity compared to the other kind of work that all of the interviewed women were familiar with: housework. (See tables A-76 and A-77.) In answer, 54 percent liked their job more, 32 percent the same, and 14 percent less. The differences among the nine groups are considerable. Only 18 percent of Group 6 (German industry) like their occupational work more than their housework, 52 percent like it as much, and as many as 30 percent like it less. Apparently this group is still strongly attached to the housewife role. At the other end of the range, 85 percent of Group 5 (U.S. office), like their job more than housework, 10 percent the same, and only 5 percent less. This group obviously is attached to its occupational role and rejects the exclusive housewife's role. Regarding the national groups, Israel and the United States show great similarity, but double the number of Germans like the work they do in their job as much as they like housework. The differences here are not only on a national level. There is a clear occupational scale, with industry at the bottom; 36 percent in this group like their work more than housework and 27 percent less, 55 percent in retail work like it more and 8 percent less, and 70 percent of office workers like it more and 8 percent less. A clear positive correlation emerges between the quality of the task of a woman's job and her preference of it over housework. The scale is obvious in all three national groups.

The third question, "If a good friend were looking for a job and there was an opening here for a job just like yours, would you advise her to apply?" invites the interviewee to evaluate her job as compared to other women's jobs. (See tables A-78 and A-79.) In the entire sample, 80 percent answered affirmatively and 20 percent negatively, including twelve women who did not know or did not answer. The range of difference among the nine groups is very small, with seven of them ranging between 77 and 82 percent in the affirmative. The two exceptions are Group 7 (German retail), with only 73 percent answering affirmatively, and Group 5 (U.S. office) with as many as 90 percent answering affirmatively. The differences among the national groups are not great either. Israel and Germany are very similar, and the Americans evaluate their jobs slightly higher. The difference among the occupational groups is different from the usual ranking, since the retail group is the lowest (although it hardly differs from the industrial group). The positive evaluation of the office group is decidedly higher. In general, the answers indicate that the evaluations provoked by the question are conditional, since the interviewee normally sees her friend as having the same limitations as herself. Those 20 percent who would not recommend their jobs to their friends thereby exhibit a considerable degree of dissatisfaction and a seriously negative attitude—in contrast with the 14 percent who declared themselves dissatisfied in response to the first and direct question.

The fourth control question, "If your daughter were looking for a job, would you advise her to apply?" invites the interviewee to evaluate her job as compared with her own occupational aspirations. (See tables A-80 and A-81.) The purpose was to enable the interviewee to take into account all the shortcomings of the job—its dreariness, the unattractive surroundings, the poor chances for promotion, and especially its low social status—because she desires only the best for her daughter. Only women who are genuinely satisfied with their job will advise their daughters to follow in their occupational footsteps. This question is thus very revealing. It is, of course, easier to answer for the woman who has a daughter of school age who will soon have to choose an occupation. Some of the interviewees whose daughters were older and who either already had another occupation or were full-time housewives mentioned this fact as a difficulty. Yet most of them made the effort and answered the question hypothetically, as did those who had no daughters, whose number is considerable. Some of the very young interviewees had great difficulties and were not pressed to answer. Thus seventy-six women (10 percent) did not answer and were excluded from the calculations.

Of the 685 women who answered, 42 percent replied affirmatively and 58 percent negatively. The range of differences among the nine groups is very wide, ranging from only 16 percent of Group 0 (Israeli industry) answering affirmatively to 79 percent of Group 5 (U.S. office). In six of the nine groups, the overwhelming majority of the women do not consider their job to be good enough for their daughters, a very pronounced manifestation of covert dissatisfaction. Within each of the three national groups, the percentage of those considering their kind of job to be fit for their daughter rises with the occupational group. Of the industrial workers, 25 percent answered affirmatively, 40 percent of the retail workers, and 61 percent of the office workers. The explanation that emerges is that the relative quality of the job, its content, and its occupational standing caused the interviewees to answer in the way they did. Yet there were also strong national differences; only 25 percent of the Israeli sample answered affirmatively compared to 44 percent of the German sample and 55 percent of the U.S. sample. This difference cannot be attributed to the objective scale of the quality of the jobs of the three national groups.

A second factor inlfuences the woman's designation of her own job to be fit for her daughter; she considers the relative social prestige of her occupation within her culture and whether it is a suitable occupation for young women with the level of education that her daughter has reached or that she hopes she will reach. There is little difference among the three national groups regarding the social prestige of factory production work, especially for women. It is regarded as being not fit for young women who have reached the popularly accepted minimal educational norm for each culture. Most Israeli and German retail workers also consider the social prestige of their work in their cultures as too low for the aspired educational level of their daughter. It does not agree with their aspirations for the upward social mobility of their children. In Israel, where large numbers of the middle class hope for a college education for sons and daughters alike, clerical work is considered unprestigious for persons with a college education. They are expected to aspire to administrative, managerial, semiprofessional, or even professional jobs instead. In the German office group, educational aspirations for daughters are lower. In the U.S. retail and office groups, where both educational level and educational aspirations for children are high, many believe that they can rise to professional or managerial jobs through additional training and through equitable promotion. The majority of these women consider their current jobs to be steps in an occupational career and therefore also suitable for their daughters. A last likely hypothesis to explain the differences among the groups (but which cannot be tested accurately with the data included in this research) is that the stronger the influence of the ideology of the women's movement, the more likely the rejection of the traditional female attitude of seeking status and achievement by proxy through husband and/or children.

The same interviewees who had difficulties in answering the previous question also had trouble with this one: "If your son were looking for a job, would you advise him to apply?" (See tables A-82 and A-83.) Seventy-seven who did not answer were excluded from the calculations, and nine who answered "don't know" were counted as negative. Only 31 percent—compared with 42 percent in the case of a daughter—of the entire sample considered their own job as fit for their sons. The factors mentioned as explanations for the results of the previous question obviously apply here too. An additional one—the acceptance of current occupational polarization and segregation along sex lines as normal, inevitable, and justified—plays an important additional role. Views on occupational segregation have been elicited within the framework of this questionnaire, and the results follow the same occupational and national lines as the results of this question.

The percentage of those rejecting the conventional sex typing sufficiently to view their own typical women's jobs as suitable for men varies from only 4 percent in Group 0 (Israeli industry) and Group 1 (Israeli retail) to 73 percent in Group 5 (U.S. office). In the three occupational groups, 17 percent of the industrial workers answered affirmatively, 27 percent of the retail workers, and 50 percent of the office employees. In the three national groups, the Israelis evaluated their jobs as most unsuitable; only 8 percent answered affirmatively compared with 35 percent of the Germans and 48 percent of the Americans.

The last control question, "If you could start your work life over once, would you choose the same kind of work?" was designed to elicit a specific kind of job satisfaction: the evaluation of its occupational aspect as compared with other jobs, whether known to the interviewee or aspired to. (See tables A-85 and A-86.) Three factors were presumed to influence the decision of each interviewee to answer this question: her level of attachment to her job as an occupation, the level of her occupational aspiration, and the range of occupational choices open to her. Obviously, her attachment to her occupation—her occupational pride—would cause her to answer affirmatively, but if her aspirations were high and she believed that another occupational choice could help her achieve her aspiration better, she would answer negatively.

Thirty-eight percent of the entire sample answered this question affirmatively and 62 percent negatively. A comparison of the three national groups shows a very small difference between Israel and the United States, 44 and 40 percent affirmatively, respectively—but the German level of identification with the choice of occupation was lower (only 30 percent). Yet the differences are insignificant. In Group 6 (German industry), just as in Group 3 (U.S. industry), 31 percent answered affirmatively; in Group 7 (German retail), 33 percent answered affirmatively, and in Group 1 (Israeli retail), 35 percent. Indeed, there is hardly any difference among the three occupational groups. There are, however, two curiosities. The first is that 53 percent of Group 0 (Israeli industry) answered affirmatively compared to only 31 percent of the other two industrial groups. It is very unlikely that all or most of these forty-five women are strongly attached to their occupation. Instead, probably many of the very young women in this group who only recently started their first job have not reached as yet a point from which they could consider an alternative choice. The other curiosity is that only 25 percent of Group 8 (German office) answered affirmatively compared to 43 and 45 percent, respectively, in the Israeli and the U.S. office groups. Apparently here, most of the older women consider the clerical and secretarial tasks that they are performing as second best and not conforming to their original choice or to the high point in their occupational careers. A considerable number of women in this group were interrupted in their training for a semiprofession by World War II or its aftermath or had temporarily experienced entrepreneurship on a small scale in the absence of their husbands.

Composite Satisfaction and Superficial Satisfaction

I have developed a composite picture of job satisfaction by using the answers to all seven questions and giving the four levels of the answer to the first and direct question double weight. (See table A-86.) My composite variable contains the various aspects of job satisfaction. Because it was considered legitimate not to have answered any of the three questions about previous job, daughter, and son, the level of satisfaction was fixed relative to the number of questions answered. The results show that the level of satisfaction of 39.3 percent of the interviewees is relatively low, of 37.7 percent medium, and of 23 percent relatively high. By the usual method I arrived at levels of satisfaction for each group:

Group 0	64.7
Group 1	74.4
Group 2	90.4
Group 3	82.6
Group 4	92.8
Group 5	119.3
Group 6	61.9
Group 7	74.1
Group 8	93.2

For the national groups, the figures are: Israel, 76.5; United States, 98.2; and Germany, 76.4. The figures for the occupational groups are: industry, 69.7; retail, 80.4; and office, 101. These results are striking. All three national groups display a clear upward scale of satisfaction from industry through retail to office. All three have a gap between retail and office greater than between industry and retail. An extraordinary similarity is evident between the three pairs of occupational groups within the Israeli and the German groups, and the average rate of satisfaction of the two groups is the same. The composite satisfaction level of the U.S. group on its three occupational subgroups is considerably higher. (For a comparison of the direct answer with the composite on, see table A-87.)

I constructed one additional composite variable from the answers to the questions about job satisfaction that I will call "superficial satisfaction." It refers to the rather frequent combination of an overt expression of satisfaction in the form of a positive answer to the direct question ("very satisfied" or "somewhat satisfied") with a negative expression in the form of a negative answer to the fourth control question about advising her daughter to apply for a similar job. Because seventy-five interviewees did not answer this question, I used instead the answer to the previous question about advising a good friend. I considered those who had exhibited this attitude, which seems to me important on account of its inconsistency, as "superficially satisfied," and the others as not. (See table A-88.) I found that 44.4 percent of the sample are superficially satisfied by this criterion. In all three national groups, the percentage of those exhibiting this attitude is by far the lowest in the office groups. In Group 5 (U.S. office), it is as low as 10.8 percent. The average incidence of superficial satisfaction for the three national groups is: Israel, 55.2; United States, 32.9; and Germany, 45.3. Its incidence in the occupational groups is: industry, 57.3; retail, 47.5; and office, 28.7.

My interest in isolating this attitude variable arose from the observation of Goldthorpe that this kind of inconsistency, superficial satisfaction, was common among "affluent" British industrial workers, whom he describes as having a pronounced instrumental attitude to their work. My purpose was to test the assumption that this kind of inconsistent, superficial job satisfaction is indeed a component of the instrumental attitude to work.

4

Theories on Work Attitudes

Theories on Work Attitudes of Men and Women

The interest in job satisfaction stems mainly from the assumption that satisfaction leads to motivation and thus to high productivity. Consequently, one of the basic aims of personnel management is to ensure, within reason, the satisfaction of each employee. A currently popular theory is the fit theory: the correct fit between the level of aspirations of the worker and the level of the task characteristics of the job will result in an overall high level of job satisfaction.

In order to test this theory, I constructed three variables: "level of initial aspiration," "level of task or content characteristics of the job," and "level of job satisfaction." The variable "level of initial aspiration" could not be based on the expression of attitudes by the interviewees because it was necessary here to use the level of aspiration of the worker at the start of her work career or at the end of the period of her schooling and/or vocational training. Because it was impossible to obtain reliable information on this point in retrospect by a direct question, I constructed the "level of initial aspiration" from our information concerning the years of schooling plus extended systematic vocational training of each interviewee. This was compared to the average or normal level of schooling or training of each of the three national groups and graded as high, medium, or low. I am aware of the defect of this procedure. The amount of actual schooling and vocational training a young person undergoes may reflect not only her or his initial level of occupational aspirations but also the level of aspirations and the socioeconomic level of the person's family and community. Similarly, high initial aspirations may not have resulted in completed studies or training. Nevertheless, this method seemed to be the best under the circumstances. (The tabulation of this variable for the nine groups is shown in table A-89.) The level of aspiration was correlated with the level of satisfaction; the level of content of the job was kept constant by calculating the correlation separately for the populations of low, medium, and high job content. The results are shown in table A-90. I also broke down the results for the populations over and under the age of thirty-five and found that the differences are not significant. With age, the number of both those highly satisfied and those poorly satisfied declines relatively, but the correlations with aspirations and content remain unchanged with age break down.

There exists a remarkable fit between aspirations and the level of content of the job. Regarding levels of aspiration, the whole population was divided into 24.8 percent low aspiration, 34.8 percent medium, and 40.3 percent high. The same population was divided regarding the content level of their jobs thus: 32.9 percent low, 45.1 percent medium, and 22.1 percent high. There are thus considerably fewer workers with low aspirations in the population than those with low-level jobs; fewer with medium aspiration than with medium-level jobs; and nearly double with high aspirations than with high-level jobs. Therefore, a perfect fit is ruled out by the classification itself. In reality, women with low aspirations contribute 40.4 percent to the group of those with low-content jobs, 23 percent to the group of those in medium-content jobs, and only 5.4 percent to the group with high-content jobs. Women with medium initial aspirations (that is, those whose schooling and vocational training are about the national norm), who comprise 34.8 percent of the entire sample, contribute 40 percent to low-content jobs, 33.2 percent to medium, and 30.4 percent to high. Finally, the high-aspiration group (the better educated), the largest group, contributes 19.6 percent to the group with low job content, 43.8 percent to medium, and 64.2 percent to high. The picture that emerges clearly indicates that more often than not, a job is beneath the level of aspiration of its holder.

We can now proceed to the analysis of the correlations in the same table. The fit hypothesis may be formulated thus; we define three levels of fit. Bad fit equals high initial aspiration and low content of the job or low initial aspiration and high content of the job. Good fit equals high initial aspiration and high job content or medium initial aspiration and medium job content or low initial aspiration and low job content. Medium fit, then, equals low initial aspiration and medium job content, or medium initial aspiration and low job content, or medium initial aspiration and high job content, or high initial aspiration and medium job content. That is to say, good fit is the same level of initial aspiration and job content, medium fit is a one degree difference between them, and bad fit is a two degree difference between them. The fit hypothesis then correlates degrees of satisfaction with degrees of fit between initial aspirations and job content.

The facts do not agree with this hypothesis. It is true that satisfaction is significantly above average when high aspirations go with high job content, and dissatisfaction is considerable when individuals with high initial aspirations have jobs with low content. But satisfaction is high, instead of average as the fit hypothesis would predict, when initial aspiration is one degree below the level of the content of the job. In other cases, the prediction is even less in accord with the facts.

Correlating Satisfaction

Having refuted the fit theory of satisfaction, we return to the question, What determines the level of satisfaction with work? There seems to be some weak correlation with the worker's initial aspiration, and a more clear one with the level of the quality of the job. (See table A-91.) It seems advisable, then, to examine and compare a variety of likely factors for the significance of their correlation with the level of satisfaction with work. There may be factors that raise or lower the level of satisfaction, others that make workers declare more strongly overt high satisfaction or dissatisfaction. Level of satisfaction and overt satisfaction are different, the first is measured by a weighted composite value of answers to seven questions, the latter is the answer to the question, Are you satisfied with your job?

One might suggest that the declared satisfaction has little to do with either the job or the work experience but is an expression of one's life conditions, including age, health, and domestic burden. It may therefore be advisable to begin with correlating these three variables with the composite and overt levels of satisfaction. Likewise, since Bruggemann and her collaborators suggest that satisfaction or dissatisfaction with work results from the work experience and the individual's way of handling it, I shall proceed to correlate the factors "level of initial aspirations" and "progress or its absence during one's work career." It may be claimed that the changes in one's expectations have a great effect on the level of satisfaction, and that therefore women workers' views and values concerning the proper role of women in the labor market may constitute a decisive factor. I will attempt this correlation next. Finally comes the obvious correlation of the aspects of the current job with satisfaction; we have already noticed the relevance of the content of the job, yet it is essential to examine the same with respect to hygiene. This is especially true because according to Herzberg, inferior hygiene characteristics are the main cause of dissatisfaction, and their improvement is essential for its removal (although not enough to create satisfaction proper). As will be seen, my data accord with his hypothesis, although in a somewhat different formulation.

Throughout my correlations I will speak of low, medium, and high level of satisfaction, meaning composite satisfaction; I shall correlate satisfaction with any of the above variables, likewise divided into three unless otherwise specified. I will report the percentile differences between low x low satisfaction and high x low satisfaction, and the percentile difference between low x high satisfaction and high x high satisfaction. I shall then check results with overt satisfaction, which is divided into four levels: very satisfied, somewhat satisfied, somewhat dissatisfied, and very dissatisfied. The two lower levels are taken together because they are so poorly populated.

The variable "age groups" divides the population into five groups, up to twenty-five, to thirty-five, to forty-five, to fifty-five, and above. The level of composite satisfaction is not a monotone function of age. Between the youngest and the oldest group, there are 7 percent more old women with low satisfaction than young, and 5.3 percent more young women with high satisfaction than old. The picture is different for overt satisfaction. With increasing age, an increasing percentage of women answer that they are very satisfied and a decreasing percentage that they are dissatisfied. Age, then, is not a significant factor in determining satisfaction with work, although it is with overt satisfaction. Since the composite satisfaction is composed of overt satisfaction plus answers to six control questions, evidently, it is these answers that are not age dependent.

Concerning health condition, the percentile difference between low health/ low satisfaction and high health/low satisfaction is −14.2; the percentile difference between low health/high satisfaction and high health/high satisfaction is +18.4. Thus, health is a significant factor. To check with overt satisfaction, it transpires that those in poor health condition prefer to describe themselves as somewhat satisfied; poor health hardly increases the disposition to express dissatisfaction.

Concerning domestic work load, there is no significant difference in satisfaction between workers with low and medium domestic work loads, but those with high domestic work loads have their low satisfaction percentile increase by 6.7, while their high satisfaction percentile decreases by 4.6. Checking this with overt satisfaction, we find that workers with a heavy domestic work load, just like those with poor health conditions, tend to declare themselves somewhat satisfied, yet, interestingly, with the rise of the domestic load there is a significant decline in the percentage of the dissatisfied, presumably from the loss of courage to be critical of their work situation.

Turning from life situation to work career, we begin with initial aspirations. The percentile difference between low aspiration/low satisfaction and high aspiration/low satisfaction is +4; that between low aspiration/high satisfaction and high aspiration/high satisfaction is +8.8. In other words, both low satisfaction and high satisfaction rise with the rise of initial aspirations. Checking with overt satisfaction, when we move from low to high aspirations, we get a considerable decline in declared high satisfaction and a rise in declared dissatisfaction. Thus, clearly, initial aspirations signify, but not in a monotone way, since the rise of high satisfaction rate with the rise of initial aspirations is due to the rise in positive answers to the control questions, signifying a higher occupational pride in, or appreciation of, the content of the job.

As to progress in work career, I combine the lower two levels—static and declining—because of the small size of the lowest group. The percentile difference between static-low satisfaction and progressive-low satisfaction is −9; and between static-high satisfaction and progressive-high satisfaction it is +8. The overt satisfaction correlation shows a significant rise of the very satisfied with progress and a significant decline of the dissatisfied. Thus, the experience of progress in one's work career has a clear, although not an overwhelming, impact on the degree of one's satisfaction, mostly as expressed in the answer to the direct question concerning satisfaction.

From life situation and work career we now come to views and values, where the picture is very interesting. There is no difference between the traditional-low satisfaction and the egalitarian-low satisfaction; the percentile difference between the traditional-high satisfaction and the egalitarian-high satisfaction is, however, +6. Checking the overt satisfaction, we find considerable differences between those who hold traditional views and the egalitarians: significantly fewer egalitarians declare themselves very satisfied, and a very significant percentage of them declare themselves dissatisfied. The conclusion from this is that egalitarian views correlate positively with many more positive answers to the control questions; which may be explained as expressions of a higher degree of identification with their work role achieved by egalitarian women than by holders of the traditional views, as well as the rise in their ability to criticize their present job.

𝑋 Finally, there are the two variables characterizing the current job, hygiene and content. The percentile difference between low hygiene/low satisfaction and high hygiene/low satisfaction is −37.5! That between low hygiene/high satisfaction and high hygiene/high satisfaction is +24.6! When we remember that 39.3 percent of the entire sample have a low degree of satisfaction and that within the group with low hygiene jobs 59.6 percent have a low degree of satisfaction, then we can easily agree with Herzberg's claim that low hygiene constitutes the great dissatisfier. This is also borne out by the figures for overt satisfaction. In the whole sample only 13.6 percent answered that they are somewhat or very dissatisfied. In the low hygiene group this figure rises to 26.5 percent, and in the high hygiene group this figure falls to 5.8 percent. Similarly, whereas in the low hygiene group only 19.7 percent declare themselves very satisfied, in the high hygiene group 58.8 percent did—the highest percentage of any subdivision in any of the correlations with satisfaction. The percentile difference in the overt satisfaction suffices to account for the shift in composite satisfaction.

Finally, there is the content of the job and its possible influence on job satisfaction. The percentile difference between low content/low satisfaction and high content/low satisfaction is −26.6, whereas that between low content/high satisfaction and high content/high satisfaction is +21.3. In agreement with Herzberg, in low satisfaction it is hygiene that plays a greater role than content and in high satisfaction they are almost equal—since even the highest content jobs in my sample are still of relatively low content. As to overt satisfaction, in the low content group, 19.6 percent declare themselves dissatisfied and in the high content group 8.9 percent do. In the low content group, 31.6 percent declare themselves very satisfied; in the high content group, 46.4 percent do. Hence, despite the considerable shift in the answers to the direct question, it is still not sufficient to account for the shift in the level of composite satisfaction. This shift, therefore, must be taken to include a considerable rise in occupational pride.

Satisfaction and Autotelic Attitudes

I have mentioned that the superficial kind of satisfaction is claimed to be a reflection of workers' resignation. In preparation for my discussion of the different kinds of satisfaction, I wish now to correlate the ordinary kinds of satisfaction, overt and composite, with some attitudes that reflect (or possibly reflect) workers' active attitudes toward their work situation, that is, emphasis on content, concern for content, interest in advancement, and concern for hygiene.

Is a worker who demands that his job be challenging, who lays emphasis on the task characteristics of his job and thereby has higher demands from his work life than one who does not share this with him, is he less satisfied or more satisfied with his job than the other? Of course, the answer depends on the task characteristics of the job in question. Still, under the conditions of jobs that are all under the semiprofessional level of skill, my data indicate that emphasis on content relates to satisfaction in this way. The percentile difference between low emphasis/low satisfaction and high emphasis/low satisfaction is −11.5, whereas for low emphasis/high satisfaction and high emphasis/high satisfaction it is +7.8. This result is very impressive. Comparing it with the correlation of emphasis on content with overt satisfaction is also interesting, since it turns out, when moving from low to high emphasis on content, the small rise in the incidence of those who declare themselves very satisfied and the small rise in the incidence of those who declare themselves dissatisfied should cancel each other out. Hence, the shift to a higher level of composite satisfaction must here be caused by more positive answers to the control questions.

Those workers who put more emphasis on the intrinsic qualities of work tend to polarize and be either overtly very satisfied or overtly dissatisfied; also, they have a higher incidence of occupational pride.

The picture is somewhat different for concern for content. With the rising concern for content, a general decline appears in composite satisfaction with work. The incidence of those with low satisfaction rises by 19.9 percent when we move from low to high concern for content. What causes this big decline? Moving from low to high concern, there is a decline of 22.1 percent in the incidence of the overtly very satisfied, and a rise of only 5.3 percent of the overtly somewhat satisfied, and a rise of 16.3 percent of the overtly dissatisfied. Hence, with the rise of concern for content there is a decided shift to overt dissatisfaction. To put it differently, 43.1 percent of the overtly dissatisfied have a high concern for content, whereas only 18.9 percent of the overtly very satisfied have it. This indicates that many of the overtly dissatisfied workers endorse an active attitude toward the content of their job.

The picture of the correlation between satisfaction and interest in advancement is different again. Here no significant difference in the incidence of low, medium, or high level of composite satisfaction occurs between those with low and high interests in advancement. Yet there is a difference in overt satisfaction: among those with high interest in advancement, the incidence of the overtly very satisfied declines by 13.7 percent, of the somewhat overtly satisfied increases by 5.9 percent, and of the overtly dissatisfied increases again—by 8.1 percent. In other words, whereas only 43.5 percent of the overtly very satisfied show high interest in advancement, 67 percent of the overtly dissatisfied do. Again, overt dissatisfaction indicates a worker's endorsement of an active attitude toward the improvement of her work situation. Why is this not reflected in the correlation with composite satisfaction? This is because more of those who show interest in advancement offer affirmative answers to the control questions, thereby exhibiting occupational pride.

To illustrate the active character of dissatisfaction, let me briefly correlate composite satisfaction with concern for the hygiene characteristics of the job, which is also considered an active attitude, although not necessarily an autotelic one. In line with the above rule, dissatisfaction raises concern here too: with high concern for hygiene we find a shift from high to low composite satisfaction by nearly 18 percent.

Are the two concerns, then, for content and for hygiene, so very different? In other words, are those concerned with the negative content characteristics of their jobs indifferent to the negative characteristics of their work conditions? And does the concern for work conditions rule out concern for content? Let us remember that while a little over one quarter of the sample are highly concerned with content, nearly one half are concerned with hygiene. My data show that among those highly concerned with hygiene, the incidence of the highly concerned for content is 32.1 percent, whereas among those indifferent to hygiene, it is only 10.8 percent. The other way around the data are even more impressive: among those highly concerned with content, the incidence of those highly concerned with hygiene is 62.1 percent as opposed to 40.4 percent among those indifferent to content.

Thus, for those who read Maslow and Herzberg to claim that concern for content and hygiene are mutually exclusive, my data constitute a refutation of this claim. In this study, I take it for granted that those actively concerned about the improvement of the content of their jobs will see no reason to neglect being actively concerned about the improvement of their work conditions. Even the converse may hold: those ready to be active about hygiene are more likely to be active about content as well.

The Instrumental Attitude

The concept of the instrumental attitude to work is central in the sociology of work yet uncomfortably vague. I shall avoid discussing its significance outside the study of work. Clearly, whoever emphasizes the task or content characteristics of her job as important contributors to the meaning of her job has an attitude that cannot be viewed as instrumental. Yet the mere absence from her of any expression of such an emphasis on content (as a desirable quality of a good job or as what would be missed if not employed) may not be due to an instrumental attitude: it can be due to inarticulateness. The question concerning the meaning of work is rather abstract, and it might be difficult for the worker to conclude about jobs in general from her limited job experience. Therefore, rather than consider the lack of emphasis on the content of work as sufficient, I inquired also about the worker's concern about what she describes as poor content characteristics of her current job. If she shows concern about them, I decide that she exhibits not the instrumental attitude but some inarticulateness. Since all of my interviewees have described some poor content characteristics, I could define the instrumental attitude as the absence of both an emphasis on content and any concern for negative content characteristics; here the second component merely serves as a check on the possibility that the absence of an expression of emphasis on content is the result of a mere inarticulateness. But I have also added a third component, whose import seems to me to be obvious: the presence or absence of interest in advancement and promotion as I have defined it. A worker ready to make an effort to obtain a more skilled, challenging, or responsible job cannot be viewed as having endorsed the instrumental attitude.

My definition, then, of the instrumental attitude is of one compounded out of three: (1) the lack of emphasis on content, (2) the lack of concern about negative content characteristics of the job, and (3) the lack of interest in advancement.

Of the whole sample, 70.7 percent do not emphasize content highly, 45.9 percent show no concern for poor content, and 47.8 percent have low interest in advancement; 36.7 percent do not put high emphasis on content and show no concern for poor content, 37.4 percent do not put high emphasis on content and have low interest in advancement, and 28.9 percent show no concern for poor content and show low interest in advancement. The instrumental attitude is exhibited by 23.4 percent of the sample. (See tables A-92 to A-94.) For the distribution of the instrumental attitude in the nine groups see table A-95. It ranges from only 6 percent in Group 5 (U.S. office) to 50 percent in Group 6 (German industry). There is a very pronounced occupational scale, with the office group having the fewest instrumentally adapted, 8.2 percent, retail having 23.5 percent, and industry, 38.4 percent. The scale is divergent from the usual pattern for the Israeli group, where the incidence of the instrumental attitude is a little lower in the very young industrial group than in the retail group. The same low incidence of the instrumental attitude in the Israeli industrial group also gives Israel a lower incidence than the United States in spite of the fact that both the U.S. retail and office groups have a lower incidence of the instrumental attitude than the corresponding Israeli groups. The German national group has the highest incidence of the instrumental attitude in all the occupational subgroups.

What are the origins of the instrumental attitude? A frequent assumption about it is that it is the outcome of a process of adaptation: at the beginning of one's work life one's attitude to work is normally autotelic, but a prolonged period of work in jobs with low content cramps opportunities for the growth of skills, for the use of initiative and judgment, and for the acceptance of responsibility. The worker is then likely to adapt to the harsh reality, and in order to avoid the pain of frustrated aspirations, he is likely to adopt an instrumental attitude to work. One interpretation of this assumption would be that adaptation means the lowering of one's initial aspirations. Whenever these initial aspirations about the desired content of the job are considerably higher than the reality of the job, workers are most likely to lower their aspirations, even drastically, in order to adapt. According to this interpretation, the highest rate of workers exhibiting the instrumental attitude will be found in groups of workers with the highest initial aspirations but in jobs with the lowest level of content.

In my discussion of the fit theory, I have observed that 65 percent of those with high initial aspirations (based on schooling and completed vocational training) work in jobs with low or medium content. Yet only 12.1 percent of those with high initial aspirations exhibit the instrumental attitude. Of those with medium initial aspirations, 15 percent work in low content jobs, yet 24.2 percent of them, double the percentage of those with high initial aspirations, exhibit the instrumental attitude. Of those with low initial aspirations, where we cannot speak of lowering of initial aspirations in this sense at all, the incidence of the instrumental attitude is by far the highest—40.7 percent.

It therefore seems that the lower the initial aspirations, the greater the likelihood of adaptation and resignation to a poor job. Yet the more decisive factor is the content level of the job. Whereas in low content jobs (these are by definition 1/3 of the jobs in the sample) the incidence of the instrumental attitude is 38 percent, in the high content jobs it is minimal, only 4.8 percent. Among the women in relatively better jobs, the incidence of emphasis on content and of concern for content is more than three times higher than among those in the poorest jobs. For both these attitudes this is the most important factor. It is important for interest in advancement too. In poor jobs, only 42 percent show interest in advancement, in better jobs, 69 percent. Yet for this attitude, the factor that is even more significant is the views and values of the women concerned. Of those with traditional views, only 21.4 percent are interested in advancement, whereas 70 percent of those with egalitarian views are. I shall discuss this ideological factor later on.

Since the instrumental attitude is more frequent with workers whose initial aspirations are low rather than high, it may appear that it is not reached by a process of adaptation at all. Yet the correlation of the instrumental attitude with age contradicts this. Whereas the incidence of the instrumental attitude among those up to thirty-five is only 13.5 percent, it is 36.3 percent for those over thirty-five. Yet the process of instrumental adaptation is not monotone; the youngest age group, those under twenty-five, have a somewhat higher incidence of the instrumental attitude, 14 percent, than the low 12.8 percent of the twenty-six to thirty-five group. The process of adaptation begins in earnest after the age of thirty-five. Among those between the ages of thirty-six and forty-five, 31.4 percent are already instrumentally adapted, and between the age of forty-six and fifty-five, it is 37.1 percent. For those between the age of fifty-six and sixty-five it reaches 46.6 percent.

Finally, there are the other life conditions, especially health conditions and domestic work load. The correlation of these two with the instrumental attitude is significant but much weaker than the correlation with content, initial aspirations, or views and values. Of women in poor health, 27.4 percent exhibit the instrumental attitude as compared with only 19 percent of those in good health. The correlation with domestic work load is stronger—only 17 percent of those with a light domestic work load are instrumentally adapted, against 31.8 percent of those with a heavy domestic work load. The same holds for the experience of progress in one's past work career—only 14.7 percent who have had progress are instrumentally adapted, yet among those whose careers have been static or regressive 30.5 percent are instrumentally adapted.

Thus, the following picture emerges. Instrumental adaptation is most likely to occur among employed women in jobs with a low content level whose views and values are traditional, whose initial aspirations were low, who have experienced no progress in their work careers, whose domestic work load is heavy, and whose health is poor.

Satisfaction and the Instrumental Attitude

Considering how central the study of work satisfaction has been in the sociology of work, it seems rather surprising how limited the usefulness of a worker's observed level of satisfaction has been for the reliable forecast of her future attitude to work. The correlation of the composite variable "satisfaction with work" with the variables "emphasis on content," "concern for content," and "interest in advancement," are useless here. Replacing the composite variable "satisfaction with work" with "overt satisfaction with work," we find a small rise in the percentage of the overtly dissatisfied with the rise of emphasis on content, of concern for content, and of interest in advancement. Yet, as only 13.6 percent of the entire sample have declared themselves dissatisfied, our knowledge of overt satisfaction or dissatisfaction is not very helpful either.

A. Bruggemann, P. Groskurth, and E. Ulich have suggested that the problem of the significance of work satisfaction or dissatisfaction for other work attitudes can be solved by viewing it as a result of the worker's processing his own work experience. Their model presents a few variants, of satisfaction and dissatisfaction, active and passive. I shall not discuss the active variants. The three passive variants they present are called "resignated satisfaction," "pseudo satisfaction," and "fixated dissatisfaction." The processes by which workers arrive at these attitudes are, respectively, the lowering of aspirations, the distortion of perception of the work situation, and desisting from all attempts to solve problems. Let me examine these assumptions.

I assume that what I call the instrumental attitude is the attitude that is shared by all three of Bruggemann's categories of passive attitudes. Since in answer to the direct question as to satisfaction with the job, 13.7 percent of the entire sample have declared themselves dissatisfied, we may inquire as to how many of these are fixated. Correlating overt satisfaction with the instrumental attitude shows that only 5.1 percent of the dissatisfied hold the threefold instrumental attitude; only 1.2 percent of the entire sample are then fixatedly dissatisfied, thus making this category extremely marginal. (See table A-96.)

The assumption of Bruggemann et al. is that the process of arriving at resignative satisfaction is that of the lowering of aspirations. As noted earlier, the incidence of the instrumental attitude in my sample is much higher among those with lower aspirations than among the rest. Hence, the assumption does not hold for individuals with especially high initial aspirations. If, however, their assumption is that normal, healthy humans tend to constantly raise their aspirations regarding their work roles, but that some do not because of prolonged frustrations, and so become resigned and declare themselves satisfied, then their assumption may very well be true.

As to their assumption that the process of distortion of one's perception of one's work situation leads one to pseudosatisfaction, my study was not designed to test this assumption, since it was designed to help the interviewees to actively describe their work situations as accurately as possible. Rather, let me mention the findings of F. den Terhog and H.P. Vossen, which point in another direction. A false perception of one's job, they say, need not be the outcome of self-deception, but the result of a limited work experience. The same women assembly workers, who previously had not perceived the negative intrinsic characteristics of their job, developed an entirely new perception of their older jobs and describe them now as monotonous and automatonlike after a year of work in restructured jobs with considerably increased degrees of skill, variety, autonomy, and responsibility. They had previously declared themselves generally satisfied despite the poor intrinsic aspects of their jobs; they became critical even of these improved aspects and demanded further improvements. Their earlier uncritical satisfaction was thus temporary and not self-deceptive. This kind of misperception of one's work conditions is missing from the model of Bruggemann et al.

To conclude, I find the model of Bruggemann et al. very limited in applicability. I therefore wish to explore the significance of my third satisfaction variable, which I call "superficial satisfaction."

Superficial Satisfaction
and Its Significance

In studying superficial satisfaction I follow the descriptions of several sociologists of work, who had described its prevalence among instrumentally adapted workers, for example, Bennett Berger's description of Californian automobile workers and Goldthorpe's description of British industrial workers.

I assume this kind of satisfaction to be superficial because of its inconsistency. This seems to me to signify a kind of resignation and readiness to be content with the second best. (Mistakes are, of course, not ruled out. Being satisfied with a job without being ready to recommend it to one's daughter usually indicates a superficial attitude. Yet it may sometimes happen to the genuinely satisfied worker who takes into account completely different aspirations or talents for her daughter.) Superficial satisfaction is fairly frequent in my sample: 44 percent exhibit it. But variations are considerable, ranging from 63.4 percent in Group 1 (Israeli retail) to 10.8 percent on Group 5 (U.S. office). (See table A-97.)

My first question was Are women who exhibit the instrumental attitude also superficially satisfied? It turns out that they often are: 55.6 percent of the instrumentally adapted are superficially satisfied, as opposed to 41 percent of those not instrumentally adapted. The correlation is significant for each component of the instrumental attitude. Thus, 34.1 percent of those who exhibit high emphasis on content are superficially satisfied, and 51.1 percent of those who exhibit low or medium emphasis; 37.4 percent of those who show high concern for content are superficially satisfied, and 51.2 percent of those who show low concern; 37 percent of those who show high interest in advancement are superficially satisfied, and 52 percent of those who show low interest are.

My second question was What does the knowledge of a worker's superficial satisfaction tell us about her other work attitudes? It turns out that those who are superficially satisfied more often exhibit significantly each of the components of the instrumental attitude than those who are not. Thus, of the superficially satisfied, 46.4 percent place no emphasis on content as compared with 35.5 percent of those who are not; of those who are superficially satisfied, 51.2 percent show no concern for content as opposed to 41.6 percent of those who are not; and 56.2 percent of the superficially satisfied show no interest in advancement as opposed to 41.1 percent of those who are not. Finally, the threefold instrumental attitude is exhibited by 29.3 percent of the superficially satisfied, but by only 18.7 percent of the rest.

Superficial satisfaction is much more widespread than the instrumental attitude, yet it seems to be akin to it. Let us, then, examine the correlations of the percentage of the incidence of superficial satisfaction with life conditions, work career, the characteristics of one's job, and views and values.

		Percent
Age	36+	57.4
	−35	34.4
Health condition	poor	49.2
	good	39.9
Domestic burden	heavy	51.1
	light	32.2
Initial aspirations	low	57.7
	high	35.5
Progress in work	static	48.7
	progressive	44.0
Content	low	51.6
	high	31.5
Views and values	traditional	54.1
	egalitarian	33.9

The incidence of superficial satisfaction rises with each of the five age groups, from only 31.6 percent for those under twenty-five to nearly 70 percent for those over fifty-five. This is clearly a variable that expresses resignation, the acceptance of the second best. The other most important factors making for superficial satisfaction are low initial aspirations, traditional views, and the low content of the job; then comes high domestic work load. The correlation with poor health is much weaker; a static past work career correlates hardly at all, and there exists no specific correlation with the hygiene characteristics of the job.

To conclude, the correlations with superficial satisfaction and with the instrumental attitude are the same (with the exception of static work career); their order of significance is, however, somewhat different.

The Instrumental Syndrome

Following the suggestion that a fully instrumentally adapted worker will also express a superficial and inconsistent satisfaction with her job, I have isolated that group of women who exhibit superficial satisfaction in addition to the instrumental attitude: only 13 percent of the sample exhibit all four attitudes together. (For their distribution in the nine groups, see table A-98.) The incidence of this joint attitude varies from 29.8 percent in Group 6 (German industry) to 1.2 percent in Group 5 (U.S. office). I define this attitude as "the instrumental syndrome." I shall examine its correlations with various factors, and use it for the examination of two hypotheses. The correlations of the percentage of the incidence of the instrumental syndrome with life conditions, characteristics of the content of the job, and views and values, are the following.

		Percent
Age	36+	22.7
	−35	5.6
Health conditions	poor	15.8
	good	9.9
Domestic burden	high	19.2
	light	6.5
Initial aspirations	low	24.9
	high	5.9
Progress in work career	static	17.0
	progressive	8.2
Content	low	21.6
	high	3.0
Hygiene	insignificant correlation	
Views	traditional	19.5
	egalitarian	6.4

For age groups, the under twenty-five and the twenty-six to thirty-five age groups show the same low incidence of the instrumental syndrome of 5.6 percent; thence it rises gradually to 32.8 percent for the over fifty-five year olds. It appears that the level of initial aspirations and the level of the content of the job are both highly important factors for the incidence of the instrumental syndrome; age, views and values, domestic burden, and the experience of progress in one's work career or its absence follows in declining importance; health is of minor importance, and the correlation with the level of hygiene of the job is insignificant. Hence, the workers with low aspirations, working on a job with low task characteristics, over thirty-five years of age, holding traditional views, having a heavy domestic work load, and having no progress in their work careers, are most likely to adopt the full instrumental syndrome.

The Origins of the Instrumental Syndrome and the Work Ethic

Although the incidence of the instrumental syndrome rises with age, it appears also in some young workers. Hulin and Blood have attempted to explain why some young industrial workers in American cities exhibit a decided instrumental attitude, and why others doing the same kind of work do not. On the basis of the demographic data of their sample, they suggested that two different kinds of work ethic exist in American society. Rural and small-town youths are socialized to seek intrinsic value in work, the traditional American work ethic, and they thus develop an autotelic attitude to work. City youths, by contrast, especially the sons of industrial workers, have already been socialized into the instrumental attitude to work. On the basis of this assumption, it has been concluded that in the case of these city-bred workers, an improvement of the task characteristics of their jobs would not result in more "motivation"; it would not alter their instrumental and unconcerned attitude to work.

I used my demographic data and the data about the work attitudes of the present sample of 761 women in relatively low-content jobs to test this theory about the impact of different processes of socialization on city workers and on rural and small-town workers. A breakdown of the data showed that 53.6 percent of the interviewees had spent their childhood in a large city and 46.4 percent in a rural village or a small town. (See table A-99 for the distribution.) Contrary to the hypothesis, city-bred women workers do not have a higher frequency of displaying the instrumental syndrome; the frequency is even slightly lower—12.3 percent as compared with 13.9 percent for the village and small-town women. Even if we look only at the women in low content jobs, the rural women have a slightly higher incidence of the instrumental syndrome.

I do not intend to deny the following two assumptions included in the theory that, as a whole, do not agree with my data. Different systems of work ethic may indeed exist at the same time in different social groupings within the same national societies that are not necessarily social classes in any accepted sense. Childhood socialization on the lines of such divergent systems of work ethic may very well be responsible for the existence of divergent work attitudes of different workers doing the same kind of job at the same time and place.

Several aspects of the work ethic and its impact have been neglected thus far. First, there is no single traditional American work ethic, just as there is no single tradition of work ethic in any other national society. Different systems of work ethic exist side by side in contemporary society, so they existed in the past. Second, work ethics are in constant flux. Third, under the conditions of modern mass communications, the values of one social group influence those of other groups, especially those of their young, and they cross class and national boundaries even more than they did in the past. As examples, we may consider the work ethic of the youth culture and of the women's movement. Fourth, socialization or resocialization into a value system concerning work does not stop with childhood's end. Finally, throughout history, all social groups explicitly or implicitly have endorsed different systems of work ethic for the two sexes.

In the present study, neither the entire work ethic of the interviewees nor their entire value systems concerning work as such, were explored. Rather, only some aspects were examined, namely, the views and values they hold about men's and women's appropriate work roles in the household and in the labor market. In the course of the discussion of the significance of these views and values for women's job attitudes, I shall discuss the importance of modern, egalitarian views and values in counteracting the process of instrumental adaptation in employed women.

The Instrumental Syndrome and the
Preference for the Domestic
Work Role

A basic assumption in calling certain attitudes toward work instrumental is that
for the instrumentally adapted worker, the job is only an instrument for the
attainment of satisfaction outside the work sphere. For an employed man,
satisfaction may lie in the family sphere, the community sphere, or an individual
concern, usually a hobby. The general assumption of classical sociology is that
the normal woman's central life interest is the family, not the community or
hobbies. Taken consistently, this theory implies that all normal employed
women see their jobs as secondary in importance to their domestic role and
would prefer the exclusive domestic role.

In work attitude studies, one standard question is asked to induce a reply to
the unasked question of instrumental adaptation: "If you had no financial
needs, would you continue to work?" When I asked the interviewees this
question, only 19.8 percent replied that they preferred to stay at home. I
assumed that those who exhibit the symptoms of the instrumental syndrome are
more disposed to stay at home than the rest, and this assumption is borne out by
the facts. Of the instrumentally adapted, 34.6 percent would stay at home were
they not financially constrained to work as opposed to 15.6 percent of those not
instrumentally adapted. Nevertheless, even among the instrumentally adapted
women, the disposition to stay at home is smaller by far than currently assumed.
The majority of those women who exhibit indifference, resignation, and
superficial satisfaction with the limitations of their employment roles, would,
nevertheless, given the chance, still not exchange it for the exclusive domestic
role.

Monotony and Pressure, the Content
of the Job, and Psychosomatic Symptoms

Up to now I have largely examined the correlation between job characteristics
and two work attitudes of instrumentality, unconcern and resignation. These
attitudes have been considered to be negative for the intellectual well being and
psychological health of the worker. I shall now deal briefly with the correlation
between job characteristics and psychosomatic symptoms.

Observations of industrial workers that started half a century ago noted the
frequent appearance among workers in mass production industries of certain
symptoms that are now considered psychosomatic, such as nervousness, sleep-
lessness, headaches, lower backaches, and upsets of the digestive system. Because
these symptoms appeared most frequently among workers on the newly
established moving production and assembly lines, attention focused on the

characteristics of this kind of work: monotony, the extreme division of labor, the constant repetition of the one short activity (which produces fatigue), and the dependence on the performance of each worker on the speedy completion of the activity by the previous performer (which produces tension and pressure, especially if the line moves quickly and the workers cannot regulate or stop it). Another kind of tension is caused by the individual incentive pay method, popularly called piecework. It is still in wide use in industry, especially in branches employing mainly women, although in Western countries few managements pay on the basis of quantity of work alone. Labor unions insist on a basic hourly rate to be paid to all workers. Those who are on piecework are paid an additional premium relative to their surpassing the norms.

The periodic fixing of the norms has become one of the central topics of bargaining. Whenever pay is based completely or largely on quantity, and premiums tend to make up a major part of one's compensation, then speed of performance becomes of utmost importance. This results in tension. The tension and pressure resulting from the mechanically moving line with its interdependence of workers and the tendency of management to try to speed up the line, as well as to impose petty restrictions on the personal freedom of line workers, are absent in the needle trade industry. In some factories, management relies largely on the individual incentive of the women to obtain the amount of production which management aims at and puts minimal pressure on them. In other organizations, especially in those most prone to a seesaw of slack and busy periods, pay by the individual incentive method is accompanied by close supervision, admonitions to increase production, and restrictions on personal freedom of movement and communication.

In my sample, although a combination of monotony with pressure was most prevalent in the jobs of the three industrial groups, it existed also in some of the retail jobs and in a small part of the office jobs. The average rate of high monotony and pressure for the industrial group is 57.3 percent, for the retail group, 24 percent, and for the office group, 16.6 percent. In retail work, the sale of small, cheap items and cashiering, especially in large supermarkets, can be rather monotonous. For the office group, the performance of routine clerical operations can be monotonous. Tension and pressure can come from management's admonition to perform at high speed, but for retail and office workers it comes more often from impatient customers. (For the distribution of psychosomatic symptoms by subgroup see table A-100.)

In order to let the effects of the job characteristics have time to manifest themselves, I limited the sample in the present case to the 488 women who had worked at least two years in their current jobs. Of this population, 13.5 percent suffer from several psychosomatic symptoms, 68.4 percent from none, and the rest from some. I then considered the correlation between monotony and pressure in the job and the incidence of psychosomatic symptoms. The data show that 19 percent of the women who have much monotony and pressure in their jobs suffer from many psychosomatic symptoms, as compared with 11.3 percent of those with little monotony and pressure. In other words, 56 percent of the 66 women who suffer from a high level of psychosomatic symptoms also have much monotony and pressure in their jobs as compared with only 16.7 percent for those who have low monotony and pressure.

These figures seem to point to monotony and pressure on the job as an important factor for those interested in the causes of psychosomatic symptoms. But the composite variable of level of the task or content characteristics of the job shows a considerably stronger correlation with psychosomatic symptoms than monotony and pressure alone. Here the rate for low-content jobs is as high as 25 percent and for high-content jobs as low as 8 percent. In other words, 63.6 percent of the 66 women with many psychosomatic symptoms work in low-content jobs, and only 12.1 percent hold high-content jobs. The data show that a low level of the task or content characteristics of the job—a composite of low skill and quality, high speed and pressure, and the lack of variety, autonomy, and responsibility—is by far the more important factor for the appearance of psychosomatic symptoms than high monotony and pressure alone. The one variable includes the other, of course: 126 of the 169 low-content jobs in this sample (74.6 percent) also have high monotony and pressure. We can disentangle the effects of monotony and pressure from the other factors contributing to low task or content characteristics by looking at the medium-content jobs that include high monotony and pressure, since 65 of the 216 medium content jobs—30 percent—fit this category. In these cases, the rate of high psychosomatic symptoms is 7.7 percent, much lower than the 25.4 percent of low-content jobs. The combination of high monotony and pressure with medium-content of the job does not make any difference as far as the rate of psychosomatic symptoms is concerned.

The data indicate that low content of the job is the most important factor for the appearance of psychosomatic symptoms.

Theories Specific to Women

Of the theories about work attitudes and about the factors that influence employment careers, several are specific to women. The two work attitudes that are problematic for women are their attachment and commitment to work and employment and their interest in advancement and promotion; I shall discuss them in detail. I shall attempt to evaluate the weight of the factors usually claimed to influence women's employment careers most, namely, their interruptions of employment and their part-time work, as well as their domestic work load. I shall present my findings concerning the import of women's views about the appropriate work role for women and then I shall present these views as a significant factor correlating with their life conditions and work attitudes.

Women's Attachment and Commitment to
Employment and Occupation

The major sociological theory that attempts to explain sex-specific differences in work attitudes is the role theory. It attempts to explain why women are supposed to have a lower attachment and commitment to employment and occupation, as well as lower interest in advancement and promotion. I shall first discuss commitment and then interest in advancement.

Several variants of the role theory are usually proposed. One variant claims that modern women play two social roles, the domestic role—which at least historically was the primary one—and the employment role. The values and norms of these two roles conflict with each other; hence employed women live in a state of constant tension; this tension keeps their attachment and commitment to the secondary role of employment and occupation weak. The second variant speaks not of a clash between values and norms, but of the double burden that the dual role tends to put on women, especially on mothers who work outside their household. This variant claims that this double burden precludes any high commitment to an occupational role for the employed mother. A third variant of the role theory claims that because of the socialization of men into the provider role, married women see no need (and/or their husbands do not want them) to earn as much as men. Thus married women are bound to treat their employment roles as secondary to those of their husbands, and they keep their attachment to employment low. Some writers endorse two of these three variants, and some endorse all of them.

I shall try to examine the explanatory power of each of the three variants of the role theory with the help of correlations of the level of commitment to employment with views and values, domestic work load, and marital status. I shall also examine correlations with other life conditions and career factors. Finally, I shall examine my own hypothesis that the attachment and commitment to employment and occupation for women—and presumably for men, too—rises with the quality of the content of the job.

The interviewees were, of course, not asked whether they suffered from any strain between the conflicting values and norms of their domestic and employment roles. Yet their responses to the statements on the appropriate roles of men and women in the family and in the labor market imply whether they accepted the traditional values and norms that make the domestic role primary for women and the provider role primary for men. I assume that in the first variant of the role theory these women will experience some role strain between their two roles. At first I therefore correlated only the positions regarding the first subgroup of views and values—those that concern male and female roles. Then I correlate the entire composite variable "views and values" with the variable of attachment and commitment to employment and occupation.

Of the entire sample, 15.6 percent have low commitment, 34.6 percent medium, and 49.8 percent high commitment. In each subgroup of views and values, the interviewees are graded into traditional and modern only, although the more complex composite variable grades them into three levels, traditional, intermediate, and egalitarian. The correlation of the subgroup of values concerning roles with commitment is significant though not very strong: of those with traditional values, 20.1 percent have low commitment; of those with modern values, only 13.2 percent; of those with traditional values, 45.7 percent have high commitment; of those with modern values, 52 percent. The correlation with commitment for the entire composite variable "views and values" (which contains, in addition to values concerning male and female roles, a wide variety of views concerning the rights and capacities of women in the occupational sphere) is considerably stronger. Of those with traditional views, 21.8 percent have low commitment; of those with egalitarian views, only 10.6 percent; of those with traditional views, 41.4 percent have high commitment, of those with egalitarian views, as many as 56.9 percent. It can therefore be concluded, first, that it is not only the acceptance of the traditional values and norms concerning the primary and secondary role of women that weakens their commitment to work but also their acceptance of the traditional justification of their de facto inferior position in the occupational sphere. Second, that the role strain on women is neither uniform nor static. It is therefore assumed that for women whose views and values about the appropriate roles, rights, and duties of men and women in the family and in the occupational sphere approach the egalitarian, the impact of the remaining role strain on their degree of commitment to employment and occupation should be minimal.

To test the second variant of the role theory, the variable domestic work load, which has three levels—light, medium, and heavy—was correlated with commitment. Of those with a heavy domestic work load, 23.4 percent have low commitment, of those with a light work load, only 9.4 percent—the greatest variance in the incidence of low commitment to work that appears in any of my correlations. Yet, whereas a light domestic work load seems to reduce the incidence of low commitment considerably, it does not increase the incidence of high commitment quite as significantly: of those with a heavy work load, 43.3 percent have high commitment; of those with a light load, 56.2 percent—a variance that, although quite significant, is somewhat smaller than that for views and values.

The third variant of the role theory assumes the impact of the presence of the provider role for men will lessen the commitment of women to employment. I have tried to test this variant by examining the level of commitment of a group of women who all have husbands present and earning and by comparing it to the level of commitment of the others in the sample. As we have already seen, the impact of the domestic work load on commitment is very considerable, I have tried to isolate a group whose members are likely to have some domestic work load, yet are unlikely to expect the birth of children in the future, or to have children under school age in their care. I chose married women between the age of thirty-five and fifty; there were 147 women in this group. Of them, 26.5 percent have low commitment compared to only 15.6 percent of the entire sample, 20.8 percent have medium commitment compared to 34.6 percent of the entire sample, and only 32.7 percent have high commitment compared to 49.8 percent of the entire sample. These figures support the view that the presence of an earning husband who is supposed to be the chief provider for his family lowers a woman's commitment to work. Nevertheless, this apparent strong negative correlation between the married state and commitment may be misleading because of two intervening variables. In my sample, married women in the specified age group work disproportionately in industry, and hence their values are disproportionately traditional—traditional views and values, we have seen, lower commitment. The other intervening variable is the low content characteristic of these women's jobs, a variable that, as we shall see, also lowers commitment to employment and occupation. In conclusion, all three variants of the role hypothesis seem to be useful when translated into significant correlations.

Let me now examine the correlation of commitment to work with the other life conditions, beginning with age. Correlating the two age groups, less than thirty-five and older than thirty-six years, with commitment we find that the incidence of low commitment is somewhat—4.7 percent—lower in the older group, whereas the incidence of high commitment rises by 17.2 percent with age. Looking at the five age groups, it turns out that the level of commitment remains nearly equal until age forty-five; thereafter high commitment rises very considerably to 63.6 percent in the age group forty-six to fifty-five and 82.8 percent for those over fifty-five. Among the group of those over fifty, we find the near disappearance of low commitment—only 5.1 percent—and 77.4 percent with high commitment. This rise of the incidence of high commitment with age can be explained by the interest of many of the older women in the sample to continue employment in order to gain favorable pensions for themselves. In this older group, there were women, especially in Group 1 (Israeli retail), who had entered employment first after the age of thirty-one and others who had very long interruptions in their employment careers. Often they still had not completed the minimum period legally required for eligibility for the basic national old age pension in their own right. The interest of another sizable group of older women in Group 3 (U.S. industry) to continue in employment is explicable by their wish to gain the full union pension: only those who have been employed for a period of twenty years in firms that are organized by the same union are eligible.

We have thus to take account of the fact that here the age factor—age fifty and up—intervenes and counteracts the impact of the traditional views on commitment.

The correlation of commitment to work with health conditions is insignificant; whereas the rate of low commitment rises somewhat with poor health—by 8.6 percent—the incidence of high level of commitment does not decline with it.

Now to career factors. The level of initial aspirations has a minimal insignificant positive correlation with commitment: high initial aspirations raise the incidence of high commitment over low initial aspirations by a mere 3.7 percent. Yet the experience of progress in one's employment career raises commitment significantly: of those with regressive or static careers, only 43 percent have high commitment and of those with progressive careers, 52.2 percent do. This correlation is significant, yet weaker than the one with views and values, domestic work load, and the presence of a husband.

Now to the characteristics of the current job. My data show that better hygiene conditions only mildly raise commitment: the rate of low commitment declines by 5.4 percent and the rate of high commitment rises by 5.4 percent with the improvement of hygiene conditions. Things are very different with the task or content characteristics of the current job. Whereas the incidence of low commitment among women with low-content jobs is 23.6 percent, among women with high-content jobs it is only 10.7 percent; and the high commitment rate rises from a mere 42 percent for low-content jobs to 58.9 percent for high-content jobs. The correlation between commitment and the quality of the current job is even stronger than that with views and values.

In conclusion, the acceptance of the values and norms of the primacy of the domestic/maternal role tends to weaken women's commitment to employment and occupation; so does a heavy domestic work load; the absence of progress in their careers also lowers commitment, but to a lesser degree. As all three conditions are still rather widespread, it is to be assumed that the average level of attachment and commitment to employment and to occupation is still lower for women than for men. The apparent trend toward the acceptance of egalitarian views and values should be expected to reduce this difference. Yet, as long as the level of the task characteristics of the jobs of women is considerably lower than that of men, any comparison between the commitment to work of men and of women will largely reflect the inferiority of the quality of women's jobs, not sex-specific differences in work attitudes. My finding of the strong correlation between the content level of the current job and the level of commitment to work makes it imperative to base any future comparative work attitude studies on detailed measurement and strict control of the level of the task characteristics of male and female interviewees' jobs.

Interest in Advancement and Promotion

It is widely assumed that women's interest in advancement and promotion is considerably lower than that of men. Just as in the case of commitment to work, my data will suffice to test a few theories of the causes of this presumed lower level, without including any data about men. Over half the sample of interviewed women have exhibited a decidedly high level of interest in advancement and promotion, yet this high incidence of high interest varies greatly—from 30.2 percent in Group 3 (U.S. industry) to 81.9 percent in Group 5 (U.S. office). Hence, it is difficult to judge whether women's level of interest in advancement and promotion is lower than that of men, except to say that, if it is the case, then it must be determined by diverse causes, and so it cannot be entirely sex specific. It is clear that were this difference sex specific, then, hopes for an equalization of the status of women and men in the occupational sphere would be doomed to failure. Two different kinds of theories claim sex-specificity of attitudes to work: bio-psychological, and functionalist sociological. If women are genetically programmed for passivity and are therefore not capable of competitiveness, and men are genetically programmed for aggressiveness and are therefore highly capable of competitiveness, then, presumably, women's interest in advancement and promotion will be permanently lower than men's—not withstanding changes in any other factor. The same holds for the classical sociological role theory which assumes that the differentiation of social sex roles is permanent, since it is functional and stabilizes the family, and since the family is essential as a stabilizing factor in any society. The very socialization of boys and girls according to different ideals of masculinity and femininity thus was also deemed unavoidable, since it was deemed functional in accordance with their future functional roles.

A different variant of the role theory pertains to changing roles, as correlated to changing socializations to fit the changing value systems and the changing ideals of masculinity and femininity; different ideals of masculinity and femininity and different kinds of socialization for them would then exist simultaneously in the same national societies, and resocialization into changed value systems would then also possibly take place in adult life. It is well known that a widely accepted traditional ideal of femininity discourages women from developing interest in advancement; a "career woman" was to be abhorred not only because having a career meant that she had to neglect her primary domestic/maternal role but also since a proper woman was supposed to be soft, compliant, adaptive, always ready for compromise, never ambitious, and never competitive with men. In particular, it was traditionally taken to be self-understood that women should never attempt to surpass, supervise, or manage men.

I shall later test the impact of this kind of traditional value on the level of interest in advancement as contrasted with more egalitarian values. First I want to examine the claim that women's apparent lower interest in advancement and promotion can be explained by the facts of the present average lower quality of women's jobs alone, without reference to their values. The fact that at present so many women's jobs are dead-end jobs that are not steps of any occupational ladder or career, whether within the present work organization or within the relevant branch of the economy, is perhaps sufficient to explain their lower interest in advancement. The significance of this factor can be examined by correlating interest in advancement and promotion with the content level of the current job or with progress or its absence in the past employment career. Another correlation is also possible. Crewley, Levitin, and Quinn have argued on the basis of their U.S. comparative study that it suffices even to hold men's and women's expectations of their chances for promotion in their current workplace constant for all—supposedly sex-specific—differences in interest in advancement to disappear. I shall therefore also correlate this factor—level of expectation of chances for promotion—for its relative significance for women's interest in advancement. In evaluating the correlations, it should be remembered that the variable interest in advancement is divided into only two levels; the variables to be correlated with it are divided into three levels unless otherwise specified. In the cases of factors with three levels, I shall leave out the percentage figure for the intermediate level.

First, let us look at the correlations that will help us test the significance of the quality of the worklife of the individual worker for the level of her interest in advancement. To begin with the level of content:

Interest in Advancement	Level of Content (percent)	
	Low	High
Low	58	31
High	42	69

There exists, then, a very significant variance between the level of interest in advancement of women working in low-content jobs and that of women working in relatively high-content jobs. This is not the case with hygiene conditions. Whereas the incidence of interest in advancement rises considerably with the rise of content characteristics, it declines insignificantly with the rise of hygiene characteristics.

Second, experience of progress in the past employment career (this variable has only two levels because the very small group of those with declining careers has been united with the group of those with static careers).

Interest in Advancement	Progress in Career (percent)	
	Static	Progressive
Low	54	40.2
High	46	59.8

Remembering that here we have a correlation with only one degree of freedom, we notice that the variance appears similarly strong.

Third, expectations of chances for promotion in the current work place, a variable with three levels.

Interest in Advancement	Expectations of Chances for Promotion (percent)	
	Poor	Good
Low	48.3	32
High	51.7	68

The effect of expectations of good chances for promotion in the current workplace on the level of interest in advancement is very similar to that of high level of content of the job; yet expectations of poor chances for advancement do not lower interest in advancement as much as poor content of the job does.

Fourth, views and values, divided into three levels.

Interest in Advancement	Views and Values (percent)	
	Traditional	Egalitarian
Low	64.1	30
High	35.9	70

It is apparent that views and values have the strongest impact on the interest in advancement. Whereas the impact of egalitarian values seems very similar to that of a (relatively) high content of the job, as well as to that of expectations of good chances for promotion, traditional values lower interest in advancement even more than either low content of the job or the expectations of poor chances for promotion.

It seems clear that the changing socialization and resocialization of women in all three national societies has a decisive effect on their level of interest in advancement. An intriguing question arises here: is the level of men's interest in advancement equally affected by the changing values concerning the male role, the changing idea of masculinity, the socialization and resocialization in their light, and the existence of varieties of male socializations within the same national society?

Let us now examine the significance of life conditions for interest in advancement. First, let us discuss age. It is commonplace that men and women alike, if they belong to occupations below the semiprofessional level, tend to consider interest in advancement futile and unrealistic once they near the mandatory or customary retirement age. As the customary retirement age is currently lower for women than for men in all three countries, a considerable decline of the interest in advancement of the women past the age of fifty was to be expected. I therefore divided the sample into three age groups:

Interest in Advancement	Age (percent)		
	−35	36-50	51+
Low	31.6	60	77.2
High	68.4	40	22.8

Whereas the extremely low level of interest in advancement for the age group of fifty-one or older was to be expected, the radical decline of interest in advancement of the thirty-six to fifty year age group as compared to the younger group is rather surprising. Hence, it might prove interesting to look at the incidence of high interest in advancement in all five age groups:

	Age				
	16-25	*26-35*	*36-45*	*46-55*	*56-65*
Percentage of women with high interest in advancement	70.4	65.6	42.9	28	10.3

The decline is uniform, but two sharp points of decline are apparent: first, around the age of forty and second, around the age of fifty. And the sharp decline in the interest in advancement of so many women at the relatively early age of forty requires explanation. Does it perhaps reflect a similar decline in the incidence of egalitarian values in the middle-aged group? The incidence of traditional and egalitarian views and values in the five age groups is as follows (with the incidence of the middle range omitted as usual here).

	Age				
	16-25	*26-35*	*36-45*	*46-55*	*56-65*
Percentage of women with: Traditional views and values	26.8	20.6	34.3	36.4	32.8
Egalitarian views and values	38.8	48.3	32.9	31.1	20.7

It is immediately apparent that there is here no sharp break between the age groups from thirty-six to forty-five and from forty-six to fifty-five. The sharp decline in the interest in advancement around the age of fifty, then, is—as expected—independent of values, although the sharp decline in interest in advancement around the age of forty seems to reflect a similarly sharp rise in the prevalence of traditional views. (I shall return later to the significance of the sharp rise in egalitarian views in the twenty-six to thirty-five age group.)

Now to the other two life conditions, health and, specifically for women, domestic work load; both variables have three levels.

It may be assumed that a person's self-image as in rather poor health would lower interest in advancement.

Interest in Advancement	Health Condition (percent)	
	Poor	*Good*
Low	53.8	39.9
High	46.2	60.1

There is a significant correlation here, yet not as strong as with the factors of the quality of the worklife and certainly considerably weaker than that with views and values.

The correlation with domestic work load is of strikingly similar significance to that of health condition.

Interest in Advancement	Domestic Work Load (percent)	
	Heavy	Light
Low	56.3	39.5
High	43.7	60.5

We notice, then, that the overly heavy domestic work load of employed women tends to depress both their commitment to their occupation and their interest in advancement.

Finally, it may be assumed that women whose initial aspirations were low and whose schooling and vocational training were below the accepted norm of their society may tend to have little hopes for any occupational advancement independent of the presence or absence of any objective chances for such advancement in their workplace, whereas those with relatively high initial aspirations may tend to consider themselves as suitable for advancement. The variable initial aspirations has three levels, and the medium level will be omitted.

Interest in Advancement	Initial Aspirations (percent)	
	Low	High
Low	67.2	37.8
High	32.8	62.2

The correlation is, indeed, quite significant; whereas the impact of a relatively high level of initial aspirations on interest in advancement is about the same as the impact of egalitarian values, low initial aspirations have a somewhat smaller impact on interest in advancement than traditional values.

Let me add one minor factor: the interviewees were divided according to their status of vocational training and its use into three groups: those who had never completed any vocational training, those who had completed their vocational training but do not use it in their current job, and the rest who were using their completed vocational training in their current job. It turns out that those who had completed vocational training but were not using it in their current job have a lower incidence of interest in advancement than those who had not completed any vocational training. Apparently, many women who have spent years in vocational training but found themselves later performing semiskilled work, tend to lose any hope that they might advance through additional vocational training.

Significance of the Relative Intensity
(Interruptions and Part-time Work)
for Employment Career

One of the most common explanations for the inferior status of women in the world of work is that they tend to interrupt their work lives more frequently and for much longer periods than men do, often extending the time to ten or fifteen or more years of absence. Further, many more employed women than employed men work part time, which means work either not full day or not full week or only part of the year.

Within the confines of this study, it was impossible to match women with men in the same occupational groups, holding constant other major factors like level of education and training and interest in advancement, and to correlate relative levels of intensity of employment career with the rate of progress in career. My only way to test the hypothesis that the cause of the low rate of progress in women's careers is low intensity—interruptions and part-time work— is to correlate these two factors for this sample of women. The variable intensity was based on information given by the interviewees about their past work careers, age of entry into work, jobs held, periods worked, interruptions, length of interruptions, and periods of part-time work. Half of each period of part-time work of twenty weekly hours or less was reckoned as interruption. Those whose interruptions were less than one-third of the time from entry into work until the time of the interview were considered as having what I will call "intensive work careers"; those with less, "medium" or "nonintensive." Because the group of nonintensive turned out to be rather small—7.4 percent—I combined them with the medium intensive as one group for the purpose of the correlation. I also combined the regressive with the static for the variable "progress in work career." The more refined cross-tabulation and even the division into groups under and over age thirty gave no significant difference. The main results show a correlation, but it is minimal and thus irrelevant (table A-101). The variance between the degree of progress for the nonintensive and the intensive is 1.8 percent. The conclusion is that at least within the range of typical basic women's jobs (and outside the professions and the semiprofessions), a high level of intensity of employment does not necessarily raise the level of progress of a career and vice versa.

The absence of progress in the employment career of 55.2 percent of the sample cannot be explained by the more frequent interruptions and/or periods of part-time work of these women. The widespread theory is false. The most obvious alternative to it is that the dead-end nature of women's job careers is a matter of discrimination—no matter whether overt or covert, conscious or unconscious, acceded to willingly or reluctantly.

Domestic Work Load

In the overall sample, 33.6 percent have a limited domestic work load of no more than ten hours per week, 29.4 percent have a medium-sized domestic work load of ten to twenty hours per week, and 34.3 percent have a high work load of twenty-three or more hours per week. (See table A-25.) The interviewees usually underestimated their domestic work load, tending to ignore any time spent working before they went out to work and also time spent during the weekend.

The sample was divided into those with and without children at home (tables A-102 and A-103). Only 15.7 percent in the latter group have a high domestic work load. And in the three office subgroups, of those with no children at home, very few women have high domestic work loads. Of those with children at home, 66.8 percent suffer from a high domestic work load. Of the nine groups, those with the heaviest work loads, both for those with and without children at home, are in Group 6 (German industry). Women in this group are in the German tradition of excessive house cleaning; moreover, they are largely rural women and thus often have additional work on the family farm or vegetable garden. Women who are employed full time (thirty-seven to forty-five hours weekly) and work at domestic tasks for twenty-three hours or more per week have an excessive work load that precludes any systematic leisure-time activity. My sample includes 663 women employed full time and 261 with a heavy domestic work load; at least 163 of the latter (possibly more) have reported a work week of over sixty hours. This figure is at least 21 percent of a population that includes many unmarried women, few of whom have a heavy domestic work load. Of the 522 ever-married interviewees, 261 have a heavy domestic work load. Of these 261, ninety-eight are part-time workers. Hence, among the 424 ever-married, fully employed women, 163—38 percent—also have a heavy domestic work load.

The answers to the question about how much help the interviewees received in the home and with the children, show that 71.9 percent receive no help at all, 7.5 percent receive between one and five hours help per week; 6.7 percent between six and nine; and a mere 13.9 percent receive ten hours per week or more, which is the minimum level which begins to count as significant (table A-104). Most of the women who have this help—7 percent of the sample—also have heavy domestic work loads. Yet most of those with a heavy domestic work load—150 women, or 19.7 percent—have no help at all.

The data show that of the options presented—paid helper, husband, sons, daughters, mother, or mother-in-law—husbands are the most frequent helpers. Of the 118 women who report receiving help from their husbands, 11.1 percent are helped fewer than six hours per week! Only 28 men (6.4 percent) help over ten hours a week. Since these are too few to study in detail, I have added to them the forty-three who help six to ten hours a week, making a population of seventy-one men, or an average of eight men for each of the nine groups. Yet Group 7 (German retail) has sixteen of them, even though only fifty-nine of the eighty-five women in this group are married, an indication that among the three national groups, the Germans have the highest percentage of husbands helping: 23.8 percent.

The next significant group of helpers are the mothers; there are fifty-two in all. They are followed by eighteen mothers-in-law. Of these seventy, forty-four (thirty-five mothers and nine mothers-in-law) offer more than ten hours of help a week. The pattern of significant help is present in all German groups and in Group 3 (U.S. industry).

There are twenty-six cases of paid help. Fifteen of these are Israeli, but only three cases are for ten hours a week or more. Most of our interviewees cannot afford this kind of help.

Finally, there is the traditional pattern of daughters helping, and here I wanted to compare daughters with sons. The traditional maxim that helping in the household suits girls but not boys seems to be on its way out, especially in the United States. In the whole sample, forty-six daughters and thirty-nine sons help. Of these, twenty-two girls and twenty-five boys—48 percent and 64 percent respectively—are Americans. One reason is that the American group has more children than the other two, but this may not be the whole story. Perhaps most of the over-eleven year olds who live at home are simply recorded as helping in some measure. What is specifically American is that more boys help than girls; in Germany, almost as many boys help as girls; only Israel shows the traditional pattern.

As to part-time work, 12.9 percent of the whole sample work part time (ninety-eight women). Of these, 3.8 percent work fewer than twenty hours per week, 7.1 percent between twenty-one and thirty-one hours, and 2 percent thirty-one hours or more but fewer than the full work week of thirty-six to thirty-eight hours. Groups 4 and 5 (U.S. industry and office) have no part-time work at all and in the three retail groups, part-time work fits into the general work schedule. Sixty-four of the ninety-eight part-time employees (65 percent) worked in retail. In Israel and Germany, part-time workers serve as bank tellers in late afternoon or on the weekend. Generally, then, part-time work is used for unusual shifts, not to suit the needs of working mothers.

Correlating the level of domestic work load with state of health (health condition) shows the following (table A-27). Of those with a low domestic work load, 40.9 percent are in a good state of health and 30.8 percent in a poor state of health as opposed to those with a heavy domestic work load, among whom 27.6 percent are in a good state of health and 47.5 percent in a poor state of health. Nearly half of the women with a heavy domestic work load have a poor state of health. Hence, the size of the domestic work load is important to the work attitudes of women through the medium of their state of health. A heavy domestic work load thus contributes directly and indirectly to the reduction of a woman's level of overall satisfaction, concern, commitment to employment, and interest in advancement. It also raises the prevalence of superficial satisfaction. As we have seen, the incidence of the threefold instrumental attitude is nearly double among those with a heavy domestic work load than among those with a light one, and the incidence of the instrumental syndrome is two-and-a-half times as much. We may conclude that a heavy domestic work load is an important contributing factor to the instrumental resignative adaptation of employed women.

Views and Values about the Rights and
Duties of Women re Domestic Work,
Occupation, and Employment

The high significance of the variable "views and values" for the work attitudes of women has already been noted in the preceding sections. I now intend to describe in some detail the composition and the meaning of the data out of which this variable is composed.

Although the views and values are part of a larger ideology concerning the appropriate roles of men and women in all areas of life, the images of masculinity and femininity, sexual morality, and the future of marriage and the family, I have tried to concentrate here only on statements expressing views and values concerning women's appropriate roles, rights, duties, capabilities, opportunities and limitations, choices, and status regarding work—whether in the household or as occupation and as employment.

The interviewees were requested to say whether they consider certain statements of views or information read to them as correct or incorrect and whether they agree or disagree with the value statements read to them. About half of the fifty statements expressed traditional views and values; the other half more egalitarian or modern ones. The statements were listed in the questionnaire at random rather than according to topics so as to achieve a spontaneous reaction from the interviewee to each statement separately. The statements were then grouped in this way:

Group A   The role of men and women in the family and in economic life

Group B   Pay

Group C   Education and vocational training

Group D   Responsibility

Group E   Managerial positions

Group F   Segregation

Group G   Skills and capabilities

Group H   Job characteristics and job behavior

Group I   Awareness of inequality

Our sample was neither random nor representative of the adult female population of the three national societies. Only between 34 and about 40 percent of the female populations of these societies are "economically active," and our three samples are taken from this very sizable and growing minority, I assume that it is fairly representative of that population. If it had been taken from the female population at large, we might have found some women who would have taken the traditional stand on all or nearly all statements. Yet in our sample, nobody took fewer than twenty modern, egalitarian stands, and only nine women took fewer than thirty. I consider those who gave between twenty and thirty-four egalitarian answers traditional, between thirty-five and thirty-nine egalitarian answers intermediate, and those who gave forty or more modern or egalitarian. There was a considerable clustering of the answers. Just as only nine women had taken less than thirty egalitarian stands, only eight took forty-one or more, yet 275 women took exactly forty egalitarian stands each. The resultant classification is that of 220 women (28.9 percent) are conservative or traditional; 258 women (33.9 percent) are intermediate; and 283 (37.2 percent) are modern or egalitarian (table A-105). The divisions among nations and occupations are shown in table A-106.

Germany shows the least polarization and the fewest traditionalists, the United States the most polarization and the most egalitarians. Israel is obviously most traditional: its industrial group has an overwhelming majority of traditionalists, and even in its better-educated office group, only a third are egalitarians, reflecting the relatively small influence of the women's movement ideology even among the collegiate young there. The division into occupational groups is clear cut. The only exception is that in Israel the rise in egalitarianism between retail and office is smaller than in the other two national groups. Among the retail groups, the American one is most influenced by the ideology of the women's movement.

The answers, broken down into subgroups A-I follows. The clusters of responses are divided into the traditional and the modern; those who have responded in a modern fashion to two-thirds of the questions were deemed modern. The breakdown enables one to study which traditional views and values persist. (For a detailed distribution, see tables A-107 through A-115).

                                                                      Percent

A. Male and female roles   35.3 traditional
                                                            63.7 modern

Percent

B. Pay   44.9 traditional
                                                       55.1 modern

C. Education and vocational training   8.9 traditional
                                                       91.1 modern

D. Responsibility   51.8 traditional
                                                       48.2 modern

E. Managerial positions   28.9 traditional
                                                       71.1 modern

F. Segregation   56.4 traditional
                                                       43.6 modern

G. Skills and capabilities   25.5 traditional
                                                       74.5 modern

H. Job characteristics and work behavior   35   traditional
                                                       65   modern

I. Awareness of inequality   49.5 traditional
                                                       50.5 modern

The most traditionally held topics are segregation (the acceptance of the justification for the sex typing of occupations) and responsibility (the endorsement of the view that women do not like positions of responsibility as a justification for their not being given them). The next two topics on which traditional views are held are awareness of inequality and discrimination and pay. Many accept the claim that women are less trained than men as a proper justification of unequal pay. The most pronounced traditional views are that since men are the breadwinners, they deserve the higher pay, and that since husbands should earn more than wives, men should be paid more. The lack of awareness of the situation is expressed, for example, in the obviously erroneous yet widespread view that most men help their wives in the home.

At the opposite extreme are education and vocational training. The vast majority of the sample agree that girls deserve the same education and vocational training as boys and that a woman needs a trade just as much as a man does. Next is the topic of capabilities. Most of the sample agree that women are as good in arithmetic as men and are as capable of machinery operation and of political activity.

I will explore now the correlations of views and values with demographic data and then recapitulate its correlations with all the work attitudes and go into more detail than before.

The correlation of views and values with marital status (table A-116) shows that the unmarried women are slightly and insignificantly less egalitarian than the married ones: 35.5 percent versus 36.9 percent. The few who live with a friend, as well as the divorced women, are the most egalitarian: 50 percent and 45.7 percent, respectively. The most traditional are the separated and the widowed: 33.3 percent each. As to age groups, I already mentioned the interesting result is that although traditionalism rises considerably after age thirty-five, as expected, it is not the youngest who are the most egalitarian but those between twenty-five and thirty-five years old (table A-117). Egalitarian views are absorbed not in the home or in schools but in college and in young adult society. The percentages of egalitarianism for the under twenty-five, for the twenty-five to thirty-five year olds, and for the thirty-five to forty-five year olds are: 38.8, 48.3, and 32.9 percent, respectively. Of the oldest—fifty-five to sixty-five years old—only 20.7 percent are egalitarian.

The attitudes to consider at this point in the correlation of views and values are satisfaction (composite, direct, and superficial), meaning of work (emphasis on content), concern for content, concern for hygiene, commitment to work, interest in advancement, self-confidence, and the two aggregates of attitudes, the instrumental attitude and the instrumental syndrome. In order to determine which of the views signifies most, I have also correlated certain views with certain attitudes, especially views on the roles of men and women in the family and economic life with commitment to work and interest in advancement, and managerial positions with interest in advancement.

The first correlation is between the three levels of views and values in general and satisfaction (table A-118 and A-119). Taking the three levels of the composite variable of satisfaction that combine the answer to the direct question concerning satisfaction with the answers to six control questions, we find that whereas only 19.5 percent of the traditional women have a high level of satisfaction, the egalitarian group contains 25.4 percent highly satisfied. The percentage of those with a low level of satisfaction among the traditionalists is almost the same as among the intermediates and the egalitarians: 38.2, 42.2, and 37.5 percent, respectively. In short, the correlation between views and values and composite satisfaction is insignificant. Not so with the direct or overt satisfaction. Correlating the frequency of egalitarianism among the different groups according to the answer to the direct question, "Are you very satisfied, somewhat satisfied, or dissatisfied with your job?" we find that the frequency of egalitarianism is 30.9 percent among the overtly very satisfied, 38.9 percent among the overtly somewht satisfied, and 49.5 percent among the overtly dissatisfied. Nearly half of the overtly dissatisfied, then, are egalitariams. Looking at the correlation the other way, we find that of the egalitarians only 32.9 percent are very satisfied as compared to 45.5 percent of the traditionalists, and 18 percent of them say they are dissatisfied as opposed to 10 percent of the traditionalists.

Next, views and values were correlated with the meaning of work or the emphasis on content. Of the women with traditional views, only 16.4 percent place high emphasis on the content of their jobs as opposed to 37.1 of the egalitarians (table A-120). Put in another way, only 29.3 percent of the sample place high emphasis on content, and 47.1 percent of those have egalitarian views.

The women who are highly concerned about the poor task characteristics or the negative aspects of the content of their jobs comprise 25.6 percent of the entire sample; they divide into 52.8 percent egalitarians, 29.7 percent intermediate, and only 17.4 percent traditionalists, as opposed to the 28.9 percent traditionalists in the entire sample. In the other direction, 31.4 percent of the egalitarians show little concern for the task characteristics of their jobs, and 36.4 percent show high concern. Among the traditionalists, 57.7 percent show little concern and only 15.5 percent show high concern for the task characteristics (table A-121).

It is clear that egalitarianism raises both the emphasis on and the concern for the task characteristics or content of the job, yet egalitarianism more often raises concern than emphasis. More than a third are concerned about content, yet only more than a fifth have come to the generalized conclusion about the significance of content in work in general. If it were the other way around, it would indicate a flagrant inconsistency.

The question arises, then, as to whether egalitarianism also influences a concern for hygiene characteristics and a readiness to be active about them. I took it for granted that the answer would be affirmative. The egalitarians would resent low pay and poor conditions no less than the others, and the traditionalists, who are ready to accept monotonous and dead-end jobs, may also be ready to accept low pay. The facts, indeed, bear me out. In the entire sample, the frequency of high concern for hygiene is higher than that for content (42.2 percent versus 25.6 percent); among the traditionalists, the frequency of high concern for hygiene is 41.4 percent; among the intermediates, it is 35.3 percent, whereas among the egalitarians it is 49.1 percent (table A-122). The data show that concern for hygiene and for content are not exclusive. The traditionalists are split equally into those concerned and unconcerned about working conditions, the intermediates are more often unconcerned, and the egalitarians are more often concerned.

The two attitudes that are especially problematic for women are commitment to work and interest in advancement and promotion. I assumed from the start that high commitment to work is susceptible to change with any changes in views and values, although I took economic need as a significant factor as well. About half of the entire sample—49.8 percent—are highly committed to work. Since only 37.2 percent of the entire population are egalitarians, it is clear that egalitarianism cannot be the sole cause of high commitment to work. Nevertheless, a significant correlation between high commitment to work and egalitarian views is apparent. Among the traditionalists, only 41.4 percent exhibit a high commitment to work and 21.8 percent a low commitment, whereas among the egalitarians, 56.9 percent show a high commitment and only 10.6 percent a low one (table A-123).

I have assumed that views on the division of labor between the sexes in the family and in employment are particularly influential in determining a woman's level of commitment to work and employment. I therefore examined the correlation of the views on this matter (Group A), with commitment to work. The results show that a large minority of the traditionalists—45.7 percent— exhibit a high commitment to work, and a small majority of the egalitarians, who constitute nearly two-thirds of the sample, do so (52 percent). By comparison, the awareness of the existence of inequality (Group I), for instance, bears no relevance to the degree of commitment to work.

Interest in advancement and promotion correlates with views and values very significantly, I had assumed, since traditionally this interest was considered unwomanly; thus traditionally oriented women would be less disposed to show interest in advancement. The facts strongly support this hypothesis. Indeed it is the strongest correlation between an attitude and views. The population divides into two almost equal parts of high and low interest in advancement: 47.8 percent low and 52.2 percent high. Of the traditionalists, 64.1 percent have a low interest in advancement and 35.9 percent have a high one. Among the egalitarians, 30 percent show a low interest in advancement and 70 percent a high interest. (See table A-124.)

Since this correlation is so strong, I wanted to pinpoint the views and values most significant as factors determining interest in advancement. The result was that the subgroup of views about the roles of the sexes in family and employment (Group A) is most influential, followed by views on women's suitability for managerial jobs (Group E). Views concerning responsibility and awareness of the existing inequalities are poorly correlated to interest in advancement and promotion. (See tables A-125 through A-127.)

There remain the correlations of views and values with the presence or absence of the instrumental attitude and of the instrumental syndrome. Important in this regard are the strong correlations between views and values, on the one hand, and components of the instrumental attitude and syndrome or its absence on the other, such as emphasis on content, concern for the low content of the job, and interest in advancement, and also superficial satisfaction due to the tendency of the egalitarians to declare themselves dissatisfied. The conclusion cannot be avoided that views and values strongly influence the presence or absence of the instrumental syndrome. Of the 23.4 percent of the total sample who exhibit the instrumental attitude (178 women), 45.5 percent of them (81 women) exhibit traditional views and values, 34.8 percent (62 women) intermediate, and only 19.7 percent (35 women) egalitarian views. Whereas 36.8 percent of the traditional women exhibit the instrumental attitude, only 12.4 percent of the egalitarians do.

The correlation between views and values and the even more stringent composite attitude "instrumental syndrome" is even stronger: 13 percent of the entire sample show this syndrome, 19.5 percent of the traditionalists and only 6.4 percent of the egalitarians.

The correlations of views and values with two additional minor attitudes to work, the strong correlation with "self-confidence," and the weaker one with the attitude "self-image as an economically active person" will be discussed in the next two sections.

Self-Confidence or Self-Worth

It is frequently assumed that women have not only a weaker interest in advancement in their employment careers than men but also a weaker sense of self-confidence in their own ability to perform more demanding work. Certainly, both attitudes are akin, although one is more specific and the other is more general. It is to be expected, then, that the response to the question concerning the ability to perform more skilled or responsible tasks is less influenced by the specific current life conditions of the interviewee and more by her general level of sense of self-worth; it may also reflect the meaning of work for her in general.

The question now arises, what are the factors that cause this presumably lower level of occupational self-confidence or self-worth in women—whether their lower average level of progress in their employment careers, their inferior schooling and vocational training, unfavorable life conditions of an overly heavy domestic work load, and/or poor health? Does self-confidence reflect the quality of the current job, or is the occupational self-confidence of women a product of their socialization, their value system concerning the ideal of femininity and the appropriate social roles of women?

Here are my findings. 84.1 percent of the entire sample had answered affirmatively the question concerning their ability to perform more challenging work; this overall relatively high level of self-confidence varied from a low of 65.9 percent in Group 1 (Israeli retail) to a high of 96.4 percent in Group 5 (U.S. office). (See table A-71.) Correlating this evidence of affirmative answers to the question of self-confidence with the various likely factors produced the following order of relative significance. Of the positive correlations, first in significance is egalitarian views and values; second, high initial aspirations; third, progressive employment career; fourth, high content of the current job; and fifth, light domestic work load. The correlation with good health is minimal. Surprisingly, there is no positive correlation between better hygiene and self-confidence, but a weak negative one. As to the difficult age factor, the age group of twenty-six to thirty-five is the one with the highest incidence of self-confidence—91.1 percent—and thereafter it declines to below the average for the total sample. Yet the decline is minimal until the age of fifty-five; only the oldest group of those over fifty-five has a much lower incidence of self-confi-dence—61 percent. We see here a marked difference between the work attitude of self-confidence as the ability to perform more challenging work and interest in advancement: high interest in advancement starts to decline at a much earlier age, apparently mainly because training and retraining are still considered by many women as appropriate only for the young. The relatively high incidence of the lack of interest in advancement among employed women about the age of forty and over seems, then, to reflect their very early perception of themselves as too old to succeed in practical attempts to obtain a better quality job—while not necessarily reflecting a general early decline in self-confidence concerning their ability to perform a more challenging job.

Finally, it was to be assumed that the incidence of self-confidence among the instrumentally adapted is relatively low. The correlation is strong indeed: of those who are instrumentally adapted only 66.9 percent express self-confidence; of the others, 89.4 percent.

Self-Image as an Economically
Active Person

The colloquial expression, "women work only for pin money" expresses the assumption that in contradistinction to the average normal adult man who sees himself as earning his own livelihood and as a provider for his family, if he has one, the average normal woman sees her economic activity outside the household, if she has one, as secondary, incidental, and marginal. I have described my attempt to probe this work attitude of self-image as an economically active person. The difficulty I had was to disentangle the impact of ideological self-image from that of the individual, practical life conditions that may have prompted interviewees to respond one way or the other. Nevertheless, it can be taken for granted that these women, 46.3 percent of the sample, who declared as their first choice that they go out to work either "in order to earn my own living" or "to earn the living of my family," do not consider their economic activity as secondary, incidental, or marginal. This attitude clearly correlates to practical economic needs yet is not completely dependent on it. I therefore tried to explore correlations with other likely factors. My findings are as follows.

The strongest correlation is with domestic work load: of women with a heavy domestic work load only 32.6 percent see themselves as basic and primary breadwinners, of those with a light one, 50.2 percent see themselves as breadwinners. The shift caused by high initial aspirations, although second in importance, is only half the shift caused by light domestic work load—12.1 percent. Content of the job is third: of women in low-content jobs, 44 percent see themselves as basic breadwinners; of women in high-content jobs, 55.4 percent do. The correlation with the ideological factor is slightly weaker, but still quite significant: traditionalists, 42.7 percent; egalitarians, 51.6 percent. There is no significant correlation with either progress in past work career or in hygiene conditions of the current job or health condition.

Now to the difficult factor of age. Here we find that of the large group of those under twenty-five there are 52 percent who see themselves as basic breadwinners, a slight decline to 47.8 percent for the twenty-six to thirty-five group, and then a steep decline to 37.9 percent of the thirty-six to forty-five group, a slight increase to 42.4 percent of the forty-six to fifty-five group and another to 45.8 percent of the over fifty-five group. Hence there is definitely no uniform decline of this attitude with age.

Finally, is the correlation between this attitude and that of the composite instrumental attitude: only 37.1 percent of those whose attitude to work is instrumental and resigned see themselves as basic breadwinners, whereas 49.1 percent of the others do.

5 Conclusion

Summaries

Let me recapitulate my findings about the impact of the various factors recorded with each of the work attitudes studied. All factors but progress are graded into three levels; all comparisons are between top and bottom level unless otherwise stated.

Let me begin with the three kinds of satisfaction with work. The direct question about satisfaction allowed four answers, two indicating dissatisfaction, two satisfaction, and I have united the two dissatisfactions, so as to have only two positive values and one negative value for the variable overt satisfaction. Some factors correlate strongly with both the increase of incidence of overt satisfaction and the decline of the incidence of overt dissatisfaction, such as good hygiene characteristics, high quality of content, progress in one's employment career, and good health condition. These factors correlate with increased satisfaction and decreased dissatisfaction to varying degrees. The strongest by far is good hygiene: the incidence of the overtly very satisfied rises from the mere 19.7 percent of those in low-hygiene jobs to 58.8 percent of those in high-hygiene jobs, and the incidence of overtly dissatisfied declines from a high 26.5 percent for low-hygiene jobs to only 5.8 percent of those in high-hygiene jobs. By comparison, the impact of the level of content is smaller, but still very strong. The incidence of overtly very satisfied increases from 31.6 percent for those in low-content jobs to 46.4 percent for those in high-content jobs, and the incidence of overtly dissatisfied declines from 19.6 percent for those in low-content jobs to 10.7 percent for those in high-content jobs. Thus, the incidence of the overtly very satisfied rises by 39.1 percent with the rise of hygiene and by 14.8 percent with the rise of content, and the incidence of the overtly dissatisfied diminishes by 20.7 percent with the rise of hygiene and by 10.7 percent with the rise of content.

Moving from poor to good health condition we find the rise of incidence of those very satisfied by 16.5 percent (a little stronger correlation than with content), and yet the decline of incidence of the dissatisfied is smaller than in the case of content: it is a mere 5.4 percent. If the small sample of those with declining careers is considered as a means for judging the impact of progress in one's career or its absence on overt satisfaction, we find a rise in the incidence of the very satisfied with the rise of incidence of progress by 23.2 percent; considering both the regressive and the static together for the same purpose, we find the figures to be 7.5 percent and 6.1 percent respectively.

117

Finally, the correlation of overt level of satisfaction with the size of the domestic work load is curious. The incidence of the overtly very satisfied increases very little, by a mere 1.1 percent, and that of the somewhat satisfied by 7.2 percent, with the move from heavy to light domestic work load. Yet the incidence of the overtly dissatisfied decreases by 9.9 percent. Apparently, the disproportionately high percentage of the very young among those who have a very light domestic work load has biased the result here, since these young workers are also disposed to be critical and to declare their dissatisfaction openly.

There are two more factors that correlate with overt satisfaction, and they correlate differently from the five already mentioned factors: views and values and initial aspirations. Among those with egalitarian views, the incidence of the very satisfied is 10.5 percent lower than among those with traditional views; that of the somewhat satisfied rises by 5 percent and that of the dissatisfied also rises by 7.5 percent; very similarly, those with relatively high initial aspirations (measured by years of schooling and training) have 10.6 percent less of the very satisfied, 4.2 percent more of the somewhat satisfied, and 6.6 percent of the more dissatisfied.

Reviewing the impact of the various factors on the three levels of composite satisfaction (overt satisfaction or dissatisfaction combined with responses to six control questions), we may notice that the contribution of the direct satisfaction/dissatisfaction is of course reflected—yet differences in the impact of the various factors on the control questions appear. We have seen that low hygiene is one of the major dissatisfiers, this is reflected in the effect high hygiene has of decreasing the low level of satisfaction by 37.5 percent; yet it increases high satisfaction less—by 24.6 percent. Hence, high hygiene does not cause a shift to positive responses to the control questions equal to the shift from overt dissatisfaction to overt satisfaction. High content reduces the low level by 26.6 percent, which is less than high hygiene, but it increases high satisfaction by 21.3 percent, which is nearly the same as high hygiene. Good health decreases low satisfaction less, by 14 percent, and raises high satisfaction by 18.4 percent, which is quite considerable. As to progress, the small number with declining careers have an overwhelming percentage of low level of composite satisfaction; therefore, the impact of the experience of decline and progress in work career on low satisfaction appears extremely strong: the low satisfaction rate declines by 40.1 percent! With the usual consideration of the declined together with the static, there still remains a decline of 9 percent, and the rise of high satisfaction remains unchanged at 8.9 percent. As to domestic work load, we find a small impact of a heavy work load in the expected direction: low satisfaction rises by 6.7 percent and high satisfaction declines by a mere 4.6 percent.

Now to the impact of views and values: whereas low satisfaction is the same for the traditionalists and the egalitarians, satisfaction is raised by 5.9 percent by egalitarian views. Remembering that egalitarian views increase the incidence of those declaring themselves dissatisfied by 7.5 percent and decrease that of those very satisfied, it follows that those with egalitarian views answer the control questions considerably more positively than those with traditional views. Higher aspirations have a polarizing effect: the incidence of low satisfaction rises by 4.0 percent and that of high satisfaction by 8.8 percent.

Now to the attitude of superficial satisfaction, an inconsistent combination of overt job satisfaction with regarding one's job as unsuitable for one's daughter (or good friend). The incidence of this kind of satisfaction is 44.4 percent of the entire sample. Four factors have a nearly equally strong correlation with its incidence: a heavy domestic burden raises its incidence by 24.9 percent; high aspirations lower it by 22.2 percent; egalitarian views lower it by 20.2 percent; and a high level of content of the job by 20.1 percent; bad health condition increases it by only 9.3 percent; and neither the level of hygiene, nor past progress or its absence have any impact of the incidence of superficial satisfaction.

As for emphasis on the content of the job, content is the most significant factor: high content decreases low emphasis by 42.3 percent and raises high emphasis by 35 percent. Next come initial aspirations: relatively high initial aspirations decrease low emphasis by 28.8 percent, and raise high emphasis by 26.9 percent. Only a little less significant are views and values: egalitarian views decrease low emphasis on content by 25.5 percent and raise high emphasis by 20.7 percent. A heavy domestic work load increases low emphasis by 18 percent and decreases high emphasis by 21.9 percent. Similarly with progress: the experience of progress (compared with declining and static work career taken together) decreases low emphasis by 16.2 percent and raises high emphasis by 18.1 percent. Poor health condition raises low emphasis by 9.4 percent and decreases high emphasis by 8.4 percent. Finally, high hygiene decreases low emphasis on content only minimally, by 4.8 percent, and it does not raise high emphasis.

Regarding concern or indifference as to negative content characteristics of the job, the level of the content is the most significant factor for this attitude, too: high content decreases low concern (indifference) by 37.4 percent and raises high concern by 28.4 percent. Only little less significant is the level of initial aspirations: high initial aspirations decrease low concern by 32.5 percent and increase high concern by 26.8 percent. Next in significance are views and values: egalitarian views decrease low concern by 26.3 percent and increase high concern by 20.9 percent. Whereas the impact of progress in one's work career is significant in decreasing low concern—by 14.6 percent—it increases high concern by only 6.7 percent. The impact of the domestic work load is still significant, a high work load increases low concern by 9.5 percent and lowers high concern by 10.3 percent: it is significant in both directions. High hygiene, by contrast, is significant in only one direction: interestingly it raises indifference by 15.7 percent but hardly decreases high concern (2.3 percent in all).

The variable "interest in advancement" has only two levels, so that the shift in one level is always the same as in the other. Views and values correlate with it more significantly than any other factor, egalitarian views increasing interest in advancement by 34.1 percent. Next in significance are initial aspirations: high initial aspirations increase high interest in advancement by 29.4 percent. High content increases incidence of high interest by 27 percent. A high domestic work load decreases the incidence of high interest in advancement by 16.8 percent. I have also correlated the interviewees' evaluations of their chances for promotion—one item of content—with interest in advancement. Since such an evaluation becomes rather irrelevant for interviewees approaching retirement age, I have excluded those over the age of fifty. The evaluation of good chances for promotion, then, appears to raise the incidence of high interest in advancement by a mere 16.3 percent. The impact of good health condition and of progress in past career are nearly the same, increasing high interest in advancement by 13.9 percent and 13.8 percent, respectively. Of those who use their vocational training in their current jobs, 8.6 percent more have a high interest in advancement than those who do not. Finally, high hygiene correlates negatively and insignificantly with high interest by 2.5 percent only.

The instrumental attitude to work, as defined here, is composed of the last three attitudes to work just discussed, namely, the lack of high emphasis on content, indifference toward negative task characteristics of the job, and the lack of interest in advancement to a more challenging job. Obviously, the factors having an impact on the three constituent attitudes, will also correlate significantly with their combination. The factors in order of significance are, content of the current job, initial aspirations, views and values, progress in the past work career, and domestic work load. In the entire sample, the incidence of the instrumental attitude to work is 23.4 percent. Among the 168 women in this sample whose jobs have a relatively high level of content, the incidence of the instrumental attitude is only 4.8 percent; high content lowers the incidence of the instrumental attitude from its incidence in low content by 33.2 percent. High initial aspirations lower it by 28.7 percent, egalitarian views by 25.8 percent, past progress in work career by 16.1 percent, evaluations of good chances for promotion by 15.6 percent, and light domestic work load by 14.8 percent.

The instrumental syndrome includes, in addition to the three attitudes comprising the instrumental attitude, superficial satisfaction attitude strengthens even more the element of resignation. The factors influencing the incidence of the instrumental syndrome are, in order of relevance, initial aspirations, content, views and values, domestic work load, progress in past work career, and health condition. The incidence of the instrumental syndrome in the entire sample is only 13 percent. Yet among those with low initial aspirations, namely, with schooling and vocational training below the national norm, it is as high as 24.9 percent; high initial aspirations lower this incidence by 19 percent. High content lowers the incidence of the syndrome by 18.6 percent, egalitarian views by 13.1 percent, a light domestic work load by 12.7 percent, progress in past work career by 8.8 percent, and good health condition by 6.7 percent.

As for attachment and commitment to employment and occupation, the difference between the impact of the major factors is not very large. First is content, with high content decreasing the incidence of low commitment by 12.9 percent and raising the incidence of high commitment by 16.9 percent. Next comes domestic work load; a light work load lowers the incidence of low commitment by 14 percent and raises the incidence of high commitment by 12.9 percent. The extent of the impact of views and values is almost the same: egalitarian views decrease the incidence of low commitment by 11.2 percent and raise the incidence of high commitment by 15.5 percent. Past experience of progress in work career lowers the incidence of low commitment and raises the incidence of high commitment equally by 9.2 percent. Three minor factors influencing commitment are hygiene, health condition, and initial aspirations. Good hygiene lowers low commitment by 5.7 percent and raises high commitment by 5.4 percent. A good health condition lowers low commitment by 8.6 percent but hardly raises high commitment. Finally, high initial aspirations lower low and raise high commitment by only 3.7 percent.

Regarding the worker's self-image as an economically active person. Of the entire sample, 46.3 percent chose the image of earning their own livelihood or that of their family as the first choice. Only four of the factors correlate significantly with this attitude: domestic work load, initial aspirations, content, and views and values. A light domestic work load has by far the strongest impact on this attitude, raising its incidence by 27.9 percent; high initial aspirations raise it by 12.1 percent, high content by 11.4 percent, and egalitarian views by 9 percent.

Looking at self-confidence as to ability to perform more challenging work, of the entire sample, 84.1 percent answered this question affirmatively. The factors influencing this self-confidence are, in order of significance: views and values, initial aspirations, progress in past work career, content, and domestic work load. Egalitarian views raise it by 14.9 percent, high initial aspirations by 13.8 percent, progressive work career by 12.3 percent, a better content job by 9.7, and a light domestic work load by 7.1 percent.

The last attitude to work, whose correlations with the same factors remains to be discussed, is concern for hygiene. Yet the only factor to correlate with it at all significantly is views and values, egalitarian views lowering indifference to poor hygiene by 9.2 percent and raising concern for it by 7.7 percent.

What then is the relative impact that the seven major factors recorded have on the work attitudes of employed women? Let me start with the simpler attitudes, that is, ones which are not combinations of other attitudes:

1. Overt satisfaction/dissatisfaction
2. Emphasis on content

3. Concern for content
4. Interest in advancement
5. Commitment
6. Self-image as economically active person
7. Self-confidence

I shall then consider the four attitudes that are combinations:

8. Composite satisfaction
9. Superficial satisfaction
10. The instrumental attitude
11. The instrumental syndrome

Considering only the four most significant factors for each of these attitudes and weighting them and ordering them according to their relative significance, we find that the factors come in almost the same order—regardless of whether we consider them for the seven simple attitudes alone, for the four combined ones alone, or for all of them together: the content level of the job is the most significant factor, appearing as one of the first four important factors for all 11 attitudes. Taking first only the seven simple attitudes, we find content as the most important factor for emphasis on content, concern for content, and commitment to work; second in importance for overt satisfaction and third for interest in advancement and self-image as an economically active person.

Following in their order of relative impact on the seven simple attitudes are the factors views and values, initial aspirations, domestic work load, progress in employment career, hygiene level of the current job and health condition. Views and values is of major significance for all seven simple attitudes, and is the most important factor for interest in advancement and for self-confidence. Initial aspirations has nearly the same weight, being the second factor in importance for five simple attitudes—emphasis on content, concern for content, interest in advancement, self-image as an economically active person, and self-confidence. Domestic work load is of major significance for four of the simple attitudes; it is first for self-image as breadwinner, but only fourth for emphasis on content, concern for content, and interest in advancement.

Progress in past employment career is among the four most significant factors affecting two simple attitudes only, namely commitment to work and self-confidence. The level of hygiene conditions of the job affects only one of the simple attitudes, overt satisfaction or dissatisfaction, and here it is the first and strongest factor. Finally, health condition although correlating significantly with several attitudes is always of relatively minor importance, being third in significance for only one simple attitude, overt satisfaction.

As for the relative impact of the seven factors on the four composite attitudes, content is the most important, affecting all four, and being the most important factor for the instrumental attitude and the second most important for composite satisfaction and for the instrumental syndrome. Initial aspirations has nearly as strong an impact on the composite attitudes as content, somewhat more than views and values; it is the first factor affecting the incidence of the instrumental syndrome and the second for superficial satisfaction and for the instrumental attitude.

Views and values affects three of the four composite attitudes as third factor, namely superficial satisfaction, the instrumental attitude, and the instrumental syndrome.

Domestic work load is the first factor affecting superficial satisfaction and fourth for the instrumental syndrome.

Progress in the employment career is the fourth factor affecting composite satisfaction and the instrumental attitude.

The level of hygiene characteristics of the job is the first factor for composite satisfaction, but it affects none of the other three composite attitudes. Health condition also affects only composite satisfaction as third most important factor.

Age is the last factor in the present discussion. Before attempting to analyze the significance of the other factors for work attitudes of employed women, it is necessary to discuss its impact on work attitudes. For, it may be suggested, that this factor may have an overriding and independent impact on any person's work attitudes, and that variations in such attitudes do not reflect the impact of the quality of the job, or the worker's values or aspirations, but simply differences in the age compositions of the subgroups of the sample studied. It is possible that age affects women's work attitudes differently from men's.

It will be impossible, within the framework of the present study, to disentangle the effects of the other factors completely from the effects of the age factor. Nor will it be possible to do so even for the incidence of the other factors. In order to clarify the picture somewhat, however, let me present now the correlations of the work attitudes here studied with age, using the five usual age groups.

1. *Overt satisfaction.* The percentage of those answering, "very satisfied" rises regularly with age. The youngest group, under age twenty-five, has by far the highest incidence of dissatisfaction—20.8 percent—and it is still high in the next group—14.4 percent—and then it declines.

2. *Composite satisfaction.* High satisfaction rises until age fifty-five, and then declines; low satisfaction remains steady, and increases only after age fifty-five.

3. *Superficial satisfaction.* The youngest group has only 31.6 percent superficially satisfied. There is a big increase in the thirty-six to forty-five group and a steady increase thereafter, reaching 69 percent for the oldest group.

4. *Emphasis on content.* There is a considerable rise in emphasis on content in the twenty-six to thirty-five group and a decline in the thirty-six to forty-five group, but no overall rise or decline.

5. *Concern for content.* Indifference rises at age thirty-six and again at age fifty-six, yet concern decreases from age forty-six onward; the twenty-six to thirty-five age group is the most concerned.

6. *Concern for hygiene.* Between those under and over thirty-five there is only a mild rise—4.1 percent—of indifference.

7. *Interest in advancement.* There is a considerable decline in the interest in advancement at thirty-six, again at forty-six and at fifty-six. Those over thirty-five have 37.3 percent less interest than those under thirty-five.

8. *Instrumental attitude.* Here the patterns of concern for content and of interest in advancement are reflected: there is a decided rise in the incidence of the instrumental attitude in the thirty-six to forty-five group and again in the oldest group. Consequently, the over thirty-five group has 2.7 times the incidence of this attitude than the under thirty-five group.

9. *Instrumental syndrome.* Here the similar age patterns of concern for content, interest in advancement and superficial satisfaction all combine. There is a decided rise in the incidence of this syndrome at thirty-six and again at fifty-six. Of the oldest age group, 32.8 percent have this syndrome. The over thirty-five group has four times the incidence of it than the under thirty-five group.

10. *Commitment.* Until age forty-five there is hardly any change. Then begins a big rise in high commitment, apparently caused by the need to gain adequate pension qualification. Consequently, the high commitment rate of the over thirty-five is 17.2 percent higher than that of the under thirty-five, whereas low commitment is declining only minimally.

11. *Self-image as economically active person.* The youngest age group sees itself most as independent breadwinners; at twenty-five there is a small decline and a much bigger one for the thirty-five to forty-six group, the group which has the greatest incidence of presently married women. Thereafter, however, a new gradual rise of this image begins. Consequently, its incidence is only 8.1 percent lower for the over thirty-five group than for the under thirty-five group.

12. *Self-confidence as to ability to perform more challenging work.* The most self-confident group is not the youngest but the twenty-six to thirty-five year olds. From then on begins a decline, mild until the age of fifty-six when it becomes sharp. Of the oldest group only 60.3 percent answered the question about self-confidence affirmatively.

13. *Views and values about the proper work role of women.* Although this item figures here as a factor influencing attitudes to work, it is itself an attitude, of course, and one which varies considerably with age. The two young groups are much more egalitarian than the others, yet the twenty-six to thirty-five age group is the most egalitarian; and at thirty-six there is a great decline, and then another at fifty-six.

It might be argued on the basis of these figures that age is the overriding factor in causing variations in work attitudes: young women are more openly critical of their jobs, demand more challenging tasks, are more interested in advancement, see themselves as earning their own living, and are self-confident and progressive. It may be claimed that it is merely age that makes workers superficially satisfied, instrumental toward their jobs, lose interest in advancement and self-confidence and become conservative. Only the attitudes of self-image as earner and of commitment to employment have a different age pattern. The self-image of a woman as a basic earner declines most in midlife because then most women are married and can rely on their husbands' income, which some of the older ones can no longer do, being separated, divorced, or widowed. Age can also be viewed as a decisive factor influencing commitment, since the nearer a woman approaches retirement the more she becomes committed to employment.

I want to reject the claim that age is a decisive factor overriding the other factors. As a counter example I want to use the attitude that seems to be most affected by age, namely interest in advancement. The incidence of high interest in advancement declines from 68.4 percent for those under thirty-five to 40 percent for those between thirty-six and fifty. (I exclude all those approaching retirement.) Nevertheless, modern views make a big difference for the older group: whereas 26.7 percent of the traditional thirty-six to fifty year olds have a high interest in advancement, 43.8 percent of the ones with modern views and values have it.

Of course, we still have to take into consideration the age factor when comparing subgroups in the sample: the consideration of two or more factors favoring the same age group may strengthen this tendency more than is reasonable. Therefore, whenever the age composition of a subgroup is disproportionate, then this may bias the comparison: the factor content of the job somewhat favors the young in this sample, as the office group has a much higher average of high-content jobs and a much higher proportion of women under thirty-five than the other groups. The factor initial aspirations also favors the younger group as all three national societies have experienced an upgrading of their public education during the last two decades. The factor views and values likewise favors the younger group: the new women's movement started in the midsixties; therefore the chances for those under thirty-five to have formed or reformed their views and values under its impact are much greater than those of the older women.

Consequently, it may be the disproportionately high incidence of better jobs, higher initial aspirations and egalitarian views among the younger group that is the cause for their higher degree of autotelic attitude to work and not their youth alone.

Of course, I do not deny the impact of age as an independent factor altogether. Resignation plays an important part in the formation of work attitudes, and resignation takes time. Instrumental adaptation takes time and is therefore rare among the very young, even when their jobs are of low quality and dead end, their education and training inferior, and their views and values traditional.

I also want to suggest that current differences between the sexes in their conception of the life cycle, the onset of aging and old age may possibly make women resign themselves earlier to poor work situations than men.

Comparisons

In designing a comparison of job attitudes of women from three occupational and three national groups it was assumed that these attitudes are influenced by some factors that belong to the occupational sphere and by others that belong to the sphere of the national culture or society. My aim was to differentiate among these influences, as well as to measure them. I have found five factors to be of major importance for the attitudes to work measured and two of minor importance. The question, then, is, Are these factors influenced by occupational or by national-cultural characteristics? Let us make a close comparison.

In comparing the incidence of these seven factors for the three national groups and the three occupational groups we see that for the three most important factors, content, views and values, and initial aspirations, there is a considerable difference among the three occupational groups, the level of these factors being two or three times higher (or more egalitarian) for the office group than for the industrial group with the retail group half way in between. The content level of the job of the U.S. group is somewhat higher than that of the other two; the views of the Israeli group are somewhat more traditional whereas its level of initial aspirations is somewhat higher. For the next two important factors, progress in past employment career and domestic work load, the difference between the three occupational groups is small and the scale is the usual one; the differences among the national groups are of the same order of magnitude. For both, the U.S. group is in a favorable position, with the highest incidence of experience of progress in past work career and of light domestic work load. For progress in past work career, the level of the German and the Israeli groups is nearly the same, whereas the German group has the highest incidence of heavy domestic work load. Now to the level of hygiene of the job, which plays a role as a major factor only for overt and composite satisfaction. Here, in each of the two sets of groups, the differences between them are nearly the same. The level of the office group is 1.4 times higher than that of the industrial group; the Israeli group has the highest level and the U.S. group, the lowest. Finally, for health condition, which plays a major though not a primary role for overt and composite satisfaction but only a minor one for superficial satisfaction, the usual occupational scale appears; the health condition of the office workers is barely better than that of the retail workers and both are considerably better than that of the industrial workers. By comparison, national differences are much more pronounced: the health level of the Israeli group is twice as high as that of the German group with that of the U.S. being nearer to that of the Israeli group than the German.

What, then, can we learn from this?

The finding of a factor that is hardly significantly different for the three national cultures but is pronouncedly different for the three occupational groups points to the probable occupational origins of that factor. If differences between the two sets are about the same, then the origin of the factor may still be in the national cultures. Yet differences between conditions in the three national societies are not reflected in any marked difference between the levels of the factor in the different national groups. For example, the Israeli office workers can employ private nurse maids but German and American ones cannot. Yet these other two office groups may have lighter domestic work loads than their respective retail and industrial groups for other reasons, each specific to its own national culture. The reason for the similarity among the three national groups may be less accidental than caused by the fact that women employed in each occupation come from similar social groups that in all three countries are similarly stratified regarding the conditions of life that are relevant to the factor considered. Some of the factors are probably influenced by both national-cultural and occupational-specific causes.

The most significant factor is the content of the job, and it is clearly occupational. The next in significance are views and values and the level of initial aspirations. These two look occupational in origin, yet they certainly are also determined by national-cultural causes. Next comes progress in past work career, which is strongly correlated with content and is thus clearly occupational, although with some national-cultural influences. Next comes domestic work load, which is more nationally than occupationally determined. Next comes the hygiene level of the job, and it is mixed, because the evaluation of conditions of work heavily reflects nationally accepted criteria. Finally, health condition which is mixed again, although it is more nationally than occupationally determined.

All this amounts to the conclusion that the occupational differences are weightier than the national-cultural ones for the sum of the factors here considered.

Comparing in a similar fashion the national and occupational differences among the twelve attitudes to work here studied, we find the following.

I begin with the three attitudes reflecting job satisfaction. In answer to the direct question concerning satisfaction, occupational differences are minor, whereas there appear to be national differences. The U.S. group is most polarized in its answers, having the highest incidence of both those who declare themselves very dissatisfied and of those who declare themselves dissatisfied. The German group has the greatest incidence of the somewhat satisfied.

Coming to composite satisfaction, we find the usual occupational scale with the office group's level being 1.4 times higher than that of the industrial group, and the retail group being somewhat nearer to the office group. The level of the Israeli and the German groups is the same, yet the level of the U.S. group is 1.3 times higher.

With superficial satisfaction, clear differentiations of both the national and the occupational groups appear, although that of the occupational groups is sharper. It is also in the usual order for the occupational groups. The incidence of superficial (inconsistent) satisfaction is twice as large for the industrial group than it is for the office group, with the retail group nearer to the industrial group. And its incidence is 1.5 times as high in the Israeli group than in the U.S. group, with the German group nearer to the Israeli group.

Now to emphasis on content. Here the occupational scale is pronounced to the extreme, with the incidence of emphasis on content being 2.5 times higher in the office group than in the industrial group. The U.S. group has a level of emphasis on content somewhat higher than that of the German and the Israeli group.

Now let us move to concern about content. Here too the occupational scale is pronounced, the level of concern of the office group being 2.2 times that of the industrial group, the retail group being nearly in the middle. The difference among the national groups is much smaller, the level of the U.S. group is lowest, that of the German group is nearly the same, but that of the Israeli group is considerably higher.

For concern about hygiene, the picture is different: here the usual occupational differentiation is rather slight, whereas the national differentiation is pronounced. The rate of concern for hygiene of the German group is 1.7 times that of the U.S. group with the Israeli group nearer to the German.

Now let us discuss interest in advancement and promotion. Here the occupational differentiation is much greater than the national one, with the office group having 1.7 times the incidence of high interest in advancement than the industrial group, yet the retail group's interest is hardly higher than that of the industrial group. The interest of the Israeli group is less than one percent higher than that of the U.S. group but the German group's interest is 1/3 lower.

The level of commitment to employment and occupation is hardly higher in the office group than in the retail group, yet it is 1/5 higher than that of the industrial group. The differentiation among the national groups is a little sharper: the commitment level of the U.S. group is highest, nearly by 1/3 higher than that of the German group; the Israeli level lies in the middle.

Now let us move to self-image as an economically active person. The incidence of self-image as basic earner is higher in the office group than in the other two occupational groups where it is equal. The incidence of the same attitude in the Israeli and the German groups is nearly equal, and in the U.S. group it is more than 1/3 higher.

For self-confidence as to ability to perform more challenging work, the level of the industrial and the retail groups is about equal (that of the industrial group is 0.5 percent higher), yet that of the office group is significantly higher. For the national groups, the differentiation is only a little more pronounced. The U.S. group sees itself nearly as often able to perform more challenging work as the entire office group, the Israeli group 1/5 less, and the German group is a little nearer to the Israeli.

Finally, the two attitudes that are combinations of simple attitudes—the instrumental attitude, which is a combination of the absence of emphasis on content, indifference toward content, and low interest in advancement, and the instrumental syndrome, which adds to these three attitudes superficial satisfaction.

There is an extreme differentiation among the occupational groups in the incidence of the instrumental attitude: its incidence is 4.8 times higher in the industrial group than in the office group. Whereas 38.5 percent of the industrial workers and 23.5 percent of the retail workers have an instrumental attitude to their work, only 8.1 percent of the office workers have it. The differentiation among the national groups is much less pronounced. The incidence of the instrumental attitude among the German group is 1.7 times that of the Israeli group. The U.S. group is somewhat nearer to the Israeli group.

The situation as to the instrumental syndrome, which signifies a more pronouncedly resignative instrumental adaptation, is similar. The incidence of this syndrome is 7.2 times higher in the industrial group than in the office group, with the retail group about half way in between. The national differentiation is much less pronounced. The incidence of this syndrome in the German group is 1.8 times higher than in the Israeli group, and that in the U.S. group is insignificantly higher.

All this amounts to the conclusion that the occupational differences are weightier for the work attitudes: emphasis on content, concern for content, interest in advancement, instrumental attitude, and instrumental syndrome and that national differences are weightier for the work attitudes: overt satisfaction/ dissatisfaction and concern for hygiene. The two are about evenly balanced for the work attitudes: composite and superficial satisfaction, commitment to work, self-image as an economically active person and self-confidence as to the ability to perform more challenging work.

The picture that emerges regarding the occupational groups, then, is clear enough. Only as to overt satisfaction is there no difference among the three occupational groups and for concern for hygiene it is very small. The office group has the highest level of composite satisfaction, emphasis on content, concern for content and for hygiene, interest in advancement, commitment to work, self-image as an economically active person, and self-confidence as to the ability to perform more challenging work. It is also lowest in the incidence of superficial satisfaction, the instrumental attitude, and the instrumental syndrome. The industrial group is clearly the lowest on composite satisfaction, emphasis on content, and concern for content, and has the highest incidence of superficial satisfaction, the instrumental attitude, and the instrumental syndrome. As for interest in advancement, commitment to work, self-image as an economically active and self-confidence as to the ability to perform more challenging work, their incidence in the industrial and the retail groups is nearly the same.

The picture that emerges regarding the national groups, however, is not that clear. The U.S. group has the highest incidence of overt and composite satisfaction, the lowest of superficial satisfaction, the highest emphasis on content, self-image as basic earner and self-confidence as to the ability to perform more challenging work. The Israeli group has the highest incidence of high concern for content. The positions of the Israeli and the U.S. groups are about equally high as to interest in advancement and commitment to work, and the incidence of the instrumental attitude and syndrome are about equally low in both. The German group has clearly the lowest incidence of overt satisfaction, interest in advancement, and commitment to work and the highest incidence of superficial satisfaction, the instrumental attitude and the instrumental syndrome. The U.S. group clearly has the lowest concern for content and for hygiene. The Israeli group clearly has the lowest self-confidence as to the ability to perform more challenging work, and, with the German group, it has equally low composite satisfaction, emphasis on content, and self-image as a basic earner.

The office group has obviously the most favorable position as to its work attitudes, being the most satisfied, consistent, autotelic, concerned with the defects they perceive in their jobs, interested in advancement and promotion to more challenging and responsible positions, committed to employment and occupation, assured of their economic worth, and more confident as to ability to perform more challenging work. This is easily explained by their advantage as to all seven factors influencing work attitudes.

The somewhat more favorable position as to work attitudes that the U.S. group has when compared with the other two national groups is explained by its advantage in the important factors of content quality, experience of progress in past employment career, and light domestic work load. It is also equally egalitarian as the German group. The seemingly comparably inferior level of initial aspirations, that is, level of education and vocational training, of the U.S. group is somewhat misleading. The reason for this is the fact that this variable was relativized to the national norm, which in the United States is by far the highest. Without this relativizing, each of the U.S. subgroups would become highest in level of initial aspirations in comparison with the two other occupational subgroups.

The less favorable position of the German group as to its work attitudes appears to be caused by the somewhat lower level of the quality of the content of their jobs, the heavier domestic work load they carry, and the poorest perception of its members of their own health condition.

The traditionalism and scanty experience of progress in past work career of the Israeli group are compensated by its members' high evaluation of the hygiene level of their jobs, their relatively high level of initial aspirations, and good health condition. And, just as the advantage of the office group is enhanced by the age factor, that is, because it is by far the youngest of the three occupational groups, so is the case with the Israeli group, which is the youngest among the national groups. Thus, its chance to be instrumentally adapted is lower than that of the German group, which is the oldest.

The overall picture that emerges is that what contributes most to the shaping of the attitudes of employed women toward work in jobs below the semiprofessional level, is the relative level of the quality of the content, the intrinsic or task characteristics, of their jobs. The longer the basic work cycle; the greater the variety; the higher the level of skill, of autonomy, and responsibility in the job; the more the worker tends to emphasize its task characteristics; to be concerned about the defects of the job; and to be committed to employment and occupation. Also, the relatively higher quality of the job acts as a strong incentive to both interest in advancement and promotion and commitment to employment. Of course the level of schooling and vocational training plays an important supporting role, and of course higher educational level strongly correlates with both higher content level of the job and more egalitarian views of the place of women in the world of work. Indeed, such egalitarian views are the strongest influence on women's interest in promotion and advancement as well as on their self-confidence as to their ability to perform more challenging work. Whereas the evolution of egalitarianism is a strong activating factor, there remains as an important factor the inhibiting force of a heavy domestic work load.

Two conclusions from this study then are significant. (1) There is no basis for the view that for women employed in the lower ranges of the occupational scale, or that for married women employed in the lower ranges of the occupational scale, the intrinsic quality of their jobs does not matter, and that therefore they would not benefit from the restructuring or humanizing of their jobs. On the contrary, this study illustrates the great benefit they may draw from it. (2) Any attempt to carefully compare work attitudes of men and women for genuinely sex-specific differences should meticulously record and consider all the factors found here to be strongly correlated to work attitudes.

Appendix: Tables

Tables

Table A-1
Age Distribution, by Subgroup

Age	0	1	2	3	4	5	6	7	8	Total/Average
					Subgroup					
16-25										
Number	50	18	40	11	31	38	28	13	21	250
Percent of row	20.0	7.2	16.0	4.4	12.4	15.2	11.2	5.2	8.4	32.9
Percent of column	58.8	22.0	48.2	12.8	36.9	45.8	33.3	15.3	23.6	
Percent of sample	6.6	2.4	5.3	1.4	4.1	5.0	3.7	1.7	2.8	
26-35										
Number	12	11	26	16	19	28	21	22	25	180
Percent of row	6.7	6.1	14.4	8.9	10.6	15.6	11.7	12.2	13.9	23.7
Percent of column	14.1	13.4	31.3	18.6	22.6	33.7	25.0	25.9	28.1	
Percent of sample	1.6	1.4	3.4	2.1	2.5	3.7	2.8	2.9	3.3	
36-45										
Number	13	17	7	12	13	8	19	32	19	140
Percent of row	9.3	12.1	5.0	8.6	9.3	5.7	13.6	22.9	13.6	18.4
Percent of column	15.3	20.7	8.4	14.0	15.5	9.6	22.6	37.6	21.3	
Percent of sample	1.7	2.2	0.9	1.6	1.7	1.1	2.5	4.2	2.5	
46-55										
Number	5	27	7	31	14	9	13	8	18	132
Percent of row	3.8	20.5	5.3	23.5	10.6	6.8	9.8	6.1	13.6	17.3
Percent of column	5.9	32.9	8.4	36.0	16.7	10.8	15.5	9.4	20.2	
Percent of sample	0.7	3.5	0.9	4.1	1.8	1.2	1.7	1.1	2.4	
56-65										
Number	4	9	3	16	7	0	3	10	6	58
Percent of row	6.9	15.5	5.2	27.6	12.1	0	5.2	17.2	10.3	7.6
Percent of column	4.7	11.0	3.6	18.6	8.3	0	3.6	11.8	6.7	
Percent of sample	0.5	1.2	0.4	2.1	0.9	0	0.4	1.3	0.8	
66+										
Number	1	0	0	0	0	0	0	0	0	1
Percent of row	100.0	0	0	0	0	0	0	0	0	0.1
Percent of column	1.2	0	0	0	0	0	0	0	0	
Percent of sample	0.1	0	0	0	0	0	0	0	0	

Table A-2
Marital Status, by Subgroup

Marital Status	Subgroup 0	1	2	3	4	5	6	7	8	Total/Average
Single										
Number	42	18	34	11	34	37	19	10	26	231
Percent of row	18.2	7.8	14.7	4.8	14.7	16.0	8.2	4.3	11.3	30.4
Percent of column	49.4	22.0	41.0	12.8	40.5	44.6	22.6	11.8	29.2	
Married										
Number	37	46	40	66	30	34	55	59	37	404
Percent of row	9.2	11.4	9.9	16.3	7.4	8.4	13.6	14.6	9.2	53.1
Percent of column	43.5	56.1	48.2	76.7	35.7	41.0	65.5	69.4	41.6	
Living with friend or fiancé										
Number	0	0	0	0	2	0	4	1	1	8
Percent of row	0	0	0	0	25.0	0	50.0	12.5	12.5	1.1
Percent of column	0	0	0	0	2.4	0	4.8	1.2	1.1	
Divorced										
Number	1	8	5	2	14	7	4	11	18	70
Percent of row	1.4	11.4	7.1	2.9	20.0	10.0	5.7	15.7	25.7	9.2
Percent of column	1.2	9.8	6.0	2.3	16.7	8.4	4.8	12.9	20.2	
Separated										
Number	0	1	0	1	1	3	1	0	2	9
Percent of row	0	11.1	0	11.1	11.1	33.3	11.1	0	22.2	1.2
Percent of column	0	1.2	0	1.2	1.2	3.6	1.2	0	2.2	
Widowed										
Number	5	9	4	6	3	2	1	4	5	39
Percent of row	12.8	23.1	10.3	15.4	7.7	5.1	2.6	10.3	12.8	5.1
Percent of column	5.9	11.0	4.8	7.0	3.6	2.4	1.2	4.7	5.6	

Table A-3
Average Age and Marital Status, by National and Occupational Groups

	National Group			Occupational Group		
	Israel	United States	Germany	Industry	Retail	Office
Average age	32	35	36	34	37	31
Percent single	37.5	32.6	21.2	28.3	24.8	38.3
Percent married	49.3	51.1	58.8	61.9	53.7	43.6

Table A-4
Number of Children

Number of Children	Subgroup									Total/Average
	0	1	2	3	4	5	6	7	8	
None										
Number	56	27	45	20	51	59	35	31	48	37
Percent of row	15.1	7.3	12.1	5.4	13.7	15.9	9.4	8.3	12.9	48.9
Percent of column	65.9	32.9	54.2	23.3	60.7	71.1	41.7	36.5	53.9	
One										
Number	12	5	14	18	12	4	27	25	22	139
Percent of row	8.6	3.6	10.1	12.9	8.6	2.9	19.4	18.0	15.8	18.3
Percent of column	14.1	6.1	16.9	20.9	14.3	4.8	32.1	29.4	24.7	
Two										
Number	9	43	21	33	5	8	14	19	13	165
Percent of row	5.5	26.1	12.7	20.0	3.0	4.8	8.5	11.5	7.9	21.7
Percent of column	10.6	52.4	25.3	38.4	6.0	9.6	16.7	22.4	14.6	
Three										
Number	4	6	3	8	3	8	5	7	4	48
Percent of row	8.3	12.5	6.3	16.7	6.3	16.7	10.4	14.6	8.3	6.3
Percent of column	4.7	7.3	3.6	9.3	3.6	9.6	6.0	8.2	4.5	
Four										
Number	2	1	0	3	7	4	2	2	1	22
Percent of row	9.1	4.5	0	13.6	31.8	18.2	9.1	9.1	4.5	2.9
Percent of column	2.4	1.2	0	3.5	8.3	4.8	2.4	2.4	1.1	

											Total
Five											
Number	1	0	0	1	3	0	1	1	1		8
Number of row	12.5	0	0	12.5	37.5	0	12.5	12.5	12.5		1.1
Number of column	1.2	0	0	1.2	3.6	0	1.2	1.2	1.1		
Six											
Number	0	0	0	1	1	0	0	0	0		2
Percent of row	0	0	0	50.0	50.0	0	0	0	0		0.3
Percent of column	0	0	0	1.2	1.2	0	0	0	0		
Seven											
Number	0	0	0	2	1	0	0	0	0		3
Percent of row	0	0	0	66.7	33.3	0	0	0	0		0.4
Percent of column	0	0	0	2.3	1.2	0	0	0	0		
Eight											
Number	1	0	0	0	0	0	0	0	0		1
Percent of row	100.0	0	0	0	0	0	0	0	0		0.1
Percent of column	1.2	0	0	0	0	0	0	0	0		
Nine											
Number	0	0	0	0	1	0	0	0	0		1
Percent of row	0	0	0	0	100.0	0	0	0	0		0.1
Percent of column	0	0	0	0	1.2	0	0	0	0		
Column Total	85	82	83	86	84	83	84	85	89		761
	11.2	10.8	10.9	11.3	11.0	10.9	11.0	11.2	11.7		100.0

Note: There are 389 mothers and 791 children, of whom 474 are at home.

Table A-5
Employed Mothers and Their Children, by Subgroup

	Subgroup								
Status	0	1	2	3	4	5	6	7	8
Number of ever-married women	43	75	65	64	50	75	49	46	63
Number of children	63	145	83	113	96	97	65	60	69
Children per one hundred married women	146	193	128	176	192	129	173	130	103
Children at home[a]	40 (11)	74 (10)	64 (9)	58 (3)	64 (4)	60 (5)	41 (18)	38 (6)	35 (6)
Children at home per one hundred married women[a]	93 (25)	99 (13)	98 (14)	91 (5)	128 (8)	80 (7)	84 (37)	83 (13)	56 (9)
Children at home per one hundred children	63	51	77	51	67	46	63	63	51

[a]The numbers in brackets are cases of young children age five and under.

Table A-6
Child Care, by Subgroup

Type of Child Care				Subgroup						Total/Average
	0	1	2	3	4	5	6	7	8	
Traditional										
Number	20	37	45	204	32	43	186	109	68	744
Percent of row	2.7	5.0	6.0	27.4	4.3	5.8	25.0	14.7	9.1	46.7
Percent of column	28.6	39.8	29.2	49.5	22.0	28.1	83.4	55.0	46.6	
Neutral										
Number	18	33	71	51	30	43	22	37	49	354
Percent of row	5.1	9.3	20.0	14.4	8.5	12.1	6.2	10.5	13.6	22.2
Percent of column	25.7	35.5	46.1	12.4	20.7	28.1	9.9	18.7	33.6	
Modern										
Number	32	23	38	157	83	67	15	52	29	496
Percent of row	6.5	4.6	7.7	31.7	16.7	13.5	2.6	10.5	14.8	31.1
Percent of column	45.7	24.7	24.7	38.1	57.2	43.8	6.7	26.3	19.9	
Total sample										
Number	70	93	154	412	145	153	223	198	146	1,594
Percent	4.4	5.8	9.7	25.8	9.1	9.6	14.0	12.4	9.2	100.0

Note: *Traditional* refers to child care by the interviewee, her mother, her mother-in-law, her sister, her daughter, or the school. *Neutral* refers to care by a neighbor in the child's home, by a nursemaid, in a private nursery school, or in an obligatory kindergarten. *Modern* refers to care by the father, a neighbor in her home, a son, a crèche or day-care center, a play center, a boarding school, or a school with a long school day.

Table A-7
Child Care, by Age of Child

Type of Child Care	0-1 year old	2-3 years old	4-5 years old	6 years to age of independence	Total/ Average
Traditional					
Number	147	158	148	291	744
Percent of row	19.8	21.2	19.9	39.1	
Percent of column	60.2	46.5	33.3	51.4	46.7
Neutral					
Number	39	67	191	57	354
Percent of row	11.0	18.9	54.0	16.1	
Percent of column	16.0	19.7	43.0	10.0	22.2
Modern					
Number	58	115	105	218	496
Percent of row	11.7	23.2	21.2	44.0	
Percent of column	23.8	33.8	26.6	38.5	31.1
Total sample					
Number	244	340	444	566	1,594
Percent	15.3	21.3	27.9	35.5	100.0

Note: See note to table A-6 for definition of types of child care.

Table A-8
Mothers with Children under Age Ten, by Subgroup

| | Subgroup | | | | | | | | | Total/ |
	0	1	2	3	4	5	6	7	8	Average
Mothers in group										
Number	29	55	38	66	33	24	49	54	41	389
Percent	34.1	67.0	45.78	76.7	39.2	28.9	58.3	63.5	46.0	51.1
Employed while at least one child was under age 10										
Number	21	21	31	63	23	20	40	43	33	295
Percent of mothers	72.4	38.1	81.5	95.4	69.6	83.3	81.6	79.6	80.4	75.1
Total women in group	85	82	83	86	84	83	84	85	89	761

Table A-9
Ethnic Status, by Subgroup

Status	Subgroup									Total/Average
	0	1	2	3	4	5	6	7	8	
Immigrant from less-favored country										
Number	36	17	9	14	5	3	1	4	6	95
Percent of row	37.9	17.9	9.5	14.7	5.3	3.2	1.1	4.2	6.3	12.5
Percent of column	42.4	20.7	10.8	16.3	6.1	3.6	1.2	4.8	6.7	
Native born with father immigrant from less-favored country										
Number	31	12	23	27	9	9	1	1	1	114
Percent of row	27.2	10.5	20.2	23.7	7.9	7.9	0.9	0.9	0.9	15.0
Percent of column	36.5	14.6	27.7	31.4	11.0	10.8	1.2	1.2	1.1	
Immigrant from favored country										
Number	15	42	15	3	4	1	6	12	14	112
Percent of row	13.4	37.5	13.4	2.7	3.6	0.9	5.4	10.7	12.5	14.8
Percent of column	17.6	51.2	18.1	3.5	4.9	1.2	7.1	14.3	15.7	
Native-born father from favored country or third generation (or more)										
Number	3	11	36	42	64	70	76	67	68	437
Percent of row	0.7	2.5	8.2	9.6	14.6	16.0	17.4	15.3	15.6	57.7
Percent of column	3.5	13.4	43.4	48.8	78.0	84.3	90.5	79.8	76.4	
Total sample										
Number	85	82	83	86	82	83	84	84	89	758
Percent	11.2	10.8	10.9	11.3	10.8	10.9	11.1	11.1	11.7	100.0

Table A-10
Stability of Employment, by Subgroup

Years in Current Job		Subgroup									Total/Average
		0	1	2	3	4	5	6	7	8	
Under 1											
	Number	38	19	26	6	34	41	9	16	6	195
	Percent of row	19.5	9.7	13.3	3.1	17.4	21.0	4.6	8.2	3.1	25.6
	Percent of column	44.7	23.2	31.3	7.0	40.5	49.4	10.7	18.8	6.7	
1-5											
	Number	22	30	26	25	29	33	29	22	40	257
	Percent of row	8.6	11.7	10.1	10.1	11.3	12.8	11.3	8.6	15.6	33.8
	Percent of column	25.9	36.6	31.3	30.2	34.5	39.8	34.5	25.9	44.9	
6-10											
	Number	15	22	17	10	8	8	19	26	26	151
	Percent of row	9.9	14.6	11.3	6.6	5.3	5.3	12.6	17.2	17.2	19.8
	Percent of column	17.6	26.8	20.5	11.6	9.5	9.6	22.6	30.6	29.2	
11-20											
	Number	6	10	10	33	10	1	20	14	17	121
	Percent of row	5.0	8.3	8.3	27.3	8.3	0.8	16.5	11.6	14.0	15.9
	Percent of column	7.1	12.2	12.0	38.4	11.9	1.2	23.8	16.5	19.1	
21+											
	Number	4	1	4	11	3	0	7	7	0	37
	Percent of row	10.8	2.7	10.8	29.7	8.1	0	18.9	18.9	0	4.9
	Percent of column	4.7	1.2	4.8	12.8	3.6	0	8.3	8.2	0	
Total sample											
	Number	85	82	83	86	84	83	84	85	89	761
	Percent	11.2	10.8	10.9	11.3	11.0	10.9	11.0	11.2	11.7	100.0

Table A-11
Years of Schooling, by Subgroup

Completed Years of Schooling	Subgroup									Total/ Average
	0	1	2	3	4	5	6	7	8	
0-4										
Number	2	1	0	0	0	0	0	0	0	3
Percent of row	66.7	33.3	0	0	0	0	0	0	0	0.4
Percent of column	2.4	1.2	0	0	0	0	0	0	0	
5-8										
Number	24	13	1	23	2	0	49	42	12	166
Percent of row	14.5	7.8	0.6	13.9	1.2	0	29.5	25.3	7.2	21.8
Percent of column	28.2	15.9	1.2	26.7	2.4	0	58.3	49.4	13.5	
9-11										
Number	47	35	32	41	10	1	35	35	48	284
Percent of row	16.5	12.3	11.3	14.4	3.5	0.4	12.3	12.3	16.9	37.3
Percent of column	55.3	42.7	38.6	47.7	11.9	1.2	41.7	41.2	53.9	
12										
Number	11	28	36	16	32	25	0	5	13	166
Percent of row	6.6	16.9	21.7	9.6	19.3	15.1	0	3.0	7.8	21.8
Percent of column	12.9	34.1	43.4	18.6	38.1	30.1	0	5.9	14.6	
13										
Number	1	0	4	3	4	10	0	3	12	37
Percent of row	0.7	0	10.8	8.1	10.8	27.0	0	8.1	32.4	4.9
Percent of column	1.2	0	4.8	3.5	4.8	12.0	0	3.5	13.5	
14 and over										
Number	0	5	10	3	36	47	0	0	4	105
Percent of row	0	4.8	9.5	2.9	34.3	44.8	0	0	3.8	13.8
Percent of column	0	6.1	12.0	3.5	42.9	56.6	0	0	4.5	
Total sample										
Number	85	82	83	86	84	83	84	85	89	761
Percent	11.2	10.8	10.9	11.3	11.0	10.9	11.0	11.2	11.7	100.0

Table A-12
Vocational Training and Its Use, by Subgroup

Vocational Training	Subgroup									Total/ Average
	0	1	2	3	4	5	6	7	8	
Did not complete training										
Number	49	61	59	76	72	67	52	34	30	500
Percent of row	9.8	12.2	11.8	15.2	14.4	13.4	10.4	6.8	6.0	65.7
Percent of column	58.0	74.4	71.1	88.4	85.7	80.7	61.9	40.0	33.7	
Completed training not in use										
Number	19	17	11	6	6	5	24	19	15	122
Percent of row	15.6	13.9	9.0	4.9	4.9	4.1	19.7	15.6	12.3	16.0
Percent of column	22.0	20.7	13.3	7.0	7.1	6.0	28.6	22.3	16.9	
Completed training in use										
Number	17	4	13	4	6	11	8	32	44	139
Percent of row	12.2	2.9	9.4	2.9	4.3	7.9	5.8	23.0	31.7	18.3
Percent of column	20.0	4.9	15.7	4.6	7.1	13.3	9.5	37.7	49.4	
Total sample										
Number	85	82	83	86	84	83	84	85	89	761
Percent	11.2	10.7	10.9	11.3	11.0	10.9	11.0	11.2	11.7	100.0

Table A-13
Completed Vocational Training and Training on the Job, by Subgroup

Group	Completed Training and Are Using It		Training on the Job		Total Percent of Subgroup Trained
	Number	Percent	Number	Percent	
0	17	20	19	22	42
1	4	5	20	24	29
2	13	16	20	24	40
3	4	5	15	16	21
4	6	7	15	18	25
5	11	13	38	46	59
6	8	10	14	17	27
7	32	38	12	14	52
8	44	49	24	27	76

Table A-14
Father's Occupation, by Subgroup

Father's Occupation	Subgroup									Total/ Average
	0	1	2	3	4	5	6	7	8	
Manual										
Number	57	30	29	73	31	39	68	47	27	401
Percent of row	14.2	7.5	7.2	18.2	7.7	9.5	17.0	11.7	6.8	52.7
Percent of column	67.1	36.6	34.9	84.9	36.9	47.1	81.0	55.3	30.3	
Sales										
Number	5	3	1	0	4	4	0	0	0	17
Percent of row	29.4	17.6	5.9	0	23.5	23.5	0	0	0	2.2
Percent of column	5.9	3.7	1.2	0	4.8	4.8	0	0	0	
Highly skilled, blue collar, clerical, or small business										
Number	11	25	27	9	15	8	15	23	37	170
Percent of row	6.5	14.7	15.9	5.3	8.8	4.7	8.8	13.5	21.8	22.3
Percent of column	12.9	30.5	32.5	10.5	17.9	9.6	17.9	27.1	41.6	
Professional and managerial										
Number	5	23	23	3	31	29	1	14	24	153
Percent of row	3.3	15.0	15.0	2.0	20.3	19.0	0.7	9.2	15.7	20.1
Percent of column	5.9	28.0	27.7	3.5	36.9	34.9	1.2	16.5	27.0	
No answer or did not know father										
Number	7	1	3	1	3	3	0	1	1	20
Percent of row	35.0	5.0	15.0	5.0	15.0	15.0	0	5.0	5.0	2.6
Percent of column	8.2	1.2	3.6	1.2	3.6	3.6	0	1.2	1.1	
Total sample										
Number	85	82	83	86	84	83	84	85	89	761
Percent	11.2	10.8	10.0	11.3	11.0	10.9	11.0	11.2	11.7	100.0

Table A-15
Intergenerational Occupational Mobility, by Subgroup

Occupational Status of Interviewee	Subgroup									Total/ Average
	0	1	2	3	4	5	6	7	8	
Lower status than father										
Number	19	43	22	12	36	26	14	32	23	227
Percent of row	8.4	18.9	9.7	5.3	15.9	11.5	6.2	14.1	10.1	30.6
Percent of column	24.4	53.1	27.5	14.1	44.4	32.5	16.7	38.1	26.1	
Same status as father										
Number	55	5	25	73	11	11	66	1	37	284
Percent of row	19.4	1.8	8.8	25.7	3.9	3.9	23.2	0.4	13.0	38.3
Percent of column	70.5	6.2	31.3	85.9	13.6	13.7	78.6	1.2	42.0	
Higher status than father										
Number	4	33	33	0	34	43	4	51	28	230
Percent of row	1.7	14.3	14.3	0	14.8	18.7	1.7	22.2	12.2	31.0
Percent of column	5.1	40.7	41.3	0	42.0	53.7	4.8	60.7	31.8	
Total sample										
Number	78	81	80	85	81	80	84	84	88	741
Percent	10.5	10.9	10.8	11.5	10.9	10.8	11.3	11.3	11.9	100.0

Note: Twenty interviewees had no information on their fathers.

Table A-16
Occupational Status Compared to Husband's, by Subgroup

Occupational Status of Interviewee	Subgroup									Total/ Average
	0	1	2	3	4	5	6	7	8	
Lower than husband's										
Number	13	36	15	15	18	17	16	40	13	183
Percent of column	31.0	59.0	31.9	20.0	39.1	41.5	26.7	56.3	21.3	36.3
Percent of row	7.1	19.7	8.2	8.2	9.8	9.3	8.7	21.9	7.1	
Equal to husband's										
Number	26	0	16	60	7	11	41	2	37	200
Percent of column	61.9	0	34.0	80.0	15.2	26.8	68.3	2.8	60.7	39.7
Percent of row	12.0	0	8.0	30.0	3.5	5.5	26.8	68.3	2.8	
Higher than husband's										
Number	3	25	16	0	21	13	3	29	11	121
Percent of column	7.1	41.0	34.0	0	45.7	31.7	5.0	40.8	18.0	24.0
Percent of row	2.5	20.7	13.2	0	17.4	10.7	2.5	24.0	9.1	
Total sample										
Number	42	61	47	75	46	41	60	71	61	504
Percent	8.3	12.1	9.3	14.9	9.1	8.1	11.9	14.1	12.1	100.0

Table A-17
Mother's Occupation, by Subgroup

Mother's Occupation	Subgroup									Total/Average
	0	1	2	3	4	5	6	7	8	
Housewife										
Number	70	64	66	45	47	41	70	59	60	522
Percent of column	83.3	80.0	80.5	52.3	56.0	50.0	85.4	69.4	67.4	69.2
Percent of row	13.4	12.3	12.6	8.6	9.0	7.9	13.4	11.3	11.5	
Manual										
Number	13	8	5	36	10	12	9	12	7	112
Percent of column	15.5	10.0	6.1	41.9	11.9	14.6	11.0	14.1	7.9	
Percent of row	11.6	7.1	4.5	32.1	8.9	10.7	8.0	10.7	6.3	
Sales										
Number	0	1	1	0	3	1	0	2	1	9
Percent of column	0	1.2	1.2	0	3.6	1.2	0	2.4	1.1	1.2
Percent of row	0	11.1	11.1	0	33.3	11.1	0	22.2	11.1	
Highly skilled blue collar, clerical, or small business										
Number	1	6	5	3	15	13	3	11	15	72
Percent of column	1.2	7.5	6.1	3.5	17.9	15.9	3.7	12.9	16.9	9.5
Percent of row	1.4	8.3	6.9	4.2	20.8	18.1	4.2	15.3	20.8	
Professional or managerial										
Number	0	1	5	2	9	15	0	1	6	39
Percent of column	0	1.2	6.1	2.3	10.7	18.3	0	1.2	6.7	5.2
Percent of row	0	2.6	12.8	5.1	23.1	38.5	0	2.6	15.4	
Total sample										
Number	84	80	82	85	84	82	82	85	89	754[a]
Percent	11.1	10.6	10.9	11.4	11.1	10.9	10.9	11.3	11.8	100.0

[a]Seven interviewees had no information on this topic. Most of them had not been brought up by their mother.

Table A-18
Health: Direct Answer, by Subgroup

Health	0	1	2	3	4	5	6	7	8	Total/ Average
					Subgroup					
Very good										
Number	55	58	63	61	75	75	32	38	44	501
Percent	64.7	70.7	75.9	70.9	89.3	90.4	38.1	44.7	49.4	65.8
Medium										
Number	22	22	19	22	8	8	49	43	41	234
Percent	25.9	26.8	22.9	25.6	9.5	9.6	58.3	50.6	46.1	30.7
Not so good										
Number	8	2	1	3	1	0	3	4	4	26
Percent	9.4	2.4	1.2	3.5	1.2	0	3.6	4.7	4.5	3.4
Total sample	85	82	83	86	84	83	84	85	89	761

Table A-19
Health, by National Group

Health	Israel	United States	Germany	Total/ Average
Very good				
Number	177	211	144	502
Percent of row	35.3	42.0	22.7	66.0
Percent of column	70.8	83.4	44.2	
Medium				
Number	62	38	133	233
Percent of row	26.6	16.3	57.1	30.6
Percent of column	24.8	15.0	51.6	
Not so good				
Number	11	4	11	26
Percent of row	42.3	15.4	42.3	3.4
Percent of column	4.4	1.6	4.3	
Total sample				
Number	250	253	258	761
Percent	32.9	33.2	33.9	100.0

Table A-20
Health by Occupational Group

Health	Industry	Retail	Office	Total/Average
Good				
Number	148	171	183	502
Percent of row	29.5	34.1	36.5	66.0
Percent of column	58.0	68.1	71.8	
Medium				
Number	93	73	67	233
Percent of row	39.9	31.3	28.8	30.6
Percent of column	36.5	29.1	26.3	
Not so good				
Number	14	7	5	26
Percent of row	53.8	26.9	19.2	3.4
Percent of column	5.5	2.8	2.0	
Total sample				
Number	255	251	255	761
Percent	33.5	33.0	33.5	100.0

Table A-21
Health, by Age

Health	−25	26-35	36-45	46-55	56-65	65+	Total/Average
Very good							
Number	195	125	71	78	33	0	502
Percent of row	38.8	24.9	14.1	15.5	6.6	0	66.0
Percent of column	78.0	69.4	50.7	59.1	56.9	0	
Medium							
Number	54	50	59	49	20	1	233
Percent of row	23.2	21.5	25.3	21.0	8.6	0.5	30.6
Percent of column	21.6	27.8	42.1	37.1	34.5	100.0	
Not so good							
Number	1	5	10	5	5	0	26
Percent of row	3.8	19.2	38.5	19.2	19.2	0	3.4
Percent of column	0.4	2.8	7.1	3.8	8.6	0	
Total sample							
Number	250	180	140	132	58	1	761
Percent	32.9	23.7	18.4	17.3	7.6	0.1	100.0

Table A-22
Health Complaints

Complaint	Percent of Sample Suffering from It	Percent of Suffering Sample Attributing Complaint to Their Work
1. Nervousness	41.5	36.4
2. Headaches	38.6	45.3
3. Backache	35.2	64.4
4. Tired eyes	28.6	64.3
5. Varicose veins (painful legs)	27.9	59.4
6. Blood pressure (too high, too low, irregular)	20.8	20.6
7. Sleeplessness	15.5	36.7
8. Stomach or digestive troubles	19.8	33.7
9. Feminine complaints	10.5	20.9
10. Hemorrhoids	8.7	32.2
11. Heart trouble	7.4	35.1
12. Skin trouble	7.1	40.8
13. Hearing trouble	7.0	41.4

Table A-23
Health Condition, by Age and National Group

Health Condition	Israel	United States	Germany	Total/ Average
	Up to 35 Years Old			
Good				
Number	82	60	28	170
Percent of row	48.2	35.3	16.5	39.5
Percent of column	52.2	42.0	21.5	
Medium				
Number	46	45	31	122
Percent of row	37.7	36.9	25.4	28.4
Percent of column	29.3	31.5	23.8	
Not so good				
Number	29	38	71	138
Percent of row	21.0	27.5	51.4	32.1
Percent of column	18.5	26.6	54.6	
Total sample				
Number	157	143	130	430
Percent	36.5	33.3	30.2	100.0

Table A-23 continued

Health Condition	Israel	United States	Germany	Total/ Average
		36 Years and Older		
Good				
Number	27	43	13	83
Percent of row	32.5	51.8	15.7	25.1
Percent of column	29.0	39.1	10.2	
Medium				
Number	25	33	25	83
Percent of row	30.1	39.8	30.1	25.1
Percent of column	26.9	30.0	19.5	
Not so good				
Number	41	34	90	165
Percent of row	24.8	20.6	54.5	49.8
Percent of column	44.1	30.9	70.3	
Total sample				
Number	93	110	128	331
Percent	28.1	33.2	38.7	100.0

Table A-24
Domestic Work Load, by National and Occupational Group

	National Group			Occupational Group			
Domestic Work Load	Israel	United States	Germany	Industry	Retail	Office	Total/ Average
Light							
Number	84	134	58	72	83	121	276
Percent of row	30.4	48.5	21	26.1	30.1	43.8	
Percent of column	33.6	53.0	22.5	28.2	33.1	47.8	33.5
Medium							
Number	77	52	95	75	68	81	244
Percent of row	34.4	23.2	42.4	33.5	30.3	36.2	
Percent of column	30.8	20.5	36.8	29.4	27.1	31.8	29.4
Heavy							
Number	89	67	105	108	100	53	261
Percent of row	34.1	25.7	40.2	41.4	38.3	20.3	
Percent of column	35.6	26.5	40.7	42.4	39.8	20.8	34.3
Total sample							
Number	250	253	258	255	251	255	761
Percent	32.8	33.2	33.9	33.5	33	33.5	100

Note: *Light* refers to ten or fewer hours per work, *medium* is from eleven to twenty-two hours per week, and *heavy* is twenty-three hours or more per week.

Table A-25
Domestic Work Load, by Subgroup

Domestic Work Load	Subgroup									Total/
	0	1	2	3	4	5	6	7	8	Average
Light										
Number	28	19	37	31	48	55	13	16	29	276
Percent of column	32.9	23.2	44.6	36.0	57.1	66.3	15.5	18.8	32.6	36.3
Percent of row	10.1	6.9	13.4	11.2	17.4	19.9	4.7	5.8	10.5	
Medium										
Number	30	22	25	20	15	17	25	31	39	224
Percent of column	35.3	26.8	30.1	23.3	17.9	20.5	29.8	36.5	43.8	29.4
Percent of row	13.4	9.8	11.2	8.9	6.7	7.6	11.2	13.8	17.4	
Heavy										
Number	27	41	21	35	21	11	46	38	21	261
Percent of column	31.8	50.0	25.3	40.7	25.0	13.3	54.8	44.7	23.6	34.3
Percent of row	10.3	15.7	8.0	13.4	8.0	4.2	17.6	14.6	8.0	
Mean hours worked (number)	17.7	20.8	14.5	21.6	14.6	12.7	23.8	23.3	17.7	
Total sample										
Number	85	82	83	86	84	83	84	85	89	761
Percent	11.2	10.8	10.9	11.3	11.0	10.9	11.0	11.2	11.7	100.0
Number of women with children at home	22	36	27	43	22	20	42	39	26	277
Number of single and not-now married women	56	19	37	31	40	55	33	16	29	316

Note: See note to table A-25 for definition of *light*, *medium*, and *heavy*.

Table A-26
Health and Health Condition, by Domestic Work Load

	Light Work Load	Medium Work Load	Heavy Work Load	Total/ Average
Health				
Good				
Number	208	147	146	501
Percent of row	41.5	29.3	29.1	65.8
Percent of column	75.4	65.6	55.9	
Medium				
Number	61	74	99	234
Percent of row	26.1	31.6	42.3	30.7
Percent of column	22.1	33.0	37.9	
Not so good				
Number	7	3	16	26
Percent of row	26.9	11.5	61.5	3.4
Percent of column	2.5	1.3	6.1	
Total sample				
Number	276	224	261	761
Percent	36.3	29.4	34.3	100.0
Health Condition				
Good				
Number	113	68	72	253
Percent of row	44.7	26.9	28.5	33.2
Percent of column	40.9	30.4	27.6	
Medium				
Number	78	62	65	205
Percent of row	38.0	30.2	31.7	26.9
Percent of column	28.3	27.7	24.9	
Not so good				
Number	85	94	124	303
Percent of row	28.1	31.0	40.9	39.8
Percent of column	30.8	42.0	47.5	
Total sample				
Number	276	224	261	761
Percent	36.3	29.4	34.3	100.0

Table A-27
Age of Starting Work, by Current Age

Age of Starting Work	Current Age of Interviewee			Total/ Average
	Under 35	35-50	51 and Over	
Under age 14				
Number	61	41	16	118
Percent	14.2	20.0	12.6	15.5
Age 15				
Number	74	25	12	111
Percent	17.2	12.2	9.5	14.6
Age 16				
Number	131	47	30	208
Percent	30.5	22.9	23.8	27.3
Ages 17-20				
Number	134	58	39	231
Percent	31.2	28.3	30.9	30.4
Ages 20-24				
Number	25	9	5	39
Percent	5.8	4.4	3.9	5.1
Ages 25-30				
Number	4	6	5	15
Percent	0.9	2.9	3.9	2.0
Ages 31 and over				
Number	1	18	19	38
Percent	0.2	8.8	15.0	5.0
No answer				
Number	0	1	0	1
Percent	0	0.5	0	0.1
Total sample				
Number	430	205	126	761
Percent	56.5	26.9	16.6	100.0

Table A-28
Mean Number of Previous Jobs Held

Group	Average Number of Jobs Held	Average Number of Jobs, Excluding Summer Jobs
National group		
Israel	1.4	1.3
United States	3.4	2.6
Germany	2.1	2.0
Occupational group		
Industry	1.6	1.5
Retail	2.6	2.3
Office	2.7	2.2
Subgroup		
Group 0	1.1	1.1
Group 1	1.8	1.7
Group 2	1.4	1.2
Group 3	2.5	2.3
Group 4	3.6	2.7
Group 5	4.0	2.8
Group 6	1.2	1.1
Group 7	2.5	2.4
Group 8	2.7	2.5

Table A-29
Reasons for Career Interruption

Reason	Motherhood	Other Family	Job Too Time-Consuming or Change of Residence	Personal[a]	Economic	Volunteer Work
Average length of interruption (in months)	59.9	59.8	9.5	9.2	7.3	3
Percent of reasons	9.0	10.0	17.0	15.0	17.0	31.0
Percent of time of all interruptions	33.0	36.0	10.0	8.0	8.0	6.0

[a]The interruption was usually the nine months of the school year between summer jobs.

Table A-30
Women with Long Interruption in Work Career, by Subgroup

					Subgroup					Total/
	0	1	2	3	4	5	6	7	8	Average
Women with interrupted work careers (number)	4	13	2	9	12	8	4	11	7	70
Women ever married, 36 years or older (percent)	19.0	38.0	12.0	17.0	43.0	50.0	13.0	23.0	19.0	25.0

Note: Includes only women who have interrupted their careers for ten years or more.

Table A-31
Hours Worked per Week, by Subgroup

Work Hours per Week	Subgroup									Total/ Average
	0	1	2	3	4	5	6	7	8	
Under 20										
Number	0	2	2	0	5	1	7	9	3	29
Percent of row	0	6.9	6.9	0	17.2	3.4	24.1	31.0	10.3	3.8
Percent of column	0	2.4	2.4	0	6.0	1.2	8.3	10.6	3.4	
21-30										
Number	3	11	3	0	7	0	8	17	5	54
Percent of row	5.6	20.4	5.6	0	13.0	0	14.8	31.5	9.3	7.1
Percent of column	3.5	13.4	3.6	0	8.3	0	9.5	20.0	5.6	
31 and over										
Number	1	6	1	0	1	0	0	6	0	15
Percent of row	6.7	40.0	6.7	0	6.7	0	0	40.0	0	2.0
Percent of column	1.2	7.3	1.2	0	1.2	0	0	7.1	0	
Full time										
Number	81	63	77	86	71	82	69	53	81	663
Percent of row	12.2	9.5	11.6	13.0	10.7	12.4	10.4	8.0	12.2	87.1
Percent of column	95.3	76.8	92.8	100.0	84.5	98.8	82.1	62.4	91.0	
Total sample										
Number	85	82	83	86	84	83	84	85	89	761
Percent	11.2	10.8	10.9	11.3	11.0	10.9	11.0	11.2	11.7	100.0

Table A-32
Progress in Employment Career, by Subgroup

Career	Subgroup									Total/Average
	0	1	2	3	4	5	6	7	8	
Regressive										
Number	3	5	1	4	8	1	8	7	2	39
Percent of row	7.7	12.8	2.6	10.3	20.5	2.6	20.5	17.9	5.1	5.1
Percent of column	3.5	6.1	1.2	4.7	9.5	1.2	9.5	8.2	2.2	
Static										
Number	61	51	31	47	27	18	60	41	45	381
Percent of row	16.0	13.4	8.1	12.3	7.1	4.7	15.7	10.8	11.8	50.1
Percent of column	71.8	62.2	37.3	54.7	32.1	21.7	71.4	48.2	50.6	
Progressive										
Number	21	26	51	35	49	64	16	37	42	341
Percent of row	6.2	7.6	15.0	10.3	14.4	18.8	4.7	10.9	12.3	44.8
Percent of column	24.7	31.7	61.4	40.7	58.3	77.1	19.0	43.5	47.2	
Total sample										
Number	85	82	83	86	84	83	84	85	89	761
Percent	11.2	10.8	10.9	11.3	11.0	10.9	11.0	11.2	11.7	100.0

Table A-33
Task Characteristics or Content, by Subgroup

Content	Subgroup									Total/ Average
	0	1	2	3	4	5	6	7	8	
Low										
Number	51	17	10	46	22	7	65	27	5	250
Percent of row	20.4	6.8	4.0	18.4	8.8	2.8	26.0	10.8	2.0	32.9
Percent of column	60.0	20.7	12.0	53.5	26.2	8.4	77.4	31.8	5.6	
Medium										
Number	31	50	45	37	43	30	16	44	47	343
Percent of row	9.0	14.6	13.1	10.8	12.5	8.7	4.7	12.8	13.7	45.1
Percent of column	36.5	61.0	54.2	43.0	51.2	36.1	19.0	51.8	52.8	
High										
Number	3	15	28	3	19	46	3	14	37	168
Percent of row	1.8	8.9	16.7	1.8	11.3	27.4	1.8	8.3	22.0	22.1
Percent of column	3.5	18.3	33.7	3.5	22.6	55.4	3.6	16.5	41.6	
Total sample										
Number	65	82	83	86	84	83	84	85	89	761
Percent	11.2	10.8	10.9	11.3	11.0	10.9	11.0	11.2	11.7	100.0

Table A-34
Skill Required and Quality of Product or Service, by Subgroup

					Subgroup					
Level	0	1	2	3	4	5	6	7	8	Total/ Average
Low										
Number	2	1	1	1	3	3	0	1	3	15
Percent of row	13.3	6.7	6.7	6.7	20.0	20.0	0	6.7	20.0	2.0
Percent of column	2.4	1.2	1.2	1.2	3.6	3.6	0	1.2	3.4	
Medium										
Number	24	18	15	20	25	10	50	27	13	202
Percent of row	11.9	8.9	7.4	9.9	12.4	5.0	24.8	13.4	6.4	26.5
Percent of column	28.2	22.0	18.1	23.3	29.8	12.0	59.5	31.8	14.6	
High										
Number	59	63	67	65	56	70	34	57	73	544
Percent of row	10.8	11.6	12.3	11.9	10.3	12.9	6.3	10.5	13.4	71.5
Percent of column	69.4	76.8	80.7	75.6	66.7	84.3	40.5	67.1	82.0	
Total sample										
Number	85	82	83	86	84	83	84	85	89	761
Percent	11.2	10.8	10.9	11.3	11.0	10.9	11.0	11.2	11.7	100.0

Table A-35
Repetitiveness, Speed, and Strain of Task, by Subgroup

Level	Subgroup									Total/Average
	0	1	2	3	4	5	6	7	8	
High										
Number	58	32	15	63	16	8	62	22	10	286
Percent of row	20.3	11.2	5.2	22.0	5.6	2.8	21.7	7.7	3.5	37.6
Percent of column	68.2	39.0	18.1	73.3	19.0	9.6	73.8	25.9	11.2	
Medium										
Number	21	35	41	17	29	18	13	29	45	248
Percent of row	8.5	14.1	16.5	6.9	11.7	7.3	5.2	11.7	18.1	32.6
Percent of column	24.7	42.7	49.4	19.8	34.5	21.7	15.5	34.1	50.6	
Low										
Number	6	15	27	6	39	57	9	34	34	227
Percent of row	2.6	6.6	11.9	2.6	17.2	25.1	4.0	15.0	15.0	29.8
Percent of column	7.1	18.3	32.5	7.0	46.4	68.7	10.7	40.0	38.2	
Total sample										
Number	85	82	83	86	84	83	84	85	89	761
Percent	11.2	10.8	10.9	11.3	11.0	10.9	11.0	11.2	11.7	100.0

Table A-36
Repetitiveness and Speed of Task, by Subgroup

| | Subgroup | | | | | | | | | Total/ |
Level	0	1	2	3	4	5	6	7	8	Average
High										
Number	54	28	16	40	16	12	52	16	15	249
Percent of row	21.7	11.2	6.4	16.1	6.4	4.8	20.9	6.4	6.0	32.7
Percent of column	63.5	34.1	19.3	46.5	19.0	14.5	61.9	18.8	16.9	
Medium										
Number	24	31	36	33	37	38	21	43	29	292
Percent of row	8.2	10.6	12.3	11.3	12.7	13.0	7.2	14.7	9.9	38.4
Percent of column	28.2	37.8	43.4	38.4	44.0	45.8	25.0	50.6	32.6	
Low										
Number	7	23	31	13	31	33	11	26	45	220
Percent of row	3.2	10.5	14.1	5.9	14.1	15.0	5.0	11.8	20.5	28.9
Percent of column	8.2	28.0	37.3	15.1	36.9	39.8	13.1	30.6	50.6	
Total sample										
Number	85	82	83	86	84	83	84	85	89	761
Percent	11.2	10.8	10.9	11.3	11.0	10.9	11.0	11.2	11.7	100.0

Table A-37
Time Span of Central Activity of Job, by Subgroup

Time Span	Subgroup									Total/Average
	0	1	2	3	4	5	6	7	8	
Less than 1 minute										
Number	34	3	4	32	4	4	20	4	1	106
Percent of row	32.1	2.8	3.8	30.2	3.8	3.8	18.9	3.8	0.9	14.0
Percent of column	40.5	3.7	4.9	37.2	4.9	4.8	23.8	4.7	1.1	
1-5 minutes										
Number	18	14	14	34	17	7	33	15	1	153
Percent of row	11.8	9.2	9.2	22.2	11.1	4.6	21.6	9.8	0.7	20.3
Percent of column	21.4	17.3	17.3	39.5	20.7	8.4	39.3	17.6	1.1	
6-10 minutes										
Number	8	28	14	3	16	13	11	26	6	125
Percent of row	6.4	22.4	11.2	2.4	12.8	10.4	8.8	20.8	4.8	16.6
Percent of column	9.5	34.6	17.3	3.5	19.5	15.7	13.1	30.6	6.7	
More than 10 minutes										
Number	24	36	49	17	45	59	20	40	81	371
Percent of row	6.5	9.7	13.2	4.6	12.1	15.9	5.4	10.8	21.8	49.1
Percent of column	28.6	44.4	60.5	19.8	54.9	71.1	23.8	47.1	91.0	
Total sample										
Number	84	81	81	86	82	83	84	85	89	755
Percent	11.1	10.7	10.7	11.4	10.9	11.0	11.1	11.3	11.8	100.0

Table A-38
Variety of Tasks Performed, by Subgroup

Level	Subgroup									Total/Average
	0	1	2	3	4	5	6	7	8	
Low										
Number	31	29	17	50	17	7	48	23	20	242
Percent of row	12.8	12.0	7.0	20.7	7.0	2.9	19.8	9.5	8.3	31.8
Percent of column	36.5	35.4	20.5	58.1	20.2	8.4	57.1	27.1	22.5	
Medium										
Number	37	24	35	23	29	34	22	36	51	291
Percent of row	12.7	8.2	12.0	7.9	10.0	11.7	7.6	12.4	17.5	38.2
Percent of column	43.5	29.3	42.2	26.7	34.5	41.0	26.2	42.4	57.3	
High										
Number	17	29	31	13	38	42	14	26	18	228
Percent of row	7.5	12.7	13.6	5.7	16.7	18.4	6.1	11.4	7.9	30.0
Percent of column	20.0	35.4	37.3	15.1	45.2	50.6	16.7	30.6	20.2	
Total sample										
Number	85	82	83	86	84	83	84	85	89	761
Percent	11.2	10.8	10.9	11.3	11.0	10.9	11.0	11.2	11.7	100.0

Table A-39
Autonomy on Job, by Subgroup

Level		0	1	2	3	4	5	6	7	8	Total/Average
								Subgroup			
Low	Number	50	25	18	30	22	10	52	25	6	238
	Percent of row	21.0	10.5	7.6	12.6	9.2	4.2	21.8	10.5	2.5	31.3
	Percent of column	58.8	30.5	21.7	34.9	26.2	12.0	61.9	29.4	6.7	
Medium	Number	29	45	41	52	48	50	28	39	55	387
	Percent of row	7.5	11.6	10.6	13.4	12.4	12.9	7.2	10.1	14.2	50.9
	Percent of column	34.1	54.9	49.4	60.5	57.1	60.2	33.3	45.9	61.8	
High	Number	6	12	24	4	14	23	4	21	28	136
	Percent of row	4.4	8.8	17.6	2.9	10.3	16.9	2.9	15.4	20.6	17.9
	Percent of column	7.1	14.6	28.9	4.7	16.7	27.7	4.8	24.7	31.5	
Total sample	Number	85	82	83	86	84	83	84	85	89	761
	Percent	11.2	10.8	10.9	11.3	11.0	10.9	11.0	11.2	11.7	100.0

Table A-40
Responsibility of Job, by Subgroup

| | Subgroup | | | | | | | | | Total/ |
Level	0	1	2	3	4	5	6	7	8	Average
Low										
Number	32	75	76	39	34	11	42	34	16	359
Percent of row	8.9	20.9	21.2	10.9	9.5	3.1	11.7	9.5	4.5	47.2
Percent of column	37.6	91.5	91.6	45.3	40.5	13.3	50.0	40.0	18.0	
Medium										
Number	49	7	5	41	35	29	38	43	41	288
Percent of row	17.0	2.4	1.7	14.2	12.2	10.1	13.2	14.9	14.2	37.8
Percent of column	57.6	8.5	6.0	47.7	41.6	34.9	45.2	50.6	46.0	
High										
Number	4	0	2	6	15	43	4	8	32	114
Percent of row	3.5	0	1.8	5.3	13.2	37.7	3.5	7.0	28.1	15.0
Percent of column	4.7	0	2.4	7.0	17.9	51.8	4.8	9.4	36.0	
Total sample										
Number	85	82	83	86	84	83	84	85	89	761
Percent	11.2	10.8	10.9	11.3	11.0	10.9	11.0	11.2	11.7	100.0

Table A-41
Evaluation of Chances of Promotion, by Subgroup

Level	Subgroup									Total/Average
	0	1	2	3	4	5	6	7	8	
Poor										
Number	42	30	20	61	34	26	72	50	65	400
Percent of row	10.5	7.5	5.0	15.3	8.5	6.5	18.0	12.5	16.2	52.6
Percent of column	49.4	36.6	24.1	70.9	40.5	31.3	85.7	58.8	73.0	
Medium										
Number	21	19	31	13	17	24	9	19	14	167
Percent of row	12.6	11.4	18.6	7.8	10.2	14.4	5.4	11.4	8.4	21.9
Percent of column	24.7	23.2	37.3	15.1	20.2	28.9	10.7	22.4	15.7	
Good										
Number	22	33	32	12	33	33	3	16	10	194
Percent of row	11.3	17.0	16.5	6.2	17.0	17.0	1.5	8.2	5.2	25.5
Percent of column	25.9	40.2	38.6	14.0	39.3	39.8	3.6	18.8	11.2	
Total sample										
Number	85	82	83	86	84	83	84	85	89	761
Percent	11.2	10.8	10.9	11.3	11.0	10.9	11.0	11.2	11.7	100.0

Table A-42
Level of Hygiene Characteristics of Job, by Subgroup

Level	\[Subgroup\] 0	1	2	3	4	5	6	7	8	Total/Average
Poor										
Number	27	17	10	35	31	22	23	27	16	208
Percent of row	13.0	8.2	4.8	16.8	14.9	10.6	11.1	13.0	7.7	27.3
Percent of column	31.8	20.7	12.0	40.7	36.9	26.5	27.4	31.8	18.0	
Medium										
Number	34	22	23	31	33	34	40	31	33	281
Percent of row	12.1	7.8	8.2	11.0	11.7	12.1	14.2	11.0	11.7	36.9
Percent of column	40.0	26.8	27.7	36.0	39.2	41.0	47.6	36.5	37.1	
Good										
Number	24	43	50	20	20	27	21	27	40	272
Percent of row	8.8	15.8	18.4	7.4	7.4	9.9	7.7	9.9	14.7	35.7
Percent of column	28.2	52.4	60.2	23.3	23.8	32.5	25.0	31.7	44.9	
Total sample										
Number	85	82	83	86	84	83	84	85	89	761
Percent	11.2	10.8	10.9	11.3	11.0	10.9	11.0	11.2	11.7	100.0

Table A-43
Financial Benefits, by Subgroup

Level	Subgroup									Total/
	0	1	2	3	4	5	6	7	8	Average
Low										
Number	34	25	12	50	41	23	45	46	23	299
Percent of row	11.4	8.4	4.0	16.7	13.7	7.7	15.1	15.4	7.7	39.3
Percent of column	40.0	30.5	14.5	58.1	48.8	27.7	53.6	54.1	25.8	
Medium										
Number	45	36	43	34	37	43	34	32	44	348
Percent of row	12.9	10.3	12.4	9.8	10.6	12.4	9.8	9.2	12.6	45.7
Percent of column	52.9	43.9	51.8	39.5	44.0	51.8	40.5	37.6	49.4	
High										
Number	6	21	28	2	6	17	5	7	22	114
Percent of row	5.3	18.4	24.6	1.8	5.3	14.9	4.4	6.1	19.3	15.0
Percent of column	7.1	25.6	33.7	2.3	7.1	20.5	6.0	8.2	24.7	
Total sample										
Number	85	82	83	86	84	83	84	85	89	761
Percent	11.2	10.8	10.9	11.3	11.0	10.9	11.0	11.2	11.7	100.0

Table A-44
Physical Conditions at Work Place, by Subgroup

| | | | | | Subgroup | | | | | Total/ |
Level	0	1	2	3	4	5	6	7	8	Average
Low										
Number	34	21	19	45	34	28	34	29	31	275
Percent of row	12.4	7.6	6.9	16.4	12.4	10.2	12.4	10.5	11.3	36.1
Percent of column	40.0	25.6	22.9	52.3	40.5	33.7	40.5	34.1	34.8	
Medium										
Number	23	30	27	17	20	17	17	15	22	188
Percent of row	12.2	16.0	14.4	9.0	10.6	9.0	9.0	8.0	11.7	24.7
Percent of column	27.1	36.6	32.5	19.8	23.8	20.5	20.2	17.6	24.7	
High										
Number	28	31	37	24	30	38	33	41	36	298
Percent of row	9.4	10.4	12.4	8.1	10.1	12.8	11.1	13.8	12.1	39.2
Percent of column	32.9	37.8	44.6	27.9	35.7	45.8	39.3	48.2	40.4	
Total sample										
Number	85	82	83	86	84	83	84	85	89	761
Percent	11.2	10.8	10.9	11.3	11.0	10.9	11.0	11.2	11.7	100.0

Table A-45
Convenience of Work Hours, by Subgroup

Level	Subgroup									Total/Average
	0	1	2	3	4	5	6	7	8	
Low										
Number	22	13	12	2	28	30	15	14	15	151
Percent of row	14.6	8.6	7.9	1.3	18.5	19.9	9.9	9.3	9.9	19.8
Percent of column	25.9	15.9	14.5	2.3	33.3	36.1	17.9	16.5	16.9	
Medium										
Number	15	13	19	10	24	22	10	12	15	140
Percent of row	10.7	9.3	13.6	7.1	17.1	15.7	7.1	8.6	10.7	18.4
Percent of column	17.6	15.9	22.9	11.6	28.6	26.5	11.9	14.1	16.9	
High										
Number	48	56	52	74	32	31	59	59	59	470
Percent of row	10.2	11.9	11.1	15.7	6.8	6.6	12.6	12.6	12.6	61.8
Percent of column	56.5	68.3	62.7	86.0	38.1	37.3	69.4	69.4	66.3	
Total sample										
Number	85	82	83	86	84	83	84	85	89	761
Percent	11.2	10.8	10.9	11.3	11.0	10.9	11.0	11.2	11.7	100.0

Table A-46
Evaluation of Social Relations on Job (Composite)

| | Subgroup | | | | | | | | | Total/ |
Level	0	1	2	3	4	5	6	7	8	Average
Low										
Number	33	15	15	39	16	26	28	30	39	241
Percent of row	13.7	6.2	6.2	16.2	6.6	10.8	11.6	12.4	16.2	31.7
Percent of column	38.8	18.3	18.1	45.3	19.0	31.3	33.3	35.3	43.8	
Medium										
Number	18	18	28	17	25	18	22	20	16	182
Percent of row	9.9	9.9	15.4	9.3	13.7	9.9	12.1	11.0	8.8	23.9
Percent of column	21.2	22.0	33.7	19.8	29.8	21.7	26.2	23.5	18.0	
High										
Number	34	49	40	30	43	39	34	35	34	338
Percent of row	10.1	14.5	11.8	8.9	12.7	11.5	10.1	10.4	10.1	44.4
Percent of column	40.0	59.8	48.2	34.9	51.2	47.0	40.5	41.2	38.2	
Total sample										
Number	85	82	83	86	84	83	84	85	89	761
Percent	11.2	10.8	10.9	11.3	11.0	10.9	11.0	11.2	11.7	100.0

Table A-47
Level of Union Performance, by Subgroup

Level	Subgroup									Unionized Total/ Average	Total/ Average
	0	1	2	3	4	5	6	7	8		
Low											
Number	1	4	7	3	3	0	4	3	5	5	30
Percent of row	13.3	13.3	23.3	10.0	10.0	0	13.3	10.0	16.7		3.9
Percent of column	1.2	4.9	8.4	3.5	3.6	0	4.8	3.5	5.6		
Medium											
Number	30	22	17	35	11	0	33	21	23	32	192
Percent of row	15.6	11.5	8.9	18.2	5.7	0	17.2	10.9	12.0		25.2
Percent of column	35.3	26.8	20.5	40.7	13.1	0	39.3	24.7	25.8		
High											
Number	46	51	43	47	28	9	43	56	59	63	382
Percent of row	12.0	13.4	11.3	12.3	7.3	2.4	11.4	14.7	15.4		50.2
Percent of column	54.1	62.2	51.8	54.7	33.3	10.8	51.2	65.9	66.3		
No answer[a]											
Number	8	5	16	1	42	74	4	5	2		157
Percent of row	5.1	3.2	10.2	0.6	26.8	47.1	2.5	3.2	1.3		20.6
Percent of column	9.4	6.1	19.3	1.2	50.0	89.2	4.8	5.9	2.2		
Total sample											
Number	85	82	83	86	84	83	84	85	89	604	761
Percent	11.2	10.8	10.9	11.3	11.0	10.9	11.0	11.2	11.7	100	100.0

[a]Generally not unionized.

Table A-48
Personal Freedom on Job, by Subgroup

| | Subgroup | | | | | | | | | Total/ |
Level	0	1	2	3	4	5	6	7	8	Average
Low										
Number	47	33	0	2	20	1	3	8	0	114
Percent of row	41.2	28.9	0	1.8	17.5	0.9	2.6	7.0	0	15.0
Percent of column	55.3	40.2	0	2.3	23.8	1.2	3.6	9.4	0	
Medium										
Number	26	15	5	29	31	9	34	22	0	171
Percent of row	15.2	8.8	2.9	17.0	18.1	5.3	19.9	12.9	0	22.5
Percent of column	30.6	18.3	6.0	33.7	36.9	10.8	40.5	25.9	0	
High										
Number	12	34	78	55	33	73	47	55	89	476
Percent of row	2.5	7.1	16.4	11.6	6.9	15.3	9.9	11.6	18.7	62.5
Percent of column	14.1	41.5	94.0	64.0	39.3	88.0	56.0	64.7	100.0	
Total sample										
Number	85	82	83	86	84	83	84	85	89	761
Percent	11.2	10.8	10.9	11.3	11.0	10.9	11.0	11.2	11.7	100.0

Table A-49
Plans for Continuation of Work, by Subgroup

Continue Until:	Subgroup									Percent of Women	Percent of Answers
	0	1	2	3	4	5	6	7	8		
Military service										1.2	1.3
Number	3	4	3	n.a.	n.a.	n.a.	n.a.	n.a.	n.a.		
Percent	3.6	4.9	3.6	n.a.	n.a.	n.a.	n.a.	n.a.	n.a.		
Marriage										5.5	5.9
Number	17	5	5	0	3	5	3	3	4		
Percent	20.0	6.2	5.9	0	3.2	5.1	3.3	3.4	4.2		
Birth of children										12.6	13.4
Number	10	5	11	4	9	25	18	7	13		
Percent	12.0	6.2	13.0	4.6	9.7	25.5	20.0	8.0	13.8		
Sufficient income of husband										6.8	7.2
Number	5	3	1	9	8	7	12	6	4		
Percent	5.9	3.7	1.2	9.4	8.6	7.1	13.3	6.9	4.2		
Material goal										10.9	11.6
Number	10	2	1	7	12	9	2	15	5		
Percent	12.0	2.5	1.2	7.3	12.9	9.2	30.0	17.2	5.3		
Retirement										56.7	60.3
Number	30	54	47	75	60	51	29	51	60		
Percent	36.0	66.7	55.9	78.1	64.5	52.0	32.2	58.6	63.8		
Volunteer work or hobby										1.2	1.3
Number	0	0	1	0	1	1	0	2	5		
Percent	0	0	1.2	0	1.1	1.0	0	2.3	5.3		
No plans										5.1	5.4
Number	9	8	13	1	0	0	1	3	6		
Percent	10.7	9.9	15.5	1.0	0	0	1.1	3.4	6.4		
Number of women	85	82	83	86	84	83	84	85	89	761	100.0
Number of answers	84	81	84	96	93	98	90	87	94	100.0	807

Table A-50
Plans for Continuation of Work, by National and Occupational Group

Continue Until:		National Group							Occupational Group				
		Israel	United States	Percent of Women	Percent of Answers	Germany	Percent of Women	Percent of Answers	Industry	Retail	Office	Percent of Women	Percent of Answers
Military service	Number	10	0			0			3	4	3		
	Percent	4.0	0	1.2	1.3	0	1.2	1.3	1.1	1.5	1.1	1.2	1.3
Marriage	Number	27	8			10			20	11	14		
	Percent	10.8	2.8	5.5	5.9	3.7	5.5	5.9	7.4	4.2	5.0	5.5	5.9
Birth of children	Number	26	38			38			32	21	43		
	Percent	10.4	13.2	12.6	13.4	14.0	12.6	13.4	11.8	8.0	15.6	12.6	13.4
Sufficient income of husband	Number	9	24			22			26	17	12		
	Percent	3.6	8.4	6.8	7.2	8.1	6.8	7.2	9.6	6.5	4.3	6.8	7.2
Material goal	Number	13	28			47			44	29	15		
	Percent	5.2	9.7	10.9	11.6	17.3	10.9	11.6	16.3	11.1	5.4	10.9	11.6
Retirement	Number	133	186			140			134	165	160		
	Percent	53.4	64.8	56.7	60.3	51.7	56.7	60.3	49.6	63.2	58.0	56.7	60.3
Volunteer work or hobby	Number	1	2			7			1	2	7		
	Percent	0.4	0.7	1.2	1.3	2.6	1.2	1.3	0.4	0.8	2.5	1.2	1.3
No plans	Number	30	2			7			11	11	19		
	Percent	12.0	0.7	5.1	5.4	2.6	5.1	5.4	4.1	4.2	6.9	5.1	5.4
Number of women		250	253			258				251	255		
Number of answers		249	287			271				261	276		

Table A-51
Alternatives to Employment Should Financial Need Cease, by Subgroup

Alternative		0	1	2	3	4	5	6	7	8	Percent of Answers	Percent of Women
							Subgroup					
Stay home	Number	19	5	4	34	12	6	33	13	17	13.8	18.8
	Percent	17.7	4.4	3.7	2.9	10.7	5.0	29.5	11.4	12.9		
Stay at present job	Number	19	52	23	18	24	20	18	26	24	21.6	29.4
	Percent	17.7	4.6	21.1	15.4	21.4	16.7	20.0	29.4	25.5		
Part-time work	Number	20	20	28	28	23	28	26	36	28	22.9	31.1
	Percent	18.7	17.7	25.7	23.9	20.5	23.3	23.2	31.5	21.2		
More interesting work	Number	8	9	21	10	23	25	6	17	12	12.9	17.2
	Percent	7.5	8.0	19.2	18.5	20.5	20.8	5.4	14.9	9.0		
Return to study or training	Number	37	26	31	20	27	37	17	13	37	23.9	32.2
	Percent	34.6	23.0	28.4	17.1	24.1	30.8	15.2	11.4	28.0		
Volunteer work	Number	1	0	1	3	0	0	1	0	0	0.6	0.8
	Percent	0.9	0	0.9	2.6	0	0	0.9	0	0		
Hobby	Number	0	1	1	4	3	4	11	9	14	4.5	6.2
	Percent	0	0.9	0.9	3.4	2.7	3.3	9.8	7.9	10.6		
All answers given		107	113	109	117	112	120	112	114	132	100.2	135.7
Number of women who gave no answer[a]		3	3	2	0	3	0	0	1	7		

Note: The 761 interviewees gave 1,036 answers; 294 women gave two answers each.

[a]Nineteen women gave no answer.

Table A-52

Alternatives to Employment Should Financial Need Cease, by National and Occupational Group

Alternative	National Group			Industrial Group		
	Israel	*United States*	*Germany*	*Industry*	*Retail*	*Office*
Return to study or training						
Number	94	84	67	74	66	105
Percent of answers	28.5	24.1	18.7	22.0	19.5	29.0
Percent of women	37.6	33.2	26.0	29.0	26.2	41.1
Part-time work						
Number	68	79	90	71	79	84
Percent of answers	20.7	22.6	25.1	21.1	23.3	23.2
Percent of women	27.2	31.2	34.9	27.8	31.5	32.9
Stay at present job						
Number	94	62	68	55	102	67
Percent of answers	28.5	17.8	18.9	16.4	30.1	18.5
Percent of women	37.6	24.5	26.4	21.6	40.6	26.3
Stay home						
Number	28	52	63	86	30	27
Percent of answers	8.5	14.8	17.6	25.6	8.8	7.5
Percent of women	11.2	20.5	24.4	33.7	11.9	10.6
More interesting work						
Number	38	58	35	24	49	58
Percent of answers	11.5	16.6	9.8	6.1	14.5	16.0
Percent of women	15.2	22.9	13.6	9.4	19.5	22.7

Note: In the Israeli group, 250 women gave 329 answers; in the U.S. group, 253 women gave 349 answers; and in the German group, 258 women gave 358 answers. In the industrial group, 255 women gave 336 answers; in the retail group, 251 women gave 399 answers; and in the office group, 255 women gave 361 answers.

Table A-53
Commitment to Work/Employment, by Subgroup

Level	Subgroup									Total/Average
	0	1	2	3	4	5	6	7	8	
Low										
Number	13	8	13	8	6	7	41	16	7	119
Percent of row	10.9	6.7	10.9	6.7	5.0	5.9	34.5	13.4	5.9	15.6
Percent of column	15.3	9.8	15.7	9.3	7.1	8.4	48.8	18.8	7.9	
Medium										
Number	45	18	36	26	29	22	16	41	30	263
Percent of row	17.1	6.8	13.7	9.9	11.0	8.4	6.1	15.6	11.4	34.6
Percent of column	52.9	22.0	43.4	30.2	34.5	26.5	19.0	48.2	33.7	
High										
Number	27	56	34	52	49	54	27	28	52	379
Percent of row	7.1	14.8	9.0	13.7	12.9	14.2	7.1	7.4	13.7	49.8
Percent of column	31.8	68.3	41.0	60.5	58.3	65.1	32.1	32.9	58.4	
Total sample										
Number	85	82	83	86	84	83	84	85	89	761
Percent	11.2	10.8	10.9	11.3	11.0	10.9	11.0	11.2	11.7	100.0

Table A-54
Use of Income from Employment, by Subgroup

Answers[a]	Subgroup								
	0	1	2	3	4	5	6	7	8
Clothes									
Number	49	19	41	49	47	31	22	30	19
Percent	12.7	5.2	11.4	12.9	15.1	9.2	6.7	9.8	6.0
Earn own living									
Number	78	81	75	93	135	142	60	59	115
Percent	20.2	20.8	20.8	24.4	43.4	42	18.2	19.2	36.8
Earn family's living									
Number	92	39	25	51	20	35	21	18	55
Percent	23.8	10.0	6.9	13.4	6.4	10.3	6.4	5.9	17.6
Add to husband's income[b]									
Number	71	110	69	109	44	67	95	91	55
Percent	18.3	28.3	19.1	28.6	14.1	19.8	28.8	29.6	27.6
To maintain essential standard of living									
Number	55	91	66	41	28	23	50	62	20
Percent	14.2	23.9	18.3	10.8	9.0	6.8	15.2	20.2	6.4
To buy extras									
Number	11	20	32	16	17	26	8	11	22
Percent	2.8	5.1	8.9	4.2	5.5	7.7	2.4	3.6	7.0
Paid help									
Number	0	0	7	3	2	0	0	0	2
Percent	0	0	1.9	0.8	0.6	0	0	0	0.6
Save for specific goal									
Number	31	28	46	19	18	14	70	36	28
Percent	8.0	7.2	12.7	4.9	5.8	4.1	21.2	11.7	8.9
Total answers	387	388	361	381	311	338	330	307	312

[a]The answers are weighted.

[b]This answer comprises 22.8 percent of all weighted answers; 53.1 percent of the sample is married.

Table A-55
Important Aspects of Job, Grading Eight of Fifteen Options, by Subgroup

Answer (Weighted)	Subgroup									Median Percent of All Groups
	0	1	2	3	4	5	6	7	8	
1. Physical conditions										
Number	70	60	49	87	72	37	107	97	79	7.7
Percent	8.2	7.0	5.4	9.2	7.5	3.8	11.0	10.0	7.5	
2. Relations with management										
Number	93	108	68	88	94	83	118	118	96	10.2
Percent	11.0	12.6	7.5	9.3	9.8	8.6	12.3	12.0	9.1	
3. Independence in work										
Number	46	50	80	48	71	95	52	76	108	7.3
Percent	5.4	5.9	8.8	5.0	7.4	9.8	5.4	7.8	10.3	
4. Convenient hours										
Number	67	73	84	91	72	46	99	97	61	8.2
Percent	7.8	8.6	9.2	9.6	7.5	4.7	10.3	10.0	5.8	
5. Relations with workmates										
Number	78	101	79	85	86	78	115	114	115	10.0
Percent	9.1	11.8	8.7	9.0	9.0	8.0	12.0	11.8	10.9	
6. Boss who knows job										
Number	47	61	63	68	43	65	44	36	35	5.5
Percent	5.5	7.1	6.9	7.2	4.5	6.7	4.6	3.7	3.3	

7. Use of skills										
Number	32	32	57	47	60	74	40	68	98	
Percent	3.7	3.7	6.3	4.9	6.3	7.6	4.1	7.0	9.3	5.9
8. Good pay										
Number	108	85	71	106	90	91	88	69	72	
Percent	12.6	9.8	7.8	11.2	9.4	9.3	9.1	71	6.8	9.2
9. Freedom of movement and talk										
Number	13	18	21	52	55	41	47	38	52	
Percent	1.5	2.1	2.3	5.5	5.7	4.2	4.9	3.9	4.9	3.9
10. Near home										
Number	70	39	33	50	46	24	74	55	63	
Percent	8.2	4.5	3.6	5.3	4.8	2.5	7.7	5.6	6.0	5.3
11. Fringe benefits										
Number	54	58	57	87	57	75	63	68	89	
Percent	6.3	6.8	6.3	9.2	5.9	7.7	6.6	7.0	8.5	7.1
12. Chance for promotion										
Number	50	38	79	31	60	91	20	33	51	
Percent	5.8	4.4	8.7	3.3	6.3	9.4	2.1	3.4	4.8	5.3
13. Easy work										
Number	38	16	6	20	12	0	23	10	2	
Percent	4.4	1.9	0.7	2.1	1.2	0	2.4	1.0	0.1	1.5
14. Interesting work										
Number	48	56	103	59	96	125	53	74	105	
Percent	5.6	6.6	11.3	6.2	10.0	12.9	5.5	7.6	10.0	8.4
15. Useful high-quality work										
Number	42	56	60	29	46	45	14	19	25	
Percent	4.9	6.6	6.6	3.0	4.8	4.6	1.5	1.9	2.3	4.0
Total answers (weighted)	856	851	910	948	960	970	957	972	1051	

Table A-56
Order of Priority of Characteristics of Job, by Subgroup

	Subgroup								
	0	1	2	3	4	5	6	7	8
1	Good pay	Friendly relations with management	Interesting work	Good pay	Interesting work	Interesting work	Good relations with management	Good relations with management	Good relations with fellow employees
2	Friendly relations with management	Friendly relations with fellow employees	Convenient work hours	Convenient work hours	Good relations with management	Independence in work	Good relations with fellow employees	Good relations with fellow employees	Independence in work
3	Friendly relations with fellow employees	Good pay	Independence in work	Good relations with management	Good pay	Good chances for promotion	Good physical conditions	Good physical conditions	Interesting work
4	Work place near to home	Convenient work hours	Friendly relations with fellow	Good physical conditions	Good relations with fellow	Good pay	Convenient work hours	Convenient work hours	Use of skills
5	Good physical conditions	A boss/super who knows his job	Good chances for promotion	Good fringe benefits	Good physical conditions	Good relations with management	Good pay	Independence in work	Good relations with management
6	Convenient work hours	Good physical conditions	Good pay	Good relations with fellow employees	Convenient work hours	Good relations with fellow employees	Work place near to home	Interesting work	Good fringe benefits
7	Good fringe benefits	Good fringe benefits	Good relations with management	Boss who knows his job	Independence in work	Good fringe benefits	Good fringe benefits	Good pay	Good physical conditions
8	Good chances for promotion	Interesting work, high-quality work	Boss who knows his job	Interesting work	Good chances for promotion	Use of skills	Interesting work	Good fringe benefits	Good pay

Table A-57

Emphasis on Task Characteristics in Job, by Subgroup

(in percent)

	Subgroup								
Answer	0	1	2	3	4	5	6	7	8
Independence in work	5.4	5.9	8.8	5.0	7.4	9.8	5.4	7.8	10.3
Interest in work	5.6	6.6	11.3	6.2	10	12.9	5.5	7.6	10.0
Use of skills	3.7	3.7	6.3	4.9	6.3	7.6	4.1	7.0	9.3
Useful high-quality work	4.9	6.6	6.6	3.0	4.8	4.6	1.5	1.9	2.3
Boss who knows his or her job	5.5	7.1	6.9	7.2	4.5	6.7	4.6	3.7	3.3
Total	25.1	29.9	39.9	26.3	33.0	41.6	21.1	28.0	35.2

Note: The answers are weighted.

Table A-58
Aspects of Job That Would Be Missed the Most, by Subgroup
(percent)

	Subgroup								
	0	1	2	3	4	5	6	7	8
	Money 37.7	Money 30.1	Money 23.8	Money 40.4	Money 34.4	Money 29.9	Money 38.2	Money 23.9	Money 29.9
	Company 14.6	Independence 18.3	Interest 19.4	Company 19.0	Independence 19.6	Independence 16.7	Company 24.2	Company 19.2	Independence 16.9
	Usefulness 12.9	Company 16.4	Independence 16.8	Independence 13.0	Usefulness 14.6	Usefulness 15.0	Usefulness 11.0	Independence 16.4	Interest 14.8
	Independence 12.7	Interest 14.1	Usefulness 14.9	Usefulness 13.0	Company 10.7	Company 14.6	Independence 10.9	Interest 15.4	Usefulness 12.6
	Advancement 9.8	Usefulness 13.7	Company 10.9	Interest 6.5	Interest 10.4	Occupation 9.7	Interest 9.0	Usefulness 15.4	Company 10.7
	Interest 7.0	Advancement 4.0	Advancement 8.7	Occupation 6.0	Occupation 6.4	Interest 7.8	Occupation 3.8	Occupation 6.8	Occupation 10.4
	Occupation 5.3	Occupation 3.3	Occupation 5.4	Advancement 2.0	Advancement 3.9	Advancement 6.0	Advancement 2.6	Advancement 1.5	Advancement 4.7

Table A-59
Emphasis on Good Relations with Workmates, by Subgroup
(in percent)

Emphasis	Subgroup								
	0	*1*	*2*	*3*	*4*	*5*	*6*	*7*	*8*
Good relations with workmates	9.1	11.8	8.7	9.0	9.0	8.0	12.0	11.8	10.9
Would miss company of workmates	14.6	16.4	10.9	19.0	10.7	14.6	24.2	19.2	10.7

Table A-60
Emphasis on Task Characteristics
(Composite)

Level	Subgroup									Total/Average
	0	*1*	*2*	*3*	*4*	*5*	*6*	*7*	*8*	
Low										
Number	53	34	15	47	33	20	56	37	12	307
Percent of column	62.4	41.5	18.1	54.7	39.3	24.1	66.7	43.5	13.5	40.3
Percent of row	17.3	11.1	4.9	15.3	10.7	6.5	18.2	12.1	3.9	
Medium										
Number	22	32	27	26	22	21	18	25	38	231
Percent of column	25.9	39.0	32.5	30.2	26.2	25.3	21.4	29.4	42.7	30.4
Percent of row	9.5	13.9	11.7	11.3	9.5	9.1	7.8	10.8	16.5	
High										
Number	10	16	41	13	29	42	10	23	39	223
Percent of column	11.8	19.5	49.4	15.1	34.5	50.6	11.9	27.1	43.8	29.3
Percent of row	4.5	7.2	18.4	5.8	13.0	18.8	4.5	10.3	17.5	
Total sample										
Number	85	82	83	86	84	83	84	85	89	761
Percent	11.2	10.8	10.9	11.3	11.0	10.9	11.0	11.2	11.7	100.0

Table A-61
Concern about Negative Task Characteristics, by Subgroup

Level of Concern	Subgroup									Total/Average
	0	1	2	3	4	5	6	7	8	
Low										
Number	41	31	24	64	34	27	59	47	22	349
Percent of row	11.7	8.9	6.9	18.3	9.7	7.7	16.9	13.5	6.3	45.9
Percent of column	48.2	37.8	28.9	74.4	40.5	32.5	70.2	55.3	24.7	
Medium										
Number	26	17	19	16	37	31	15	31	25	217
Percent of row	12.0	7.8	8.8	7.4	17.1	14.3	6.9	14.3	11.5	28.5
Percent of column	30.6	20.7	22.9	18.6	44.0	37.3	17.9	36.5	28.1	
High										
Number	18	34	40	6	13	25	10	7	42	195
Percent of row	9.2	17.4	20.5	3.1	6.7	12.8	5.1	3.6	21.5	25.6
Percent of column	21.2	41.5	48.2	7.0	15.5	30.1	11.9	8.2	47.2	
Total sample										
Number	85	82	83	86	84	83	84	85	89	761
Percent	11.2	10.8	10.9	11.3	11.0	10.9	11.0	11.2	11.7	100.0

Table A-62
Concern about Financial Benefits, by Subgroup

Level of Concern	Subgroup									Total/Average
	0	1	2	3	4	5	6	7	8	
No concern										
Number	3	3	3	27	24	3	4	7	2	76
Percent of row	3.9	3.9	3.9	35.5	31.6	3.9	5.3	9.2	2.6	10.0
Percent of column	3.5	3.7	3.6	31.4	28.6	3.6	4.8	8.2	2.2	
Neutral										
Number	9	12	8	20	18	19	16	10	10	122
Percent of row	7.4	9.8	6.6	16.4	14.8	15.6	13.1	8.2	8.2	16.0
Percent of column	10.6	14.6	9.6	23.3	21.4	22.9	19.0	11.8	11.2	
Concerned										
Number	73	67	72	39	42	61	64	68	77	563
Percent of row	13.0	11.9	12.8	6.9	7.5	10.8	11.4	12.1	13.7	74.0
Percent of column	85.9	81.7	86.7	45.3	50.0	73.5	76.2	80.0	86.5	
Total sample										
Number	85	82	83	86	84	83	84	85	89	761
Percent	11.2	10.8	10.9	11.3	11.0	10.9	11.0	11.2	11.7	100.0

Table A-63
Concern about Physical Conditions of Work Place, by Subgroup

Level of Concern	Subgroup									Total/
	0	1	2	3	4	5	6	7	8	Average
No concern										
Number	4	3	6	7	5	3	3	4	0	35
Percent of row	11.4	8.6	17.1	20.0	14.3	8.6	8.6	11.4	0	4.6
Percent of column	4.7	3.7	7.2	8.1	6.0	3.6	3.6	4.7	0	
Neutral										
Number	31	45	49	43	38	46	27	31	45	355
Percent of row	8.7	12.7	13.8	12.1	10.7	13.0	7.6	8.7	12.7	46.6
Percent of column	36.5	54.9	59.0	50.0	45.2	55.4	32.1	36.5	50.6	
Concerned										
Number	50	34	28	36	41	34	54	50	44	371
Percent of row	13.5	9.2	7.5	9.7	11.1	9.2	14.6	13.5	11.9	48.8
Percent of column	58.8	41.5	33.7	41.9	48.8	41.0	64.3	58.8	49.4	
Total sample										
Number	85	82	83	86	84	83	84	85	89	761
Percent	11.2	10.8	10.9	11.3	11.0	10.9	11.0	11.2	11.7	100.0

Table A-64
Concern about Work Hours, by Subgroup

| | Subgroup | | | | | | | | | Total/ |
Level of Concern	0	1	2	3	4	5	6	7	8	Average
No concern										
Number	35	25	20	49	28	22	26	21	16	242
Percent of row	14.5	10.3	8.3	20.2	11.6	9.1	10.7	8.7	6.6	31.8
Percent of column	41.2	30.5	24.1	57.0	33.3	26.5	31.0	24.7	18.0	
Neutral										
Number	32	37	36	24	38	47	33	26	41	314
Percent of row	10.2	11.8	11.5	7.6	12.1	15.0	10.5	8.3	13.1	41.3
Percent of column	37.6	45.1	43.4	27.9	45.2	56.6	39.3	30.6	46.1	
Concerned										
Number	18	20	27	13	18	14	25	38	32	205
Percent of row	8.8	9.8	13.2	6.3	8.8	6.8	12.2	18.5	15.6	26.9
Percent of column	21.2	24.4	32.5	15.1	21.4	16.9	29.8	44.7	36.0	
Total sample										
Number	85	82	83	86	84	83	84	85	89	761
Percent	11.2	10.8	10.9	11.3	11.0	10.9	11.0	11.2	11.7	100.0

Table A-65
Concern about Social Relations, by Subgroup

Level of Concern	Subgroup									Total/Average
	0	1	2	3	4	5	6	7	8	
No concern										
Number	13	8	17	42	25	23	24	24	18	194
Percent of row	6.7	4.1	8.8	21.6	12.9	11.9	12.4	12.4	9.3	25.5
Percent of column	15.3	9.8	20.5	48.8	29.8	27.7	28.6	28.2	20.2	
Neutral										
Number	46	59	46	37	49	42	44	44	43	410
Percent of row	11.2	14.4	11.2	9.0	12.0	10.2	10.7	10.7	10.5	53.9
Percent of column	54.1	72.0	55.4	43.0	58.3	50.6	52.4	51.8	48.3	
Concerned										
Number	26	15	20	7	10	18	16	17	28	157
Percent of row	16.6	9.6	12.7	4.5	6.4	11.5	10.2	10.8	17.8	20.6
Percent of column	30.6	18.3	24.1	8.1	11.9	21.7	19.0	20.0	31.5	
Total sample										
Number	85	82	83	86	84	83	84	85	89	761
Percent	11.2	10.8	10.9	11.3	11.0	10.9	11.0	11.2	11.7	100.0

Table A-66
Concern about Negative Hygiene or Working Conditions (Composite), by Subgroup

Level of Concern	Subgroup									Total/Average
	0	1	2	3	4	5	6	7	8	
Low										
Number	28	31	27	54	45	34	29	25	22	295
Percent of row	9.5	10.5	9.2	18.3	15.3	11.5	9.8	8.5	7.5	38.8
Percent of column	32.9	37.8	32.5	62.8	53.6	41.0	34.5	29.4	24.7	
Medium										
Number	14	12	20	17	15	24	13	15	15	145
Percent of row	9.7	8.3	13.8	11.7	10.3	16.6	9.0	10.3	10.3	19.1
Percent of column	16.5	14.6	24.1	19.8	17.9	28.9	15.5	17.6	16.9	
High										
Number	43	39	36	15	24	25	42	45	52	321
Percent of row	13.4	12.1	11.2	4.7	7.5	7.8	13.1	14.0	16.2	42.2
Percent of column	50.6	47.6	43.4	17.4	28.6	30.1	50.0	52.9	58.4	
Total sample										
Number	85	82	83	86	84	83	84	85	89	761
Percent	11.2	10.8	10.9	11.3	11.0	10.9	11.0	11.2	11.7	100.0

Table A-67
Concern about Union Performance, by Subgroup

Level of Concern	Subgroup							Total/Average
	0	1	2	3	6	7	8	
No concern								
Number	27	21	25	1	24	47	16	161
Percent	31.8	25.9	30.1	1.2	28.6	56.0	18.0	27
Neutral								
Number	43	42	29	20	26	21	24	195
Percent	50.6	51.9	34.9	23.5	29.8	25.0	27.0	33
Concerned								
Number	15	18	29	64	34	16	49	225
Percent	17.6	22.2	34.9	75.3	40.5	19.0	55.0	38
Total sample								
Number	85	81	83	85	84	84	89	591[a]
Percent								

Note: Groups 4 and 5 are excluded because of their low degree of unionization.
[a]Three did not answer.

Table A-68
Concern for Personal Freedom on the Job, by Subgroup

Level	Subgroup									Total/ Average
	0	1	2	3	4	5	6	7	8	
Unconcerned										
Number	27	32	29	59	56	36	37	43	18	337
Percent of row	8.0	9.5	8.6	17.5	16.6	10.7	11.0	12.8	5.3	44.3
Percent of column	31.8	39.0	34.9	68.6	66.7	43.4	44.0	50.6	20.2	
No answer[a]										
Number	18	23	37	14	16	42	24	25	52	251
Percent of row	7.2	9.2	14.7	5.6	6.4	16.7	9.6	10.0	20.7	33.0
Percent of column	21.2	28.0	44.6	16.3	19.0	50.6	28.6	29.4	58.4	
Concerned										
Number	40	27	17	13	12	5	23	17	19	173
Percent of row	23.1	15.6	9.8	7.5	6.9	2.9	13.3	9.8	11.0	22.7
Percent of column	47.1	32.9	20.5	15.1	14.3	6.0	27.4	20.0	21.3	
Total sample										
Number	85	82	83	86	84	83	84	85	89	761
Percent	11.2	10.8	10.9	11.3	11.0	10.9	11.0	11.2	11.7	100.0

aNo restrictions.

Table A-69
Readiness to Apply for a More Skilled or Responsible Job in Same Work Place, by Subgroup

Answer	Subgroup									Total/Average
	0	1	2	3	4	5	6	7	8	
Yes										
Number	52	37	60	44	52	66	46	40	59	456
Percent of row	11.4	8.1	13.2	9.6	11.4	14.5	10.1	8.8	12.9	59.9
Percent of column	61.2	45.1	72.3	51.2	61.9	79.5	54.8	47.1	66.3	
No										
Number	28	44	20	41	26	17	37	44	27	284
Percent of row	9.9	15.5	7.0	14.4	9.2	6.0	13.0	15.5	9.5	37.3
Percent of column	32.9	53.7	24.1	47.7	31.0	20.5	44.0	51.8	30.3	
Don't know										
Number	2	0	1	1	0	0	0	0	2	6
Percent of row	33.3	0	16.7	16.7	0	0	0	0	33.3	0.8
Percent of column	2.4	0	1.2	1.2	0	0	0	0	2.2	
No answer										
Number	3	1	2	0	6	0	1	1	1	15
Percent of row	20.0	6.7	13.3	0	40.0	0	6.7	6.7	6.7	2.0
Percent of column	3.5	1.2	2.4	0	7.1	0	1.2	1.2	1.1	
Total sample										
Number	85	82	83	86	84	83	84	85	89	761
Percent	11.2	10.8	10.9	11.3	11.0	10.9	11.0	11.2	11.7	100.0

Table A-70
Interest in Advancement and Promotion, by Subgroup

Interest	0	1	2	3	Subgroup 4	5	6	7	8	Total/ Average
Low										
Number	34	52	21	60	35	15	54	54	39	364
Percent of row	9.3	14.3	5.8	16.5	9.6	4.1	14.8	14.8	10.7	47.8
Percent of column	40.0	63.4	25.3	69.8	41.7	18.1	64.3	63.5	43.8	
High										
Number	51	30	62	26	49	68	30	31	50	397
Percent of row	12.8	7.6	15.6	6.5	12.3	17.1	7.6	7.8	12.6	52.2
Percent of column	60.0	36.6	74.7	30.2	58.3	81.9	35.7	36.5	56.2	
Total sample										
Number	85	82	83	86	84	83	84	85	89	761
Percent	11.2	10.8	10.9	11.3	11.0	10.9	11.0	11.2	11.7	100.0

Table A-71
Self-Confidence, by Subgroup

| | Subgroup | | | | | | | | | Total/ |
	0	1	2	3	4	5	6	7	8	Average
Yes										
Number	63	54	75	75	76	80	64	68	80	635
Percent of row	9.9	8.5	11.8	11.8	12.0	12.6	10.1	10.7	12.6	83.4
Percent of column	74.1	65.9	90.4	87.2	90.5	96.4	76.2	80.0	89.9	
No										
Number	20	19	4	11	4	3	19	14	8	102
Percent of row	19.6	18.6	3.9	10.8	3.9	2.9	18.6	13.7	7.8	13.4
Percent of column	23.5	23.2	4.8	12.8	4.8	3.6	22.6	16.5	9.0	
Don't know										
Number	0	1	1	0	0	0	0	1	0	3
Percent of row	0	33.3	33.3	0	0	0	0	33.3	0	0.4
Percent of column	0	1.2	1.2	0	0	0	0	1.2	0	
No longer										
Number	0	0	0	0	0	0	0	1	0	1
Percent of row	0	0	0	0	0	0	0	100.0	0	0.1
Percent of column	0	0	0	0	0	0	0	1.2	0	
No answer										
Number	2	8	3	0	4	0	1	1	1	20
Percent of row	10.0	40.0	15.0	0	20.0	0	5.0	5.0	5.0	2.6
Percent of column	2.4	9.8	3.6	0	4.8	0	1.2	1.2	1.1	
Total sample										
Number	85	82	83	86	84	83	84	85	89	761
Percent	11.2	10.8	10.9	11.3	11.0	10.9	11.0	11.2	11.7	100.0

Table A-72
Job Satisfaction (Direct Question), by Subgroup
(in percent)

					Subgroup					
Satisfaction	*0*	*1*	*2*	*3*	*4*	*5*	*6*	*7*	*8*	*Average*
Very satisfied	35.3	47.6	43.8	57.0	36.9	41.0	28.6	35.3	29.2	39.6
Dissatsfied or don't know	24.7	6.1	10.8	12.8	21.4	21.7	7.1	9.4	12.4	13.5
Somewhat satisfied	40.0	46.3	43.4	30.2	41.7	37.3	64.3	55.3	58.4	46.9
Total not very satisfied	64.7	52.4	54.2	43.0	63.1	59.0	71.4	64.7	70.8	60.4

Table A-73
Job Satisfaction (Direct Question), by National and Occupational Group
(in percent)

Satisfaction	National Group			Industrial Group		
	Israel	*United States*	*Germany*	*Industry*	*Retail*	*Office*
Very satisfied	42.9	45.0	31.0	40.3	40.0	38.7
Dissatisfied or don't know	13.9	18.6	9.6	14.9	12.3	15.0
Somewhat satisfied	43.2	36.4	59.4	44.8	47.7	46.3
Total not very satisfied	57.1	55.0	69.0	59.7	60.0	61.3

Table A-74
Comparison with Previous Job, by Subgroup

| | | | | Subgroup | | | | | Total/ |
Comparison	0	1	2	3	4	5	6	7	8	Average
Better										
Number	28	32	31	44	58	61	35	46	56	391
Percent	56.0	56.0	65.0	62.0	74.0	74.0	65.0	61.0	71.0	65.8
Same or not as good[a]										
Number	22	25	17	27	20	21	19	29	23	203
Percent	44.0	44.0	35.0	38.0	26.0	26.0	35.0	39.0	29.0	34.2
Number who held previous job	50	57	48	71	78	82	54	75	79	594

Note: One hundred sixty-seven women gave no answer and are not included.

[a]This category is broken down further: 136 women (22.9 percent) said their current job was the same as the previous one, and 67 (11.1 percent) said their current job was not as good. The total is 203 women (34.0 percent).

Table A-75
Comparison with Previous Job, by National and Occupational Group

Comparison	National Group			Industrial Group		
	Israel	United States	Germany	Industry	Retail	Office
Better						
Number	81	163	137	107	136	148
Percent	59.0	70.0	66.0	61.0	65.0	70.0
Same or not as good						
Number	64	68	71	68	74	61
Percent	41.0	30.0	34.0	39.0	35.0	29.2
Number who held previous job	155	231	208	175	210	209

Note: One hundred sixty-seven women gave no answer and are not included.

Table A-76
Present Job Compared with Housework, by Subgroup

Comparison	Subgroup									Total/ Average
	0	1	2	3	4	5	6	7	8	
Better										
Number	46	51	57	32	58	71	15	28	51	409
Percent	54.0	62.0	69.0	37.0	69.0	85.0	18.0	33.0	57.0	54.0
Same										
Number	19	24	16	31	19	8	44	50	31	242
Percent	22.0	29.0	19.0	36.0	23.0	10.0	52.0	59.0	34.0	32.0
Not as good										
Number	20	7	10	23	7	4	25	7	7	110
Percent	24.0	8.0	12.0	27.0	8.0	5.0	30.0	8.0	8.0	14.0
Total number	85	82	83	86	84	83	84	85	89	761

Note: Twelve women answered "don't know" or did not answer at all. These replies were included in the "not as good" category.

Table A-77
Present Job Compared with Housework, by National and Occupational Group

Comparison	National Group			Industrial Group		
	Israel	United States	Germany	Industry	Retail	Office
Better						
Number	154	61	94	93	137	139
Percent	61.0	64.0	36.0	36.0	55.0	70.0
Same						
Number	59	58	125	94	93	55
Percent	24.0	23.0	48.0	37.0	37.0	22.0
Not as good						
Number	37	34	39	68	21	21
Percent	15.0	13.0	15.0	27.0	8.0	8.0
Total number	250	253	258	255	251	255

Note: Twelve women answered "don't know" or did not answer at all. These replies were included in the "not as good" category.

Table A-78
Recommendation of Present Job to a Friend, by Subgroup

Recommendation	Subgroup									Total/ Average
	0	1	2	3	4	5	6	7	8	
Would recommend job										
Number	67	65	65	69	65	75	65	62	73	606
Percent	79.0	79.0	78.0	80.0	77.0	90.0	77.0	73.0	82.0	80.0
Would not recommend job										
Number	18	17	18	17	19	8	19	23	16	155
Percent	21.0	21.0	22.0	20.0	23.0	10.0	23.0	27.0	18.0	20.0
Total number	85	82	83	86	84	83	84	85	89	761

Note: Twelve women answered "don't know" or gave no answer. These were counted as "would not recommend job."

Table A-79
Recommendation of Present Job to a Friend, by National and Occupational Group

Recommendation	National Group			Industrial Group		
	Israel	United States	Germany	Industry	Retail	Office
Would recommend job						
Number	197	209	200	201	192	213
Percent	79.0	83.0	78.0	79.0	76.0	84.0
Would not recommend job						
Number	53	44	58	54	59	42
Percent	21.0	17.0	22.0	21.0	24.0	16.0
Total number	250	253	258	255	251	255

Note: Twelve women answered "don't know" or gave no answer. These were counted as "would not recommend job."

Table A-80
Recommendation of Present Job to a Daughter, by Subgroup

Recommendation	Subgroup									Total/Average
	0	1	2	3	4	5	6	7	8	
Would recommend job										
Number	11	17	25	25	45	64	20	28	54	288
Percent	16.0	24.0	29.0	29.0	59.0	79.0	26.0	36.0	64.0	42.0
Would not recommend job										
Number	57	55	60	60	31	17	53	49	30	397
Percent	84.0	76.0	71.0	71.0	41.0	21.0	73.0	64.0	36.0	58.0
Total number	68	72	85	85	76	81	73	77	84	685

Note: Seventy-six women gave no answer and are not included. The four women who answered "don't know" were counted as "would not recommend job."

Table A-81
**Recommendation of Present Job to a Daughter, by National and
Occupational Group**

Recommendation	National Group			Industrial Group		
	Israel	United States	Germany	Industry	Retail	Office
Would recommend job						
Number	52	134	102	56	90	142
Percent	25.0	55.0	44.0	25.0	40.0	61.0
Would not recommend job						
Number	157	108	132	170	135	92
Percent	75.0	45.0	56.0	75.0	60.0	39.0
Total number	209	242	234	226	225	234

Note: Seventy-six women gave no answer and are not included. The four women who
answered "don't know" were counted as "would not recommend job."

Table A-82
Recommendation of Present Job to a Son, by Subgroup

Recommendation		Subgroup								Total/
	0	1	2	3	4	5	6	7	8	Average
Would recommend job										
Number	45	29	36	27	36	37	26	28	22	286
Percent	53.0	35.0	43.0	31.0	43.0	45.0	31.0	33.0	25.0	38.0
Would not recommend job										
Number	40	53	47	59	48	46	58	57	67	475
Percent	47.0	65.0	57.0	69.0	57.0	55.0	69.0	67.0	75.0	62.0
Total number	85	82	83	86	84	83	85	89	761	

Note: Seventy-seven women gave no answer and are not included. The nine women who answered "don't know" were counted as "would not recommend job."

Table A-83
Recommendation of Present Job to a Son, by National and Occupational Group

	National Group			Industrial Group		
Recommendation	Israel	United States	Germany	Industry	Retail	Office
Would recommend job						
Number	17	115	82	38	59	117
Percent	8.0	48.0	35.0	17.0	27.0	50.0
Would not recommend job						
Number	190	127	153	190	163	117
Percent	92.0	52.0	65.0	83.0	73.0	50.0
Total number	207	242	235	228	222	234

Note: Seventy-seven women gave no answer and are not included. The nine women who answered "don't know" were counted as "would not recommend job."

Table A-84
Readiness to Choose Same Work Career Again, by Subgroup

Choice	Subgroup									Total/ Average
	0	1	2	3	4	5	6	7	8	
Would choose same job										
Number	45	29	36	27	36	37	26	28	22	286
Percent	53.0	35.0	43.0	31.0	43.0	45.0	31.0	33.0	25.0	38.0
Would not choose same job										
Number	40	53	47	59	48	46	58	57	67	475
Percent	47.0	65.0	57.0	69.0	57.0	55.0	69.0	67.0	75.0	62.0
Total number	85	82	83	86	84	83	84	85	89	761

Note: Seven women answered "don't know," and fourteen gave no answer. These were counted as "would not choose same job."

Table A-85
Readiness to Choose Same Work Career Again, by National
and Occupational Group

Choice	National Group			Industrial Group		
	Israel	United States	Germany	Industry	Retail	Office
Would choose same job						
Number	110	100	76	98	93	95
Percent	44.0	40.0	30.0	38.0	37.0	37.0
Would not choose same job						
Number	140[a]	153	182	157	158	160
Percent	56.0	60.0	70.0	62.0	63.0	63.0
Total number	250	253	258	255	251	255

Note: Seven women answered "don't know," and fourteen gave no answer. These were counted as "would not choose same job."

[a]Ten percent answered "don't know" or gave no answer.

Table A 86
Satisfaction with Work (Composite), by Subgroup

Satisfaction	Subgroup									Total/Average
	0	1	2	3	4	5	6	7	8	
Low										
Number	38	39	31	31	33	20	38	40	29	299
Percent of row	12.7	13.0	10.4	10.4	11.0	6.7	12.7	13.4	9.7	39.3
Percent of column	44.7	47.6	37.3	36.0	39.3	24.1	45.2	47.1	32.6	
Medium										
Number	39	25	29	39	24	27	40	27	37	287
Percent of row	13.6	8.7	10.1	13.6	8.4	9.4	13.9	9.4	12.9	37.7
Percent of column	45.9	30.5	34.9	45.3	28.6	32.5	47.6	31.8	41.6	
High										
Number	8	18	23	16	27	36	6	18	23	175
Percent of row	4.6	10.3	13.1	9.1	15.4	20.6	3.4	10.3	13.1	23.0
Percent of column	9.4	22.0	27.7	18.6	32.1	43.4	7.1	21.2	25.8	
Total sample										
Number	85	82	83	86	84	83	84	85	89	761
Percent	11.2	10.8	10.9	11.3	11.0	10.9	11.0	11.2	11.7	100.0

Note: This table is a composite of tables A-73 through A-86.

Table A-87
Correlation of Direct with Composite Satisfaction

Satisfaction (Direct Answer)	Satisfaction (Composite)			Total/ Average
	Low	Medium	High	
Satisfied				
Number	9	132	160	301
Percent of row	3.0	43.9	53.2	39.6
Percent of column	3.0	46.0	91.4	
Medium				
Number	188	154	15	357
Percent of row	52.7	43.1	4.2	46.9
Percent of column	62.9	53.7	8.6	
Not satisfied				
Number	102	1	0	103
Percent of row	99.0	1.0	0	13.5
Percent of column	34.1	0.3	0	
Total sample				
Number	299	287	175	761
Percent	39.3	37.7	23.0	100.0

Table A-88
Superficial Satisfaction, by Subgroup

Superficial Satisfaction	Subgroup									Average/Total
	0	1	2	3	4	5	6	7	8	
Yes										
Number	46	52	40	51	24	9	49	43	24	338
Percent of column	54.1	63.4	48.2	59.3	28.6	10.8	58.3	50.6	27.0	44.4
Percent of row	13.6	15.4	11.8	15.1	7.1	2.7	14.5	12.7	7.1	
No										
Number	39	30	43	35	60	74	35	42	65	423
Percent of column	45.9	36.6	51.8	40.7	71.4	89.2	41.7	49.4	73.0	55.6
Percent of row	9.2	7.1	10.2	8.3	14.2	17.5	8.3	9.9	15.4	
Total sample										
Number	85	82	83	86	84	83	84	85	89	761
Percent	11.2	10.8	10.9	11.3	11.0	10.9	11.0	11.2	11.7	100.0

Table A-89
Level of Initial Aspiration,[a] by Subgroup

Initial Aspiration	Subgroup									Total/ Average
	0	1	2	3	4	5	6	7	8	
Low										
Number	27	21	4	59	11	1	38	21	7	189
Percent of row	14.3	11.1	2.1	31.2	5.8	0.5	20.1	11.1	3.7	24.8
Percent of column	31.8	25.6	4.8	68.6	13.1	1.2	45.2	24.7	7.9	
Medium										
Number	44	24	26	22	34	28	28	34	25	265
Percent of row	16.6	9.1	9.8	8.3	12.8	10.6	10.6	12.8	9.4	34.8
Percent of column	51.8	29.3	31.3	25.6	40.5	33.7	33.3	40.0	28.1	
High										
Number	14	37	53	5	39	54	18	30	57	307
Percent of row	4.6	12.1	17.3	1.6	12.7	17.6	5.9	9.8	18.6	40.3
Percent of column	16.5	45.1	63.9	5.8	46.4	65.1	21.4	35.3	64.0	
Total sample										
Number	85	82	83	86	84	83	84	85	89	761
Percent	11.2	10.8	10.9	11.3	11.0	10.9	11.0	11.2	11.7	100.0

[a]Based on years of schooling and training.

Table A-90
The Fit Theory: Correlation of Aspiration with Satisfaction and Content

Aspiration	Satisfaction			Total/ Average
	Low	Medium	High	
		Low Content		
Low				
Number				
Under 35	21	19	3	43
35 and over	26	28	4	58
Total	47	47	7	101
Percent of column	37.3	48.5	25.9	40.4
Percent of row	46.5	46.5	7.0	
Medium				
Number				
Under 35	21	27	12	60
35 and over	26	10	4	40
Total	47	37	16	100
Percent of column	37.3	38.1	59.3	40.0
Percent of row	47.0	37.0	16.0	
High				
Number				
Under 35	21	7	3	31
35 and over	11	6	1	18
Total	32	13	4	49
Percent of column	25.4	13.4	14.8	19.6
Percent of row	65.3	26.5	8.2	
Total sample				
Number	126	97	27	250
Percent of sample	50.4	38.8	10.8	32.9
		Medium Content		
Low				
Number				
Under 35	8	9	9	26
35 and over	14	24	15	53
Total	22	33	24	79
Percent of column	16.5	28.4	25.5	23.0
Percent of row	27.8	41.8	30.4	
Medium				
Number				
Under 35	27	26	15	68
35 and over	16	14	14	46
Total	45	40	29	114
Percent of column	33.8	34.5	30.8	33.2
Percent of row	39.5	35.1	25.4	
High				
Number				
Under 35	41	27	23	91
35 and over	25	16	18	59
Total	66	43	41	150
Percent of column	49.6	37.1	43.6	43.8
Percent of row	44.0	28.7	27.3	

Table A-90 continued

| Aspiration | Satisfaction | | | Total/ |
	Low	Medium	High	Average
Total sample				
Number	133	116	94	343
Percent of sample	38.3	33.8	27.4	45.1

High Content

	Low	Medium	High	Total/Average
Low				
Number				
Under 35	0	4	0	5
35 and over	1	3	1	4
Total	1	7	1	9
Percent of column	2.5	9.5	1.8	5.4
Percent of row	11.1	77.8	11.1	
Medium				
Number				
Under 35	7	14	14	35
35 and over	4	7	5	16
Total	11	21	19	51
Percent of column	27.5	28.4	35.2	30.4
Percent of row	21.6	41.2	37.2	
High				
Number				
Under 35	17	31	23	71
35 and over	11	15	11	37
Total	28	46	34	108
Percent of column	70.0	62.1	63.0	64.2
Percent of row	25.9	42.6	31.5	
Total sample				
Number	40	74	54	168
Percent of sample	23.8	44	32.2	22.1

Analysis

| | Initial Aspiration | Content Level | Satisfaction | | |
			Low	Medium	High
Bad fit	High	Low	65.3	26.5	8.2
	Low	High	11.1	77.8	11.1
Medium fit	Low	Medium	27.8	41.8	30.4
	Medium	Low	47.0	37.0	16.0
	Medium	High	21.6	41.2	37.2
	High	Medium	38.3	33.8	27.4
Good fit	Low	Low	46.5	46.5	7.0
	Medium	Medium	39.5	35.1	25.4
	High	High	25.9	42.6	31.5
Average			39.3	37.7	23.0

Table A-91
Correlation of Level of Satisfaction (Composite) with Level of Content

	Level of Content			
Satisfaction	Low	Medium	High	Total/ Average
Low				
Number	126	133	40	299
Percent of row	42.1	44.5	13.4	39.3
Percent of column	50.4	38.8	23.8	
Medium				
Number	97	116	74	287
Percent of row	33.8	40.4	25.8	37.7
Percent of column	38.8	33.8	44.0	
High				
Number	27	94	54	175
Percent of row	15.4	53.7	30.9	23.0
Percent of column	10.8	27.4	32.1	
Total sample				
Number	250	343	168	761
Percent	32.9	45.1	22.1	100.0

Table A-92
Correlating Emphasis on Content with Concern for Content

	Concern for Content			
Emphasis on Content	Low	Medium	High	Total/ Average
Low and medium				
Number	284	143	111	538
Percent of row	81.4	65.9	56.9	70.7
Percent of column	52.8	26.6	20.6	
Percent of sample	37.3	18.8	14.6	
High				
Number	65	74	84	223
Percent of row	18.6	34.1	43.1	29.3
Percent of column	29.1	33.2	37.7	
Percent of sample	8.5	9.7	11.0	
Total sample				
Number	349	217	195	761
Percent	45.9	28.5	25.6	100.1

Table A-93
Correlating Emphasis on Content with Interest in Advancement

| | Interest in Advancement | | Total/ |
Emphasis on Content	Low	High	Average
Low and Medium			
Number	279	259	538
Percent of column	76.6	65.2	70.7
Percent of row	51.9	48.1	
Percent of sample	36.7	34.0	
High			
Number	85	138	223
Percent of column	23.4	34.8	29.3
Percent of row	34.1	61.9	
Percent of sample	11.2	18.1	
Total sample			
Number	364	397	761
Percent	47.8	52.2	100.1

Table A-94
Correlating Concern for Content with Interest in Advancement

| | Interest in Advancement | | Total/ |
Concern for Content	Low	High	Average
Low			
Number	220	129	349
Percent of column	60.4	32.5	45.9
Percent of row	63.0	37.0	
Percent of sample	28.9	17.0	
Medium			
Number	82	135	217
Percent of column	22.5	34.0	28.5
Percent of row	37.8	62.2	
Percent of sample	10.8	17.7	
High			
Number	62	133	195
Percent of column	17.0	33.5	25.6
Percent of row	31.8	68.2	
Percent of sample	8.1	17.5	
Total sample			
Number	364	397	761
Percent	47.8	52.2	100.0

Table A-95
The Instrumental Attitude, by Subgroup

Instrumental Attitude	Subgroup									Total/ Average
	0	1	2	3	4	5	6	7	8	
Yes										
Number	18	20	6	38	14	5	42	25	10	178
Percent of column	21.2	24.4	7.2	44.2	16.7	6.0	50.0	29.4	11.2	23.4
Percent of row	10.1	11.2	3.4	21.3	7.9	2.8	23.6	14.0	5.6	
No										
Number	67	62	77	48	70	78	42	60	79	583
Percent of column	78.8	75.6	92.8	55.8	83.3	94.0	50.0	70.6	88.8	76.6
Percent of row	11.5	10.6	13.2	8.2	12.0	13.4	7.2	10.3	13.6	
Total sample										
Number	85	82	83	86	84	83	84	85	89	761
Percent	11.2	10.8	10.9	11.3	11.0	10.9	11.0	11.2	11.7	100.0

Table A-96
Correlating the Instrumental Attitude with Overt Satisfaction/Dissatisfaction

Instrumental Attitude	Overt Satisfaction			Total/ Average
	Very Satisfied	Somewhat Satisfied	Dissatisfied	
Yes				
Number	91	78	9	178
Percent of column	30.2	21.9	8.7	23.4
Percent of row	51.1	43.8	5.1	
Percent of sample	12.0	10.2	1.2	
No				
Number	210	278	95	583
Percent of column	69.8	78.1	91.3	76.6
Percent of row	36.0	47.7	16.3	
Percent of sample	27.6	36.5	12.5	
Total sample				
Number	301	356	104	761
Percent	39.6	46.8	13.7	100.0

Table A-97
Superficial Satisfaction, by National Group and Occupational Group

Superficial Satisfaction	National Groups			Occupational Groups			Average/ Total
	Israel	U.S.	Germany	Industry	Retail	Office	
Yes							
Number	138	84	116	146	119	73	338
Percent of row	40.8	24.9	34.3	43.2	25.2	21.6	44.4
Percent of column	55.2	32.9	45.3	57.3	47.5	28.7	
No							
Number	112	169	142	109	132	182	423
Percent of row	26.5	40	33.5	25.8	25.3	43.1	55.6
Percent of column	44.8	67.1	54.7	42.7	52.5	71.3	
Total number	250	253	258	255	251	255	761

Table A-98
The Instrumental Syndrome, by Subgroup

Instrumental Syndrome	Subgroup									Total/
	0	1	2	3	4	5	6	7	8	Average
Yes										
Number	10	12	3	22	5	1	25	17	4	99
Percent of column	11.8	14.6	3.6	25.6	6.0	1.2	29.8	20.0	4.5	13.0
Percent of row	10.1	12.1	3.0	22.2	5.1	1.0	25.3	17.2	4.0	
No										
Number	75	70	80	64	79	82	29	68	85	662
Percent of column	88.2	85.4	96.4	74.4	94.0	98.8	70.2	80.0	95.5	87.0
Percent of row	11.3	10.6	12.1	9.7	11.9	12.4	8.9	10.3	12.8	
Total sample										
Number	85	82	83	86	84	83	84	85	89	761
Percent	11.2	10.8	10.9	11.3	11.0	10.9	11.0	11.2	11.7	100.0

Table A-99
Instrumental Syndrome, by Community of Socialization

Instrumental Syndrome	City	Small Town or Village	Total/ Average
Yes			
Number	50	49	99
Percent of row	50.5	49.5	13.0
Percent of column	12.3	13.9	
No			
Number	358	304	662
Percent of row	54.1	45.9	87.0
Percent of column	87.7	86.1	
Total sample			
Number	408	353	761
Percent	53.6	46.4	100.0

Table A-100
Psychosomatic Symptoms, by Subgroup

Psychosomatic Symptoms	Subgroup									Total/Average
	0	1	2	3	4	5	6	7	8	
None										
Number	57	71	70	48	64	53	50	59	64	536
Percent of row	10.6	13.2	13.1	9.0	11.9	9.9	9.3	11.0	11.9	70.4
Percent of column	67.1	86.6	84.3	55.8	76.2	63.9	59.5	69.4	71.9	
Some										
Number	13	9	11	23	15	15	17	17	14	134
Percent of row	9.7	6.7	8.2	17.2	11.2	11.2	12.7	12.7	10.4	17.6
Percent of column	15.3	11.0	13.3	26.7	17.9	18.1	20.2	20.0	15.7	
Many										
Number	15	2	2	15	5	15	17	9	11	91
Percent of row	16.5	2.2	2.2	16.5	5.5	16.5	18.7	9.9	12.1	12.0
Percent of column	17.6	2.4	2.4	17.4	6.0	18.1	20.2	10.6	12.4	
Total sample										
Number	85	82	83	86	84	83	84	85	89	761
Percent	11.2	10.8	10.9	11.3	11.0	10.9	11.0	11.2	11.7	100.0

Table A-101
Correlating Progress in Past Employment Career with Intensity of
Past Employment Career

Intensity	Progress		Total/ Average
	Regressive or Static	*Progressive*	
Not intensive and medium intensive			
Number	149	115	264
Percent of row	56.4	43.6	34.7
Percent of column	35.5	33.7	
Intensive			
Number	271	226	497
Percent of row	54.5	45.5	65.3
Percent of column	64.5	66.3	
Total sample			
Number	420	341	761
Percent	55.2	44.8	100.0

Table A-102
Domestic Work Load: No Children at Home, by Subgroup

Domestic Work Load	Subgroup									Total/Average
	0	1	2	3	4	5	6	7	8	
Low										
Number	27	17	35	21	45	50	10	14	27	246
Percent of row	11.0	6.9	14.2	8.5	18.3	20.3	4.1	5.7	11.0	50.8
Percent of column	42.9	37.0	62.5	48.8	72.6	79.4	23.8	30.4	42.9	
Medium										
Number	24	16	15	12	12	11	19	22	31	162
Percent of row	14.8	9.9	9.3	7.4	7.4	6.8	11.7	13.6	19.1	33.5
Percent of column	38.1	34.8	26.8	27.9	19.4	17.5	45.2	47.8	49.2	
High										
Number	12	13	6	10	5	2	13	10	5	76
Percent of row	15.8	17.1	7.9	13.2	6.6	2.6	17.1	13.2	6.6	15.7
Percent of column	19.0	28.3	10.7	23.3	8.1	3.2	31.0	21.7	7.9	
Total sample										
Number	63	46	56	43	62	63	42	46	63	484
Percent	13.0	9.5	11.6	8.9	12.8	12.0	8.7	9.5	13.0	100.0

Table A-103
Domestic Work Load: Children at Home, by Subgroup

Domestic Work Load	Subgroup									Total/Average
	0	1	2	3	4	5	6	7	8	
Low										
Number	1	2	2	10	3	5	3	2	2	30
Percent of row	3.3	6.7	6.7	33.3	10.0	16.7	10.0	6.7	6.7	10.8
Percent of column	4.5	5.6	7.4	23.3	13.6	25.0	7.1	5.1	7.7	
Medium										
Number	6	6	10	8	3	6	6	9	8	62
Percent of row	9.7	9.7	16.1	12.9	4.8	9.7	9.7	14.5	12.9	22.4
Percent of column	27.3	16.7	37.0	18.6	13.6	30.0	14.3	23.1	30.8	
High										
Number	15	28	15	25	16	9	33	28	16	185
Percent of row	8.1	15.1	8.1	13.5	8.6	4.9	17.8	15.1	8.6	66.8
Percent of column	68.2	77.8	55.6	58.1	72.7	45.0	78.6	71.8	61.5	
Total sample										
Number	22	36	27	43	22	20	42	39	26	277
Percent	7.9	13.0	9.7	15.5	7.9	7.2	15.2	14.1	9.4	100.0

Table A-104
Hours of Help and Domestic Work Load

Domestic Work Load	Hours of Help				Total Average
	0	1-5	6-9	10 or More	
Low					
Number	231	13	10	22	276
Percent of row	83.7	4.7	3.6	8.0	36.3
Percent of column	42.2	22.8	19.6	20.8	
Medium					
Number	166	14	13	31	244
Percent of row	74.1	6.3	5.8	13.8	29.4
Percent of column	30.3	24.6	25.5	29.2	
High					
Number	150	30	28	53	261
Percent of row	57.5	11.5	10.7	20.3	34.3
Percent of column	27.4	52.6	54.9	50.0	
Total sample					
Number	547	57	51	105	761
Percent	71.9	7.5	6.7	13.9	100.0

Table A-105
All Views and Values, by Subgroup

Views and Values	Subgroup									Total/ Average
	0	1	2	3	4	5	6	7	8	
Traditional										
Number	52	27	15	39	19	9	31	21	7	220
Percent of row	23.6	12.3	6.8	17.7	8.6	4.1	14.1	9.5	3.2	28.9
Percent of column	61.2	32.9	18.1	45.3	22.6	10.8	36.9	24.7	7.9	
Intermediate										
Number	24	33	41	26	24	21	32	29	28	258
Percent of row	9.3	12.8	15.9	10.1	9.3	8.1	12.4	11.2	10.9	33.9
Percent of column	28.2	40.2	49.4	30.2	28.6	25.3	38.1	34.1	31.5	
Egalitarian										
Number	9	22	27	21	41	53	21	35	54	283
Percent of row	3.2	7.8	9.5	7.4	14.5	18.7	7.4	12.4	19.1	37.2
Percent of column	10.6	26.8	32.5	24.4	48.8	63.9	25.0	41.2	60.7	
Total sample										
Number	85	82	83	86	84	83	84	85	89	761
Percent	11.2	10.8	10.9	11.3	11.0	10.9	11.0	11.2	11.7	100.0

Table A-106
Views and Values, by National and Occupational Group
(in percent)

Views	National Group			Industrial Group		
	Israel	*United States*	*Germany*	*Industry*	*Retail*	*Office*
Traditional	37.4	26.2	10.9	47.8	26.7	12.3
Intermediate	39.3	28.1	46.8	32.2	34.4	35.3
Egalitarian	23.3	45.7	42.3	20.0	38.9	52.4

Table A-107
Views and Values: Male and Female Roles, by Subgroup

	Subgroup									Total/Average
Responses	0	1	2	3	4	5	6	7	8	
Traditional										
Number	44	27	12	54	25	18	44	30	15	269
Percent of row	16.4	10.0	4.5	20.1	9.3	6.7	16.4	11.2	5.6	35.3
Percent of column	51.8	32.9	14.5	62.8	29.8	21.7	52.4	35.3	16.9	
Egalitarian										
Number	41	55	71	32	59	65	40	55	74	492
Percent of row	8.3	11.2	14.4	6.5	12.0	13.2	8.1	11.2	15.0	64.7
Percent of column	48.2	67.1	85.5	37.2	70.2	78.3	47.6	64.7	83.1	
Total sample										
Number	85	82	83	86	84	83	84	85	89	761
Percent	11.2	10.8	10.9	11.3	11.0	10.9	11.0	11.2	11.7	100.0

Table A-108
Views and Values: Pay, by Subgroup

| Responses | Subgroup | | | | | | | | | Total/ |
	0	1	2	3	4	5	6	7	8	Average
Traditional										
Number	64	43	39	47	30	11	55	37	16	342
Percent of row	18.7	12.6	11.4	13.7	8.8	3.2	16.1	10.8	4.7	44.9
Percent of column	75.3	52.4	47.0	54.7	35.7	13.3	65.5	43.5	18.0	
Egalitarian										
Number	21	39	44	39	54	72	29	48	73	419
Percent of row	5.0	9.3	10.5	9.3	12.9	17.2	6.9	11.5	17.4	55.1
Percent of column	24.7	47.6	53.0	45.3	64.3	86.7	34.5	56.5	82.0	
Total sample										
Number	85	82	83	86	84	83	84	85	89	761
Percent	11.2	10.8	10.9	11.3	11.0	10.9	11.0	11.2	11.7	100.0

Table A-109
Views and Values: Education and Vocational Training, by Subgroup

Responses	Subgroup									Total/
	0	1	2	3	4	5	6	7	8	Average
Traditional										
Number	16	10	7	11	11	3	7	3	0	68
Percent of row	23.5	14.7	10.3	16.2	16.2	4.4	10.3	4.4	0	8.9
Percent of column	18.8	12.2	8.4	12.8	13.1	3.6	8.3	3.5	0	
Egalitarian										
Number	69	72	76	75	73	80	77	82	89	693
Percent of row	10.0	10.4	11.0	10.8	10.5	11.5	11.1	11.8	12.8	91.1
Percent of column	81.2	87.8	91.6	87.2	86.9	96.4	91.7	96.5	100.0	
Total sample										
Number	85	82	83	86	84	83	84	85	89	761
Percent	11.2	10.8	10.9	11.3	11.0	10.9	11.0	11.2	11.7	100.0

Table A-110
Views and Values: Responsibility, by Subgroup

	Subgroup									Total/
Responses	0	1	2	3	4	5	6	7	8	Average
Traditional										
Number	50	45	44	53	45	38	52	35	32	394
Percent of row	12.7	11.4	11.2	13.5	11.4	9.6	13.2	8.9	8.1	51.8
Percent of column	58.8	54.9	53.0	61.6	53.6	45.8	61.9	41.2	36.0	
Egalitarian										
Number	35	37	39	33	39	45	32	50	57	367
Percent of row	9.5	10.1	10.6	9.0	10.6	12.3	8.7	13.6	15.5	48.2
Percent of column	41.2	45.1	47.0	38.4	46.4	54.2	38.1	58.8	64.0	
Total sample										
Number	85	82	83	86	84	83	84	85	89	761
Percent	11.2	10.8	10.9	11.3	11.0	10.9	11.0	11.2	11.7	100.0

Table A-111
Views and Values: Managerial Positions, by Subgroup

| | Subgroup | | | | | | | | | Total/ |
Response	0	1	2	3	4	5	6	7	8	Average
Traditional										
Number	17	26	26	21	12	12	24	36	46	220
Percent of row	7.7	11.8	9.5	5.5	5.5	5.5	10.9	16.4	20.9	28.9
Percent of column	20.0	31.7	31.3	24.4	14.3	14.5	28.6	42.4	51.7	
Egalitarian										
Number	68	56	57	65	72	71	60	49	43	541
Percent of row	12.6	10.4	10.5	12.0	13.3	13.1	11.1	9.1	7.9	71.1
Percent of column	80.0	68.3	68.7	75.6	85.7	85.5	71.4	57.6	48.3	
Total sample										
Number	85	82	83	86	84	83	84	85	89	761
Percent	11.2	10.8	10.9	11.3	11.0	10.9	11.0	11.2	11.7	100.0

Table A-112
Views and Values: Occupational Segregation, by Subgroup

Response	Subgroup									Total/Average
	0	1	2	3	4	5	6	7	8	
Traditional										
Number	74	56	57	55	22	21	58	51	35	429
Percent of row	17.2	13.1	13.3	12.8	5.1	4.9	13.5	11.9	8.2	56.4
Percent of column	87.1	68.3	68.7	64.0	26.2	25.3	60.0	60.0	39.3	
Egalitarian										
Number	11	26	26	31	62	62	26	34	54	332
Percent of row	3.3	7.8	7.8	9.3	18.7	18.7	7.8	10.2	16.3	43.6
Percent of column	12.9	31.7	31.3	36.0	73.8	74.7	31.0	40.0	60.7	
Total sample										
Number	85	82	83	86	84	83	84	85	89	761
Percent	11.2	10.8	10.9	11.3	11.0	10.9	11.0	11.2	11.7	100.0

Table A-113
Views and Values: Skills and Capabilities, by Subgroup

	Subgroup									Total/
Responses	0	1	2	3	4	5	6	7	8	Average
Traditional										
Number	36	33	19	33	18	15	8	18	14	194
Percent of row	18.6	17.0	9.8	17.0	9.3	7.7	4.1	9.3	7.2	25.5
Percent of column	42.4	40.2	22.9	38.4	21.4	18.1	9.5	21.2	15.7	
Egalitarian										
Number	49	49	64	53	66	68	76	67	75	567
Percent of row	8.6	8.6	11.3	9.3	11.6	12.0	13.4	11.8	13.2	74.5
Percent of column	57.6	59.8	77.1	61.6	78.6	81.9	90.5	78.8	84.3	
Total sample										
Number	85	82	83	86	84	83	84	85	89	761
Percent	11.2	10.8	10.9	11.3	11.0	10.9	11.0	11.2	11.7	100.0

Table A-114
Views and Values: Work Behavior, by Subgroup

| Responses | Subgroup | | | | | | | | | Total/ |
	0	1	2	3	4	5	6	7	8	Average
Traditional										
Number	53	39	35	25	26	17	26	23	22	266
Percent of row	19.9	14.7	13.2	9.4	9.8	6.4	9.8	8.6	8.3	35.0
Percent of column	62.4	47.6	42.2	29.1	31.0	20.5	31.0	27.1	24.7	
Egalitarian										
Number	32	43	48	61	58	66	58	62	67	495
Percent of row	6.5	8.7	9.7	12.3	11.7	13.3	11.7	12.5	13.5	65.0
Percent of column	37.6	52.4	57.8	70.9	69.0	79.5	69.0	72.9	75.3	
Total sample										
Number	85	82	83	86	84	83	84	85	89	761
Percent	11.2	10.8	10.9	11.3	11.0	10.9	11.0	11.2	11.7	100.0

Table A-115
Views and Values: Awareness of Inequality, by Subgroup

Responses	\multicolumn{9}{c}{Subgroup}									Total/ Average
	0	1	2	3	4	5	6	7	8	
Traditional										
Number	57	49	47	52	41	32	48	34	17	377
Percent of row	15.1	13.0	12.5	13.8	10.9	8.5	12.7	9.0	4.5	49.5
Percent of column	67.1	59.8	56.6	60.5	48.8	38.6	57.1	40.0	19.1	
Egalitarian										
Number	28	33	36	34	43	51	36	51	72	384
Percent of row	7.3	8.6	9.4	8.9	11.2	13.3	9.4	13.3	18.8	50.5
Percent of column	32.9	40.2	43.4	39.5	51.2	61.4	42.9	60.0	80.9	
Total sample										
Number	85	82	83	86	84	83	84	85	89	761
Percent	11.2	10.8	10.9	11.3	11.0	10.9	11.0	11.2	11.7	100.0

Table A-116
All Views and Values: Response by Marital Status

Response	Single	Married	Living with Friend	Divorced	Separated	Widowed	Total/Average
Traditional							
Number	66	121	1	16	5	11	220
Percent of row	30.0	55.0	0.5	7.3	2.3	5.0	28.9
Percent of column	28.6	30.0	12.5	22.9	55.6	28.2	
Intermediate							
Number	83	134	3	22	1	15	258
Percent of row	32.2	51.9	1.2	8.5	0.4	5.8	33.9
Percent of column	35.9	33.2	37.5	31.4	11.1	38.5	
Egalitarian							
Number	82	149	4	32	3	13	283
Percent of row	29.0	52.7	1.4	11.3	1.1	4.6	37.2
Percent of column	35.5	36.9	50.0	45.7	33.3	33.3	
Total sample							
Number	231	404	8	70	9	39	761
Percent	30.4	53.1	1.1	9.2	1.2	5.1	100.0

Table A-117
All Views and Values: Response by Age

Response	−25	26-35	36-45	46-55	56-65	66+	Total/ Average
Traditional							
Number	67	37	48	48	19	1	220
Percent of row	30.5	16.8	21.8	21.8	8.6	0.5	28.9
Percent of column	26.8	20.6	34.3	36.4	32.8	100.0	
Intermediate							
Number	86	56	46	43	27	0	258
Percent of row	33.3	21.7	17.8	16.7	10.5	0	33.9
Percent of column	34.4	31.1	32.9	32.6	46.6	0	
Egalitarian							
Number	97	87	46	41	12	0	283
Percent of row	34.3	30.7	16.3	14.5	4.2	0	37.2
Percent of column	38.8	48.3	32.9	31.1	20.7	0	
Total sample							
Number	250	180	140	132	58	1	761
Percent	32.9	23.7	18.4	17.3	7.6	0.1	100.0

Table A-118
Correlation of All Views with Level of Satisfaction (Composite)

Views	Satisfaction			Total/ Average
	Low	Medium	High	
Traditional				
Number	84	93	43	220
Percent of row	38.2	42.3	28.9	28.9
Percent of column	28.1	32.4	24.6	
Intermediate				
Number	109	89	60	258
Percent of row	42.2	34.5	23.3	33.9
Percent of column	36.5	31.0	34.3	
Egalitarian				
Number	106	105	72	283
Percent of row	37.5	37.1	35.4	37.2
Percent of column	35.5	36.6	41.1	
Total sample				
Number	299	287	175	761
Percent	39.3	37.7	23.0	100.0

Table A-119
Correlation of All Views with Level of Overt Satisfaction

| | Level | | | Total/ |
View	Satisfied	Medium Satisfied	Unsatisfied	Average
Traditional				
Number	100	98	22	220
Percent of row	45.5	44.5	10.0	28.9
Percent of column	33.2	27.5	21.4	
Intermediate				
Number	108	120	30	258
Percent of row	41.9	46.5	11.6	33.9
Percent of column	35.9	33.6	29.1	
Egalitarian				
Number	93	139	51	283
Percent of row	32.9	49.1	18.0	37.2
Percent of column	30.9	38.9	49.5	
Total sample				
Number	301	357	103	761
Percent	39.6	46.9	13.5	100.0

Table A-120
Correlation of All Views with Emphasis on Content

| | Emphasis on Content | | Total/ |
All Views	Low	High	Average
Traditional			
Number	198	22	220
Percent of row	90.0	10.0	28.9
Percent of column	30.9	18.3	
Intermediate			
Number	215	43	258
Percent of row	83.3	16.7	33.9
Percent of column	33.5	35.8	
Egalitarian			
Number	228	55	283
Percent of row	80.6	19.4	37.2
Percent of column	35.6	45.8	
Total sample			
Number	641	120	761
Percent	84.2	15.8	100.0

Table A-121
Correlation of All Views with Concern for Content

| | Concern for Content | | | Total/ |
View	Little	Medium	High	Average
Traditional				
Number	127	29	34	220
Percent of column	36.4	27.2	17.4	28.9
Percent of row	57.7	26.8	15.5	
Intermediate				
Number	133	67	58	258
Percent of column	38.1	30.9	29.7	33.9
Percent of row	51.6	26.0	22.5	
Egalitarian				
Number	89	91	103	283
Percent of column	25.5	41.9	52.8	37.2
Percent of row	31.4	32.2	36.4	
Total sample				
Number	349	217	195	761
Percent	45.9	28.5	25.6	100.0

Table A-122
Correlation of All Views with Concern for Hygiene

| | Concern for Hygiene | | | Total/ |
Views	Passive	Neutral	Active	Average
Traditional				
Number	91	38	91	220
Percent of column	30.8	26.2	28.3	28.9
Percent of row	41.4	17.3	41.4	
Intermediate				
Number	113	54	91	258
Percent of column	38.3	37.2	28.3	33.9
Percent of row	43.8	20.9	35.3	
Egalitarian				
Number	91	53	139	283
Percent of column	30.8	36.6	43.3	37.2
Percent of row	32.2	18.7	49.1	
Total sample				
Number	295	145	321	761
Percent	38.8	19.1	42.2	100.0

Table A-123
Correlation of All Views with Commitment to Work

Views	Commitment to Work			Total/ Average
	Low	Medium	High	
Traditional				
Number	48	81	91	220
Percent of column	40.3	30.8	24.0	28.9
Percent of row	21.8	36.8	41.4	
Intermediate				
Number	41	90	127	258
Percent of column	34.5	34.2	33.5	33.9
Percent of row	15.9	34.9	49.2	
Egalitarian				
Number	30	92	161	283
Percent of column	25.2	35.0	42.5	37.2
Percent of row	10.6	32.5	56.9	
Total sample				
Number	119	263	379	761
Percent	15.6	34.6	49.8	100.0

Table A-124
Correlation of All Views with Interest in Advancement

View	Interest in Advancement		Total/ Average
	Low	High	
Traditional			
Number	141	79	220
Percent of column	38.7	19.9	28.9
Percent of row	64.1	35.9	
Intermediate			
Number	138	120	258
Percent of column	37.9	30.2	33.9
Percent of row	53.5	46.5	
Egalitarian			
Number	85	198	283
Percent of column	23.4	49.9	37.2
Percent of row	30.0	70.0	
Total sample			
Number	364	397	761
Percent	47.8	52.2	100.0

Table A-125
Correlation of Views on Role with Interest in Advancement

| | Interest in Advancement | | Total/ |
View	Low	High	Average
Traditional			
Number	169	100	269
Percent of column	46.4	25.2	35.3
Percent of row	62.8	37.2	
Modern			
Number	195	297	492
Percent of column	53.6	74.8	64.7
Percent of row	39.6	60.4	
Total sample			
Number	364	397	761
Percent	47.8	52.2	100.0

Table A-126
Correlation of Views on Women's Suitability for Managerial Positions with Interest in Advancement

| | Interest in Advancement | | Total/ |
Views	Low	High	Average
Traditional			
Number	137	83	220
Percent of column	37.6	20.9	28.9
Percent of row	62.3	20.9	
Modern			
Number	227	314	541
Percent of column	61.4	79.1	71.1
Percent of row	42.0	58.0	
Total sample			
Number	364	397	761
Percent	47.8	52.2	100.0

Table A-127
Correlation of Awareness of Inequality with Interest in Advancement

Views	Interest in Advancement		Total/ Average
	Low	*High*	
Traditional			
Number	204	173	377
Percent of row	56.0	43.6	49.5
Percent of column	54.1	45.9	
Modern			
Number	160	224	384
Percent of row	44.0	56.4	50.5
Percent of column	41.7	58.3	
Total sample			
Number	364	397	761
Percent	47.8	52.2	100.0

Bibliography

Agassi, Judith Buber. "Beyond Equality." In Jean Lipman-Blumen, and Jessie Bernard, eds., *Social Policy and Sex Roles.* Beverly Hills: Sage, 1979, 355-61.

———. "The Quality of Women's Working Life." In L.E. Davis and A.B. Cherns, eds., *The Quality of Working Life,* 1:280-298. New York: Free Press, 1975.

———. "The Unequal Occupational Distribution of Women in Israel." *Signs* 2 (1977), 888-894.

Benninghaus, Hans. "Arbeitssituation und Arbeitszufriedenheit." *Kölner Zeitschrift für Soziologie und Sozialpsychologie* 30 (1978):514-547.

Blauner, Robert. *Alienation and Freedom.* Chicago: University of Chicago Press, 1964.

Blaxall, M., and Reagan, B. *Women and the Workplace.* Chicago: Chicago University Press, 1976.

Bruggemann, A. "Zur Unterscheidung verschiedener Formen von 'Arbeitszufriedenheit.' " *Arbeit und Leistung* 28 (1974):281-284.

Bruggemann, A.; Groskurth, P.; Ulich, B. *Arbeitszufriedenheit.* Bern, Stuttgart, Wien: Verlag Hans Huber, 1975.

Crewley, Joan F.; Levitin, Teresa E.; and Quinn, Robert P. "Facts and Fiction about the American Working Woman." Ann Arbor: Survey Research Center, University of Michigan, 1973.

Davis, L.E. "Job Satisfaction Research: The Post-Industrial Views." *Industrial Relations* 10 (1971):176-193.

Davis, L.E., and Cherns, A.B., eds. *The Quality of Working Life.* 2 vols. New York: Free Press, 1975.

Davis, L.E., and Taylor, J.E., eds. *Design of Jobs.* Hammondsworth: Penguin, 1972.

Dubin, R. "Industrial Workers' Worlds: A Study of the Central Life Interests of Industrial Workers." *Social Problems* 3 (1956):131-142.

Fogarty, Michael P.; Rapoport, Rhona; and Rapoport, Robert H. *Sex, Career, and Family.* Beverly Hills: Sage, 1971.

Friedmann, Georges. *The Anatomy of Work: Labor, Leisure, and the Implications of Automoation.* New York: Free Press, 1964.

Gardell, Bertil. "Alienation and Mental Health in the Modern Industrial Environment," in Lennart Levi, ed., *Psychosocial Environment and Psychosomatic Diseases.* Oxford, 1970, pp. 148-180.

Goldthorpe, J.H.; Lockwood, D.; Bechhofer, F.; and Platt, J. *The Affluent Worker.* London: Cambridge University Press, 1968.

Hackman, J.R., and Lawler, E.E. "Employee Reaction to Job Characteristics." *Journal of Applied Psychology* 55 (1975):259-286.

Hackman, J.R., and Oldham, G.R. "The Job Diagnostic Survey: An Instrument for the Diagnosis of Jobs and the Evaluation of Job Redesign Projects." Technical Report 4. New Haven: Department of Administrative Science, Yale University, 1974.

Havens, Elizabeth M. "Marital Patterns of Female Workers." *American Journal of Sociology* 78 (1972):975-981.

Hertog, Friso J. den. "Work Structuring." In Peter Warr, ed., *Personal Goals and Work Design*, pp. 43-65. New York: John Wiley, 1978.

Herzberg, F. *Work and the Nature of Man*. New York: World, 1966.

Herzberg, F.; Mausner, B.; and Snyderman, B.B. *The Motivation to Work*. New York: John Wiley, 1959.

Hochschild, Arlie Russell. "A Review of Sex Role Research." *American Journal of Sociology* 78 (1972):1012-1029.

Hulin, C.L., and Blood, M.R. "Job Enlargement, Individual Differences, and Worker Responses." *Psychological Bulletin* 69 (1968):41-55.

Maccoby, E. *The Development of Sex Differences*. London: Tavistock, 1967.

Maslow, Abraham H. *The Farthest Reaches of Human Nature*. Hammondsworth: Penguin, 1973.

_____. *Motivation and Personality*. Rev. ed. New York: Harper and Row, 1970.

Oppenheimer, Valerie Kincade. "Demographic Influence on Female Employment." *American Journal of Sociology* 78 (1972):946-961.

Parsons, Talcott. "Age and Sex in the Social Structure of the United States." *American Sociological Review* 7 (1942):605-616.

Pross, Helge. *Gleichberechtigung im Beruf*. Frankfurt: Athenaeum, 1973.

Rapoport, Rhona, and Rapoport, Robert. "Work and Family in Contemporary Society." *American Sociological Review* 30 (1965):380-394.

Roethlisberger, F.J., and Dickson, W.J. *Management and the Worker*. Cambridge: Harvard University Press, 1939.

Rossi, Alice. "Equality between the Sexes: An Immodest Proposal." *Daedalus* 93 (1964):607-652.

Shepard, Jon W. "Technology, Alienation, and Job Satisfaction." *Annual Review of Sociology* 3 (1977):1-21.

Sheppard, H.L., and Herrick, N. *Where Have All the Robots Gone?* New York: Free Press, 1972.

Sullerot, Evelyne. *Women, Society and Change*. New York: McGraw-Hill, 1971.

Szalai, Alexander. "The Situation of Women in the Light of Contemporary Time-Budget Research." Background paper to U.N. Conference No. E Cnf. 66/BP/6. 1975.

Turner, A.N., and Lawrence, P.R. *Industrial Jobs and the Worker*. Cambridge: Harvard University Press, 1965.

University of Michigan. *Quality of Employment Survey*. Ann Arbor, 1972-73.

United States. Department of Health, Education and Welfare. *Work in America*. Cambridge: MIT Press, 1973.

Walker, C.R., and Guest, R.H. *The Man on the Assembly Line.* Cambridge: Harvard University Press, 1952.

Yankelovich, D. *Changing Youth Values in the Seventies.* New York: McGraw-Hill, 1974.

_____ . "The Meaning of Work." In J.M. Rosow, ed., *The Worker and the Job*, New Jersey: Prentice-Hall, 1974.

Index of Names

Index of Subjects

About the Author

Judith Buber Agassi was born in Germany in 1924. Her grandfather was Martin Buber; her mother is Margarete Buber-Neumann, then Buber's daughter-in-law. She graduated from the Hebrew University of Jerusalem in 1950 with an M.A. in history, sociology, and education; and from the University of London, London School of Economics, in 1960 with a Ph.D. in political science. She is married, with a daughter and a son. She has worked as a research assistant in London and in Stanford and has taught in the University of Hong Kong, the University of Illinois at Urbana, Simmons College, Boston College, and Bentley College in Boston, and in the Israeli universities of Haifa, Tel Aviv, and Jerusalem. She conducted research for two years in the MIT Center for International Studies on mass media and political concepts in Indonesia. Her present study is the result of years of work including a two-year fellowship at the Radcliffe Institute and two years of research funded by the German Research Foundation. She has published over twenty papers and a few monographs in English, Hebrew, and German on the topics of the sociology of work and leisure, the restructuring of work, women's work, sex roles, and the status of women. She is now studying the work attitudes of a male control sample, and is a guest professor at the Research Institute for the Humanities and the Social Sciences at Siegen, West Germany.